T3-BNU-501

The Cambridge Controversies in Capital Theory

A controversy in capital theory dominated economics in the 1960s and 1970s. Economists based in Cambridge, England detected flaws in the production model of neoclassical economics, associated with Cambridge, America. This debate established that the aggregate measure K for capital could not be used except in very special cases despite its still common usage in real business cycle theory today.

The Cambridge Controversies in Capital Theory discusses the main contributions to the controversy in a series of case studies. It gradually develops a methodological model of idealizations that explains both the progress of the debate and the historical ironies surrounding it, revealing that the surrounding confusion was due to the internal dynamics of the debate rather than to ideological differences. Economists were mainly engaged in attempts to solve local problems, often of a highly technical nature. This, plus the use of mathematics, led them to confuse different kinds of idealizations and to drift away from the global problems that were at stake. The main methodological result is a model describing the development of theories by a particular type of generalization: correspondence. The direction in which theories are expanded is ruled by the logical presupposition relationship between the core of a research programme and its corresponding models. This framework is used to assess Cartwright's account of scientific explanation, to solve Friedman's problem of assumptions and the problem of methodological pluralism.

This book will be of use to academics and advanced students with an interest in theoretical economics, history of economic thought, economic methodology and the philosophy of science.

Jack Birner is Professor of Economics at the University of Trento.

Routledge studies in the history of economics

The Cambridge Controversies in Capital Theory

A study in the logic of theory development

HB
501
B433
2001
WEB

Jack Birner

London and New York

First published 2002
by Routledge
11 New Fetter Lane, London EC4P 4EE

Simultaneously published in the USA and Canada
by Routledge
29 West 35th Street, New York, NY 10001

Routledge is an imprint of the Taylor & Francis Group

© 2002 Jack Birner

Typeset in 10/12 pt Times by
Newgen Imaging Systems (P) Ltd., Chennai, India
Printed and bound in Great Britain by MPG Books Ltd., Bodmin

All rights reserved. No part of this book may be reprinted or
reproduced or utilised in any form or by any electronic,
mechanical, or other means, now known or hereafter
invented, including photocopying and recording, or in any
information storage or retrieval system, without permission in
writing from the publishers.

British Library Cataloguing in Publication Data
A catalogue record for this book is available
from the British Library

Library of Congress Cataloging in Publication Data
Birner, Jack, 1951–
    Cambridge Controversies in capital theory / Jack Birner.
        p. cm.
    Includes bibliographical references and index.
        1. Capital. 2. Neoclassical school of economics. I. Title: Strategies and programmes in
    captial theory. II. Title.

HB501 .B526 2001
332′.041–dc21   00-047059

ISBN 0-415-07348-0

Contents

Illustrations

Figures

Table

Preface

The Cambridge controversies in capital theory: a remote memory for ageing economists, a completely unknown episode for most of their junior colleagues. Yet quite a bit has been written about it in the past. So why another study? As far as I know, no full-scale methodological analysis of the debate exists. One is provided here. It is based on a detailed exposition of the moves and countermoves of the most important participants. That is necessary, because it is one of my theses that models and formal methods of analysis determined to a great extent the direction and the outcome of the debate. The internal dynamics of the scientific problem solving process were more important than global theoretical ideas or ideological convictions. The thesis can be generalized to the better part of modern theoretical economics (the demonstration would require a series of similar studies). The book is also partly historical. It shows that the controversy is characterized by a series of historical ironies, which the methodological analysis helps to explain. It also corrects a few commonly accepted ideas, one of which has to do with Sraffa's role.

Most of the text was finished a dozen or so years ago, while various bits and pieces have been published more recently. As far as I know, nothing that adds anything of substance to the debate itself or its historiography has been published since, and the same goes for the methodological apparatus I use and extend. Discussions with the late Athanasios Asimakopoulos, Pierangelo Garegnani, Geoffrey Harcourt, Paul Samuelson and Robert Solow provided me with factual information and insights that I would not have acquired otherwise. I want to thank these prominent economists for their kind cooperation. I would also like to thank Neil de Marchi, Rob de Vries, Bert Hamminga and Geert Woltjer. Financial support by the Dutch organization for scientific research NWO and by Royal Dutch Shell Company is gratefully acknowledged.

Trento, October 2001
Jack Birner

Acknowledgements

The authors and publishers would like to thank the following for granting permission to reproduce material in this work:

Taylor and Francis Ltd for permission to reprint 'Cambridge Histories True and False' by Jack Birner, originally published in C. Marcuzzo, L. Pasinetti and A. Roncaglia (eds), *The Economics of Joan Robinson*, 1996, http://www.tandf.co.uk/journals/

Rodopi Press for permission to reprint 'Idealizations and Theory Development in Economics. Some History and Logic of the Logic of Discovery' by Jack Birner, originally published in Bert Hamminga and Neil B. de Marchi (eds), *Idealization in Economics*, volume 38, Idealization Subseries, Poznan Studies, 1994 and 'Idealizations and the Development of Capital Theory' by Jack Birner, originally published in J. Brzazinski, F. Coniglione, T. A. F. Kuipers and Leszek Novak (eds), *General Problems*, Volume 19, Idealization Series, Poznan Studies, 1990.

American Economic Association for permission to reprint Figure 10.1, originally published in L. Gallaway and V. Shukla, 'The Neoclassical Production Function', *American Economic Review*, 1974, p. 352.

MIT Press for permission to reproduce Figure 1 (p. 507) from Luigi L. Pasinetti, 'Changes in the Rate of Profit and Switches of Techniques', *The Quarterly Journal of Economics*, 80(4), 503–17. ©1966 by the President and Fellows of Harvard College.

MIT Press for permission to reproduce Figures 2, 5 and 6 (pp. 553, 548, 549) from Michael Bruno, Edwin Burmeister and Eytan Sheshinski, 'The Nature and Implications of the Reswitching of Techniques', *The Quarterly Journal of Economics*, 80(4), 526–53. ©1966 by the President and Fellows of Harvard College.

Wolters-Noordhoff for permission to reproduce Figures 5.9, 5.11 and 5.13 (pp. 135, 142, 145) from B. Compaijen, *Kapitaal, rendement en tijd*, Wolters-Noordhoff, Amsterdam, 1981. ©Wolters-Noordhoff Groningen, The Netherlands.

Figures 2, 3, 4 and 5 (pp. 102, 103, 105, 106) from C. E. Ferguson and R. F. Allen, 'Factor prices, commodity prices, and switches of technique', *Western Economic Journal*, 1970, by permission of Oxford University Press.

Review of Economics for permission to reproduce on p. 93 of 'The Production Function and the Theory of Capital' by J. Robinson, 1953.

Review of Economic Studies for permission to reproduce the figure that appeared on page 118 of 'The Production Function and the Theory of Capital: A Comment' by D. G. Champernowne, 1953.

Review of Economic Studies for permission to reproduce the figure that appeared on page 203 of 'Parable and Realism in Capital Theory' by P. Samuelson, 1962.

Every effort has been made to contact the copyright holders for permission to reprint material in this book. The publishers would be grateful to hear from any copyright holder who is not here acknowledged and will undertake to rectify any errors or omissions in future editions of this book.

Jack Birner

Introduction

Insiders are sometimes the slaves of silly ideas.   Solow (1988: 311)

1   The *K* that wouldn't go away

Real business cycle theory is a branch of modern economics that explains the occurrence of business cycles from real shocks. An important instrument of that theory is the production function. It explains the level of national production from the joint application of labour, capital, and technology: $Y = F(L, K, A)$. Many economists spend much of their time estimating the contribution of technology. Real business cycle theory also studies the intertemporal substitution of labour. Capital – with a capital K – is the key tool for both types of research; apparently, K is uncontroversial.

That used to be very different. Four decades ago the best minds in economics were engaged in a confrontation which the entire profession followed in the pages of the leading journals almost as if it were a soccer match. It has become customary to distinguish two opposing groups of economists to the debate. On one side are those who criticized the neoclassical production model. They are generally identified with Cambridge, England. The other side is made up of those who defended the model. Their intellectual abode is commonly considered to be Cambridge, Massachussetts, in America. Many economists thought they were witnessing the downfall of the theory that had dominated their discipline for almost a century – neoclassical economics. Whether or not that expectation was justified will not be discussed right now. What I do want to draw attention to is that the conclusions reached in that debate constitute a rare example of a set of formally proven, uncontestable, undeniably true and reliable results in economics. I will discuss these results in detail later in the book. They can be summarized by saying that the K of the production function that modern economists so confidently and fully rely on for their theoretical and empirical work can only be used in conditions where there is only a single, homogeneous capital good. One does not need to have a degree in economics to know that in reality this is not the case. The economy consists of a bewildering variety of buildings, machines, software, skills and ways of organizing production. And as everyone who has filed a corporate tax declaration knows, it is not even possible to give more than a rather inexact estimate of their value. In other words, not only is there no intuitive justification for the use of aggregate, homogeneous K, we have proofs by Nobel-calibre economists assisted by 100 per cent certain mathematical techniques that demonstrate without a shred of doubt that this K cannot and should not be used for the objectives it is currently used for. Nevertheless, economists go about their business as if these proofs did not exist. That some of them are the very same people who produced these proofs earlier makes things even more curious. The fact that production functions with the same aggregate K figure prominently in *all* current textbooks of macroeconomics is worse than curious: it is deeply worrying.

True, even though the critical results are now quite clear to those who care to look them up, at the time the debate was raging, several of the economists involved in it said they did not know very well what it was about. Robert Solow, for instance, observed: 'I find earlier discussions [in capital theory] terribly confusing and occasionally incomprehensible to a contemporary economist. Indeed, I suppose I should confess I sometimes feel much the same way about the current discussion even though – even when – I take part in it myself.' (Solow 1963: 9–10). Hindsight has not had the usual illuminating effect upon Solow, for two decades later he still expresses 'a continuing doubt as to what the controversy was *about...*' (Solow 1983: 181). His bewilderment is shared by other participants. The most authoritative commentator of the debate, Geoffrey Harcourt, writes that 'there seem to be legitimate doubts as to whether one side really understands what the other is saying.' (Harcourt 1972: 89). The question of whether or not their confusion explains the continued use of K in the face of its disavowal is interesting, but it will not be addressed in the book – at least not directly. One of the issues it concentrates on instead is the explanation of this confusion, because it shows the way in which economists work and economics develops.

So, the book gives a methodological analysis of the controversy known as the Cambridge versus Cambridge controversy, or the reswitching and capital reversing debate. When I started to work on it, my hypothesis was that the sense of confusion was a direct consequence of the highly abstract level on which the discussion took place, which is shown by the idealizing character of the models used. I also thought that the confusion was due to a failure to distinguish different types of idealizations. It turned out that idealizations are indeed of prime importance as factors that influence the way in which the debate evolved. But in the attempt to give more definite content to the original hypothesis, I discovered that the explanation of the confusion was even more complicated than I had thought.

2   The sleepwalker effect

One comment by former participants is that they had been talking at cross purposes. This, together with their sense of confusion, reminded me of the sleepwalkers that Arthur Koestler speaks of in his study of cosmology: 'The history of cosmic theories ... may without exaggeration be called a history of collective obsessions and controlled schizophrenias; and the manner in which some of the most important individual discoveries were arrived at reminds one more of a sleepwalker's performance than an electronic brain's.' (Koestler 1964: 11). In order to shed light on the matter, I decided to go and talk to some of the participants. One of them was Paul Samuelson, another central character and Solow's next-door neighbour at MIT. He told me about a model he had proposed (and which will be discussed later): 'until you know a subject perfectly, you always are in a state where you believe in A and you also believe in non-A.' In other words, Samuelson 'was in two minds', but apparently without being at a complete loss. Now this is exactly what Koestler calls 'controlled schizophrenia',[1] and Samuelson's comment seems to corroborate the sleepwalker hypothesis. In the work of yet another prominent participant, Joan Robinson, we find another example of such a split-mind condition. A point of criticism that occurs time and again in her early work is that the use of comparative statics for analysing processes and change is illicit. Nevertheless, she herself fails to see the prime importance of this for capital theory. It was not until the early 1970s that she turned this into her main criticism.[2]

Koestler continues: 'I shall not be sorry if, as an accidental by-product, the inquiry helps to counteract the legend that Science is a purely rational pursuit....' (ibid.). We have to bear in mind that Koestler is interested in the psychology of discovery, or in his words, 'to inquire into the obscure workings of the creative mind'. (ibid.: 11). Though I share his concern of trying to find general features which account for the sleepwalking behaviour, I think psychological factors are not enough to account for it (apart from the practical impossibility of reconstructing the subjective states of mind of people after so many years). Koestler belongs to a tradition in the philosophy of science, one of whose lasting contributions is the distinction between the context of discovery and the context of justification. An unfortunate consequence of this distinction was that the study of the process of discovery was declared out of bounds for philosophers of science; it was relegated to psychology. Philosophers were supposed to restrict their attention to the logical analysis of the products of scientific discovery, theories, because there one moves on the supposedly firmer ground of the context of justification. Whoever studied science had to choose between logic and psychology, and who, like Koestler, felt that logic did not take into account the fact that doing science is a human activity, opted for an analysis in psychological terms.

The consequence of this projection of the dichotomy between psychology and logic on the dichotomy between discovery and justification was that it held up progress in the analysis of the logic of scientific discovery, or heuristics, for decades.[3] What I want to do is to develop a logic of scientific discovery that is capable, among other things, of explaining scientific sleepwalking. Samuelson and Robinson belong to different theoretical traditions, yet they suffered from the same lack of focus and did not know for quite some time what conclusions to draw. This constitutes a counterexample to the idea that scientists are led by instant rationality, or learn very fast from their mistakes.[4] It seems reasonable to assume that if such eminent economists do not fit the instant rationality model, lesser figures will do so even less. But even without bothering with others, the example by itself is significant enough to suggest that we look for an explanation in terms of the context of Samuelson's and Robinson's theoretical activities rather than their psychological constitutions (which everybody will admit are very different indeed). So, my objective is different from Koestler's. Yet, like him, I will be satisfied if I can raise doubts about the legend that science is completely rational, if this legend is taken to refer to the idea that scientists always act in the full knowledge of what they are doing, and why they are doing it. For if scientists were always fully, unboundedly rational, then why did Champernowne's 1953 article (which will be discussed in Chapter 3) remain without any influence whatever? Not only was Champernowne the first to discuss reswitching and capital reversing very clearly, he also used the same model that was the main vehicle of analysis a decade later. Champernowne proved that a specific hidden assumption in the neoclassical analysis of production was the cause that these phenomena (considered to be 'anomalous') had not been predicted by the model – something others did not discover until a decade later. Champernowne generalized his results – as others did only a decade later. He also made it clear that the anomalies were only anomalies if a comparative-static model was used to describe processes in time – something other economists did not begin to suspect until two decades later. With hindsight, it is not difficult to see that 'objectively' the main elements of the later debate were all present in the early 1950s. But *at the time* no one seemed to notice. How to explain this? Psychological theories and theories of instant rationality would have great difficulties in producing a non *ad hoc* explanation. The behaviour of the economists in the debate looks more like an instance of the general human condition as summarized by the late William Bartley: 'I learnt from Popper that we never know what we are talking about, and I learnt from Hayek that we never know what we are doing.' (Bartley 1984: 19, italics deleted).

3   Levels and problems

I will look for an explanation along the following two lines. The first is what Popper calls the method of situational analysis or the logic of the situation.[5] A basic assumption of situational analysis is that people try to solve the problems that confront them as best they can. Given this assumption, explanations of human behaviour, including their behaviour as scientists,[6] have to rely on a systematic analysis of the problem situation rather than on the psychology of the problem solver. For an analysis of problem solving in science, it is useful to introduce the distinction between two levels of scientific discussion. The first is the *local* level, that of specific models and their analysis. Locally, scientists are engaged in the solving of detailed and often technical (even highly technical) problems, or puzzles, that are posed by particular models or by a particular apparatus of analysis. Solutions to such problems may give rise to the need for adaptations of models or techniques of analysis. Scientists usually have the choice among different strategies of model development, a point that will be discussed later in great detail. The second is the *global* level, or the domain of theories and research programmes.[7] Global analysis deals with what we may call the characteristic propositions of a particular theory, i.e. the propositions that enable us to distinguish one theory from another. The class of a theory's characteristic propositions consists of its premises (or 'assumptions') and its most exemplary predictions. One of the outcomes of the Cambridge debate was a differentiation within the class of characteristic propositions of neoclassical production theory: what are premises, and what are predictions.

One of the reasons why it is useful to distinguish between these two levels is that it keeps the methodologist from missing important clues for understanding the dynamics of a debate. For instance, the capital theory debate has sometimes been depicted as a clash between two opposed ideologies.[8] Ideological considerations belong to the global level. It can very well be argued that neoclassical economists and their critics subscribed to different ideologies. But this is not all there is to the debate. Both neoclassical economists and their critics are involved in discussing the same models and the same problems of detail. Apparently, their differing ideologies do not dictate that they should deal with different problems, or give different solutions to the same problems. It is hard to see how ideologies could serve as sets of instructions, or a heuristic, for solving such problems as arise in the construction, testing and adaptation of specific models.[9] Too rash an appeal to ideology risks having us overlook what is a major driving force in scientific debates: attempts to solve local problems.[10]

One of the things I will show is how economists, though coming from different theoretical backgrounds, tried to solve the same local, technical puzzles which were in part generated by the model that had somehow become the standard instrument of analysis. This local puzzle solving provided the impetus for the debate. Rarely, if ever, was anyone's local conduct directly and unequivocally guided by immediate global, programmatic or theoretical considerations. Perhaps the only exception is Garegnani. The only other author who might have influenced the debate by immediate global considerations was Sraffa, but I will argue later that, contrary to what is commonly thought, his influence was no more than indirect. All the others, even those who felt sympathy for, or reckoned themselves to belong to, a theoretical tradition that was critical of neoclassical economics – Robinson and Pasinetti come to mind – went through a painstaking process of local puzzle solving before turning their results into a global attack on neoclassical economics.

As I will explain later, the relationship between the local and the global level is quite complicated. On the one hand, the logical relation between the idealizing theories and models of a lower degree of idealization makes it impossible for the local results, which are obtained with the latter kind of models, to be used for rejecting the former. On the other hand, mathematical arguments play a very peculiar role in the relation between local and global levels. All of this can only be dealt with after an analysis of the characteristics of idealizing models and of the role of technical, mathematical arguments in the debate.

Besides the distinction between the global and local levels of discussion, I will distinguish two kinds of problems. It is a well-known fact that attempts to solve problems invariably create further problems, as has often been argued by Popper.[11] One tries to solve a problem *P* by a tentative solution or tentative theory

TT. When checking whether the solution is adequate, or when testing the theory by confronting its predictions with the evidence E, one runs into new problems which require to be solved, and so on. This can be shown in the scheme

$$P \rightarrow TT \rightarrow E \rightarrow P' \rightarrow TT' \rightarrow \cdots$$

However, the scheme is too coarse for an analysis of problem solving in science. In the course of the development of every scientific discipline two types of problems may arise, which I will call *internally generated* and *externally generated*.[12] Externally generated problems in the sense used here are problems that arise out of a theory's confrontation with its empirical domain or with other scientific or metaphysical theories. Examples in economics are: how to explain unemployment; what are the relations between inflation and the balance of payment; how are monetarist and Keynesian theories of the business cycle related? Internally generated problems are problems that arise out of the use of a particular apparatus of analysis within a particular theoretical tradition. Thus, the introduction of a particular econometric technique for estimating parameter values may create a host of mathematical and statistical problems; and the translation of an economic theory or model into an econometric model entails identification problems. It seems that in comparison to other disciplines economics has a rather high proportion of internally generated problems, problems that have to do with the characteristics or special features of the apparatus of analysis. A further discussion of how the two distinctions, the one between local and global levels of analysis, the other between internally and externally generated problems, are related will be postponed till Chapter 12.

4   Idealizations and the method of economics: some historical background

Any methodological analysis of capital theory has to take seriously the fact that it is one of the most abstract branches of economics. Idealizing theories and models are the primary vehicles of analysis. This makes capital theory an ideal object for the study of idealizations in economics. Moreover, capital theory makes much use of mathematical techniques. Though the mathematization of economics is relatively recent, the method associated with it has its roots in the history of economic thought. I am referring to the deductive systematization of economic knowledge obtained by the construction and manipulation of idealized models of reality. The method was introduced in the hope of promoting economics from the status of a collection of practical rules for public policy to the cognitive status of Euclidean geometry and Newtonian physics. According to Halévy, James Mill was the first to introduce the Euclidean metaphor in economics (in the Edinburgh Review of 1809).[13] Mill speaks of the deductive proof of consequences, like Euclidean theorems, from the laws of human nature. The French economist Jean-Baptiste Say had the similar purpose of improving upon the body of classical economics by systematizing it. In the Introduction of his *Traité d'économie politique*, Say writes: 'The celebrated work of Dr Adam Smith can only be considered as an immethodical assemblage of the soundest principles of political economy, supported by luminous illustrations . . .'.[14] The Newtonian method, or what Say believed to be that method, was his shining example. He wanted to apply it in order to integrate economic knowledge into one system and to discover new economic knowledge. The Newtonian influence is reflected by Say's terminology: 'Political economy, in the same manner as the exact sciences, is composed of a few fundamental principles, and of a great number of corollaries or conclusions, drawn from these principles. It is essential, therefore, for the advancement of this science that these principles should be strictly *deduced from observation* . . .'.[15]

In the Preface to his *Principles of Political Economy* of 1809, David Ricardo expresses his admiration for Say's method. It is mainly through Ricardo that it gained a foothold in economics and that economics took a new turning in that it started looking for laws: 'Thus political economy, which was for Adam Smith a branch of politics and legislation, has become for Ricardo the theory of the laws of the natural distribution of wealth.' (Halévy 1972: 267). Ricardo was also influenced by James Mill, who had taken over the Newtonian principle of finding the smallest possible number of general laws to 'enable all the detail of phenomena to be explained by a synthetic and deductive method' (ibid.: 6). Bentham, too, adopted the new method. In the words of Halévy, his 'Utilitarianism, or Philosophical Radicalism, can be defined as nothing but an attempt to apply the principles of Newton to the affairs of politics and of morals.' (ibid.: 6).

The Newtonian method that entered economics through Ricardo is part of a tradition that is much older than Newton. It is known as the method of analysis and synthesis (or resolution and composition). Hintikka and Remes give the following description of the Newtonian method.[16] It consists of

1   an analysis of a certain situation into its ingredients and factors;
2   an examination of the interdependencies between these factors;
3   a generalization of the relationships so discovered to all similar situations; and
4   the deductive applications of these general laws to explain and to predict other situations.

The aim of the method was to discover fundamental causes and to gain conceptual or theoretical control of the complex world. According to Zabarella, a predecessor of Galilei,

> [t]he end of the demonstrative method is perfect science, which is knowledge of things through their causes; but the end of the resolutive method is discovery rather than science; since by resolution we seek causes from their effects so that we may afterwards know effects from their causes, not so that we may rest in a knowledge of the causes themselves.
>
> (Randall 1962, Book 2: 294)

Zabarella did not insist that the principles of natural science be mathematical. It was not until Galilei that the method was put into practice in a mathematical form which actually allowed scientists to make calculations of the effects of various factors.

With this mathematical emphasis added to the logical methodology of Zabarella, there stands completed the 'new method' for which men had been so long seeking. By the mathematical analysis of a few simple instances we find the principle involved in them. From that principle we deduce further consequences, which we find illustrated and confirmed in experience . . . . This is the method called by Euclid and Archimedes a combination of 'analysis' and 'synthesis', and by the Paduans and Galileo, 'resolution' and 'composition'.

(Randall 1962, Book 1: 307)

In the history of science, the method of analysis and synthesis was not only a method of proof, it was also a method of discovery.[17] Thus, according to Newton, apart from giving rules for confirming already known hypotheses, the analytic procedure served as 'a rational method of finding these hypotheses and theories in the first place.' (Hintikka and Remes 1974: 110). Indeed, this was the case for all those who used or described this method throughout its 2000 years of existence. With the separation between context of discovery and context of justification, introduced by Reichenbach into modern philosophy of science, the idea that proof and invention can be combined in one methodological framework was abandoned.

The method of analysis and synthesis allowed a deductive systematization of knowledge and, as a consequence, a vastly increased control of the world. At the same time, it created a philosophical problem: how to account for the relationship between idealized theories and empirical reality. Or, stated perhaps more correctly, how are idealizing theories related to models that are closer to reality. The realization of the Euclidean ideal of a strictly deductively organized body of knowledge in science came at a cost: 'one had to pay for each step which increased rigour in deduction by the introduction of a new and fallible translation.' (Lakatos 1978b: 90).

Even though Say had made himself the spokesman of the new (or rather, in view of the preceding discussion, 'new') method in economics, the first detailed description of it was given by the Austrian economist Carl Menger. He did so in a defence of his own book on economics. Menger's objective in *Investigations Into Method* of 1883 was to show that the economic theory that he had developed in the *Principles* of 1871 was superior to the economics of the rival Historical School. According to Menger his *Principles* succeeds in formulating a general, universally valid theory, i.e. a theory that is true without exceptions, because it follows the Galilean method. Both requirements, generality and universal validity, can only be met by idealizing theories of a particular kind. In his methodology Menger distinguishes two 'directions of theoretical research': the *exact* orientation, which studies the laws governing *ideal* economic phenomena, and the *realistic-empirical* branch of theoretical science, which studies the regularities in the succession and coexistence of *real* phenomena. This distinction leaves him with the problem of clarifying the nature of the relationship between empirical and exact theoretical research.

Like most methodological principles, Menger's are partly based on ontological considerations. Menger believes in the existence of different fundamental motives for human behaviour. The particular drives that he mentions are the economic drive, which he considers by far the most important, 'Gemeinsinn', by which is meant 'moral sentiments' in the sense of Adam Smith, altruism, and the sense of justice. Menger firmly believes in the necessity for causal explanation: 'Scire est per causas scire'. (Menger 1883: 87). Ultimately, all social phenomena can be reduced to the fundamental human drives which are the ultimate causes in social science. The basic drives delineate the boundaries between scientific disciplines: economics, social philosophy (or perhaps sociology), ethics, and jurisprudence. Each of these disciplines studies human behaviour under one of these different aspects to the exclusion of the others.

Within each discipline, the influence of one fundamental drive can be studied in various degrees of purity, i.e. by abstracting to a greater or lesser degree from disturbing factors which are operative in reality. The more disturbing factors are abstracted from, the stronger the operation of the relevant fundamental drive manifests itself. Following Wieser, we may call the separation of fundamental drives from one another *isolating abstraction* and omitting disturbing factors *emphasizing abstraction*.[18] For Menger, this distinction is the basis of his analytic-compositive method. Through analysis or resolution one finds single fundamental causes. But the mere isolation of a single fundamental cause is not sufficient for studying it in its pure form. For that purpose, we have to abstract from factors which inhibit the full working of that single cause. Exact theoretical science thus involves both types of abstraction.

Menger specifically mentions four disturbing factors which have to be abstracted from if we are to find the exact laws of economics: ignorance, error, external force, and the measure in which people let themselves be guided by a specific fundamental drive (in the case of economics it is the degree to which people attend to their economic interests; I shall call the absence of it 'neglect'). This leads to the following classification, which underlies Menger's attempt to explain how exact and empirical theoretical science are related:[19]

Basic drives (isolating abstraction):*

Economic drive Morality Altruism Justice etc.

Disturbing factors (emphasizing abstraction):
Error
Ignorance
Force
Neglect

* Within each of the disciplines defined by one particular basic drive, the operation of that drive can be studied on various levels of emphasizing abstraction. Gradually abstracting from error, ignorance, etc., recurs in each of the disciplines.

The theoretical sciences study one or several aspects of reality or basic drives in isolation from others. Moreover, the exact theoretical sciences abstract from disturbing factors, whereas the empirical theoretical sciences do not. So, exact theories are even more idealized than empirical theories; they are about *isolated* aspects of *ideal* phenomena. According to Menger, attempting to test the predictions of exact laws empirically involves a category mistake and is a methodological absurdity (cf. Menger 1883: 54). Exact laws cannot be refuted by the results of empirical analysis. The consequence that has to be drawn from a negative test result must be not that the exact law is false, but that it is not applicable. This is an instrumentalist conclusion. Nevertheless, Menger is a scientific realist. He maintains that both empirical and exact theories are descriptions of reality, which is why *Principles* is put forward as a theory which is to provide practically involved people with a scientific foundation for their conduct by laying bare the real causal laws of economics (cf. Menger 1871, Preface).

Menger does not give a satisfactory account of the relation between exact and empirical analysis. This is because for him, as for his contemporaries (with the possible exception of Whewell), the problem of the relation between exact and empirical theory is a problem about the justification of knowledge: how can empirical-theoretical and exact-theoretical knowledge be given a foundation that is true beyond doubt. Knowledge is certain knowledge, or has to be reducible, by infallible means, to certain knowledge. The method by which knowledge about the world is to be achieved is the method of induction. For Menger, context of discovery and context of justification are not separated. How true one's knowledge is, is fully determined by the method one uses in obtaining it. The exact method guarantees the truth of exact laws:

> The goal of this orientation, which henceforth we will call the *exact* one, and which is pursued in the same way in all domains of the world of phenomena, is the determination of strict laws of the phenomena, of regularities in the succession of phenomena. Not only do these laws appear to us as being without exceptions; by virtue of the epistemic ways by which we have arrived at them, they even bear the guarantee of being without exceptions.
>
> (Menger 1883: 8; my translation)

In Menger's justificationist and inductivist theory of knowledge, abstraction is conceived as a *process* rather than as a set of hypotheses with particular properties, regardless of how they are arrived at.[20] But Menger is not a naive inductivist. He is well aware of the logical problem that arises if one maintains that general, universally valid laws can be derived from a finite number of observation statements.[21] His distinction between exact and empirical science would collapse if this were possible, and with it his case against the Historical School. Still, for a justificationist the recognition of the impossibility of inductively justifying universal laws raises the problem that he has to explain how universal laws *are* to be justified. Either exact laws are about empirical reality (but then they must have been derived from it in some way) or their basis is not empirical (but then they cannot be about empirical reality). Menger finds himself in a predicament that makes it impossible for him to solve the problem of the relation between exact and empirical laws.

5 The way forward

A model is now available that enables us to solve Menger's problem. It was developed by the Polish philosophers of science Wladyslaw Krajewski and Leszek Nowak. I adopt their analysis in this book. My principal objective is to examine how features that are characteristic of idealizing theories and models influence the development of the debate. It will turn out that the Polish model, as I will call it, has to be modified if it is to come to grips with the economic models used in the debate. An adaptation of a proposal by Alan Musgrave will be used for that purpose.

My methodological analysis of the capital theory debate is based on detailed historical research. A number of publications that were important in the reswitching and capital reversing debate will be discussed and attention will be paid to the details of the strategies, tactics, and weapons used by participants in their arguments and proofs. These case studies serve as the empirical material with which to test and improve the methodological framework, which is designed for an analysis of the structure and development of idealizing theories. More specifically, the detailed analysis has two goals. The first is a methodological reconstruction of the methods that participants typically follow, and how these influence the development of the debate. The second is an analysis of the considerations that guided participants' behaviour in the debate. In this context, attention will be paid both to economic-theoretical and to purely formal, mathematical considerations, and how these are related to each other.

The case studies consist of a number of sequences of articles that are closely related. Each batch of articles will be followed by a round of methodological analysis. In that way, I will gradually, to the extent that the empirical material requires, refine my methodological apparatus. Let me also make clear what I do *not* want to do. It is not my purpose to offer a comprehensive account of the debate. Harcourt has set a standard[22] that is difficult to emulate. My objective is different; it is to develop a methodological apparatus that gives us a better understanding of the dynamics of the debate. Hence my choice of discussing a limited number of publications in detail rather than a great number that could only have been treated more superficially. Let me hasten to add, however, that my sample is not rigged so as to yield certain predetermined conclusions. To a large extent, the results of my analysis were a surprise to me, too. Of course, subjective surprise is no justification. Should anyone look for one, or want to challenge my choice, I suggest he count the number of times the articles in the sample are quoted in others, or compare its composition to the several studies that Harcourt devoted to the debate.

The publications that will be discussed in detail, ordered as to date of publication,[23] are the following:

Robinson, J., 1953, 'The Production Function and the Theory of Capital', *Review of Economic Studies*.

Champernowne, D. G., 1953, ' The Production Function and the Theory of Capital: A Comment', *Review of Economic Studies*.

Robinson, J., 1956, *The Accumulation of Capital*, MacMillan.

Samuelson, P., 1962, 'Parable and Realism in Capital Theory: The Surrogate Production Function', *Review of Economic Studies*.

Levhari, D., 1965, 'A Nonsubstitution Theorem and Switching of Techniques', *Quarterly Journal of Economics*.

Hicks, J., 1965, *Capital and Growth*, Oxford University Press.

Pasinetti, L., 1966, 'Changes in the Rate of Profit and Switches of Techniques', *Quarterly Journal of Economics*.

Bruno, M., Burmeister, E. and Sheshinski, E., 1966, 'The Nature and Implications of the Reswitching of Techniques', *Quarterly Journal of Economics*.

Garegnani, P., 1966, 'Switching of Techniques', *Quarterly Journal of Economics*.

Brown, M., 1969, 'Substitution–Composition Effects, Capital Intensity Uniqueness and Growth', *Economic Journal*.

Garegnani, P., 1970, 'Heterogeneous Capital, the Production Function and the Theory of Distribution', *Review of Economic Studies*.

Ferguson, C. E. and Allen, R. F., 1970, 'Factor Prices, Commodity Prices, and Switches of Technique', *Western Economic Journal*.

Gallaway, L. and Shukla, V., 1974, 'The Neoclassical Production Function', *American Economic Review*.

Sato, K., 1976, 'The Neoclassical Production Function: Comment', *American Economic Review*.

Garegnani, P., 1976, 'The Neoclassical Production Function: Comment', *American Economic Review*.

Before going into the details of the proofs and arguments that made up the debate, and the methodological analysis, I will offer some help to the reader in understanding what I will talk about. For that purpose I give a brief exposition, in Chapter 1, of what the debate is about, namely reswitching and capital reversing. This is followed, in Chapter 2, by a sketch of the theoretical background of the debate, what Popperians call the problem situation of the economists who started it.

Notes

1 Alternatively known as *enkekalymmenos* or 'the veiled one'. Although this is usually called a logical fallacy, it is an epistemological allegory, as Steven Saylor's Hieronymus correctly points out. Cf. Saylor (2000: 167).

2 Another symptom of Robinson's confusion is the fact that in her book on capital accumulation (Robinson 1956) she calls particular phenomena anomalies in the framework of the same theory that she uses to explain them. See Chapter 3 below. One should have thought that the objective of explanations is to divest phenomena of their anomalous character.

3 Cf. Lakatos (1976: 143, n. 2).

4 Cf. Lakatos (1978: 87).

5 See Popper (1967).

6 The whole of Popper's philosophy of science may be considered to be an exercise in situational analysis.

7 The distinction between global and local as I use it in the present context is related, though not identical, to the use that Lakatos makes of it in *Proofs and Refutations* (Lakatos 1976).

8 Cf. Harcourt (1972: 119): 'The controversies arise because of political and ideological differences between the two sides . . . .'

9 There is nothing to exclude the possibility that scientists who are working in different theoretical traditions or who belong to different research programmes discuss the same local problems; or that on the basis of the same local results they come to entirely different global conclusions. It also happens that scientists from the same theoretical background find different solutions to local problems. Chapter 10 discusses an instance of this, the exchange between Sato, and Gallaway and Shukla.

10 On the point of the barrenness of an exclusively ideological analysis, I am in basic agreement with Hahn: 'To make matters worse the controversy has been overlaid by ideological clap-trap: the neoclassical theorist is said to be justifying the status quo while his opponent is the harbinger of progress. This makes good after-dinner conversation, but hinders serious progress and study . . . . The thing to do is to get the purely technical argument right.' (Hahn 1972: 2).

11 See, for instance, Popper (1976, Chapter 29).

12 This is a different distinction from the almost homonymous distinction that is used to separate scientific from non-scientific (for instance social) influences.

13 Cf. Halévy (1972: 272).

14 P. xix of Say (1880), which is the American translation of the 4th edition of the *Traité*.

15 Say (1880: xxvi, emphasis added). Say uses the Newtonian expression 'deducing consequences from facts' frequently. For an excellent discussion of Newton's method, see Worrall (2000).

16 Hintikka and Remes (1974: 110).

17 For an excellent history of the method, see Randall (1961) and Randall (1962, Vol. i, Book 2, II).

18 These are my translations of Wieser's 'isolierende' and 'hervorhebende Abstraktion'. See Wieser (1914: 134–5).

19 This classification cannot be found explicitly in Menger. It is the result of a reconstruction of his methodology. Cf. Birner (1990), part of which is reproduced in the text.

20 This idea is still widely diffused. Cf. 'This difficult phase of idealization and abstraction precedes the construction of any theory and any attempt to explanations . . .' (M. Piattelli-Palmarini, 1998, 'Introduction' to J. Uriagereke, *Rhyme and Reason. An Introduction to Minimalist Syntax*, MIT Press). One of my conclusions will be that idealizations are not established before a theory is constructed, but that the identification of idealizations and theory development go hand in hand.

21 Cf. Menger (1883: 34–5).

22 In Harcourt (1972) and a number of later publications. See the Bibliography.

23 And not necessarily in the order in which they will be discussed. In the case studies, the notation of the original articles will be taken over as much as possible to make it easier to refer back to the originals.

1 A brief exposition of reswitching and capital reversing

[O]n this problem, the whole theory of capital seems to have been caught in the trap of an old mode of thinking.

Pasinetti (1966: 516)

Pathology illuminates healthy physiology.

Samuelson (1966: 582)

1 A warning

Hindsight, 'that most important of all the instruments of the historian' (Finley 1977: 104–5), enables us to show in a few paragraphs what took economists, some of them the best of the profession, years to discover. That is an advantage for us now. But a brief exposition of these matters also carries a danger with it. It may falsify the historical picture to such an extent that, no matter how much time and effort is spent on the details of the actual development of the reswitching and capital reversing debate, the reader will remain permanently blinded. While I am convinced that it is important to give the reader as good an impression as possible of what was involved in the debate, I first want to spend a couple of lines in an effort to diminish that danger.

Reswitching and capital reversing are phenomena, or, rather, theoretical possibilities, which are often said to contradict certain fundamental propositions of neoclassical production and capital theory. This may easily create the impression that all of these propositions had been clearly spelled out. This, however, was not the case. The very debate in which these phenomena were introduced and developed, mainly by critics of neoclassical economics, forced neoclassical economists to decide which propositions they considered to be typically neoclassical. The debate even served to make a distinction within the class of propositions considered, or discovered, to be characteristic of neoclassical production and capital theory: those that were predictions of that theory, and those that had the status of axioms or assumptions. So, when I speak about characteristic propositions of neoclassical production and capital theory in this chapter, I can only do so because the debate helped us reconstruct a more or less coherent outline of that theory.

Sometimes the names of John Bates Clark and Frank P. Ramsey are mentioned as economists in whose work we can actually find the theory in a complete form.

This may or may not be the case. In this chapter I am not concerned with matters of history, development, or methodology. Rather, I want to clarify some of the issues that were at stake, and how they hang together. The debate centred on one particular type of model, a two-sector fixed-coefficients production model with heterogeneous capital. I will first describe the model and some of the associated assumptions, and then show how some of the characteristic propositions of neo-classical production theory follow from it. This should provide the reader with a frame of reference for understanding what the phenomena that lent their name to the debate are counterexamples against. Only at that stage will the phenomena themselves be introduced.

2 The model[1]

There are two factors of production, labour (L) and capital (K), and two products, consumer goods (C) and capital goods or machinery (M). It is assumed that both factors are fully employed. This gives

$$a_{LM}M + a_{LC}C = L, \tag{1}$$

$$a_{KM}M + a_{KC}C = K, \tag{2}$$

which says that the labour needed for producing machines, a_{LM}, plus the labour for producing consumer goods, a_{LC}, is equal to the total amount of labour, and the capital needed for producing machines, a_{KM}, plus the capital needed for producing consumer goods, a_{KC}, equals the total quantity of capital.

Capital and labour are applied in fixed proportions to obtain one particular level of output. The technical production functions, sometimes called 'activities', for capital and consumer goods that together define one particular technique are

$$M = \min\left(\frac{1}{a_{KM}}K_M, \frac{1}{a_{LM}}L_M\right), \tag{3}$$

$$C = \min\left(\frac{1}{a_{KC}}K_C, \frac{1}{a_{LC}}L_C\right). \tag{4}$$

A different level of output may be produced by choosing a different proportion of capital and labour in either sector. This is tantamount to using a different production technique, involving a different capital good (hence the heterogeneity of capital).

Different techniques, sometimes called 'blueprints', are described by the same equations with different values for the input (or production) coefficients. The entire range of techniques is sometimes called 'the book of blueprints'; it is the set of all pairs of production functions for capital and consumer goods that differ by at least one input coefficient.

Introducing factor prices w (the wage rate) and r (the rate of profit) and product prices p_M and p_C, and assuming perfect competition so that production cost equals output price, yields

$$a_{LM}wM + a_{KM}rp_MM = p_MM, \tag{5}$$

$$a_{LC}wC + a_{KC}rp_MC = p_CC. \tag{6}$$

Without loss of generality we may take the price of consumer goods as the numéraire ($p_C = 1$; as there is only one price variable left, the subscript M may be dropped from p_M), and we may rewrite the equations in costs and prices per unit:

$$a_{LM}w + a_{KM}rp = p, \tag{7}$$

$$a_{LC}w + a_{KC}rp = 1. \tag{8}$$

This is the basic model describing a technique of production. It is assumed that it describes an economy in stationary equilibrium, i.e. no growth, the rate of interest is equal to the rate of profit, and the value of total output is entirely absorbed by the factor shares. Depreciation is disregarded, i.e. it is assumed that capital goods are infinitely durable. Given the assumptions, and assuming that net output of a technique consists of one product only, net final (or national) product per head equals[2]

$$\frac{C}{L_C} = w + \frac{K_C}{L_C}rp,$$

or

$$q = w + rpk, \quad \text{with } q = C/L_C \text{ and } k = K_C/L_C. \tag{9}$$

As will be shown shortly, the model is used to analyze the choice of production techniques, the relation between the rate of profit and the capital intensity of the production technique, and the relation between the rate of profit and the net final product (i.e. the net output of the consumer good) per head. It may also be used to derive a more usual type of production function, one which relates the output of consumer goods per worker (or net final product) to the amount of capital per worker.

The relative capital intensity of the two production sectors is measured by $(a_{LM}/a_{KM})/(a_{LC}/a_{KC})$.

From the model we may derive the relation between w and r:

$$w = \frac{1 - a_{KM}r}{a_{LC} + Dr}, \tag{10}$$

where $D = a_{LM}a_{KC} - a_{LC}a_{KM}$ is the determinant of the coefficient matrix:

$$\begin{vmatrix} a_{LM} & a_{KM} \\ a_{LC} & a_{KC} \end{vmatrix}.$$

This relation is central to the entire analysis, especially in its graphical representation. It is drawn in Figure 1.1 for the case where both sectors have equal factor intensities ($D = 0$).

The intercept with the w-axis is $1/a_{LC} = w_{max}$, the net output of the consumption good per head or labour productivity C/L_C. When $r = 0$, all output goes to wages, and $q = w_{max}$ (see (9)). Given the assumption of stationary equilibrium

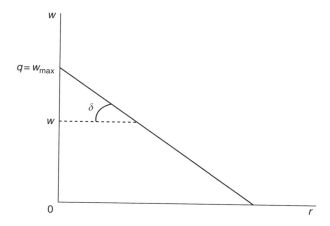

Figure 1.1 The fundamental relationship.

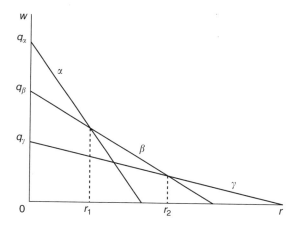

Figure 1.2 Several production techniques.

and the existence of one consumption good, $q = w_{max} = 1/a_{LC}$ for all r. I will call the w–r graph for one technique the wage-profit frontier or wpf. The wpf is always downward sloping ($dw/dr < 0$). Each technique of production has its own wpf.

The value of capital per head pk, or the capital intensity of a production technique may be read off the graph as follows. From (9)

$$pk = \frac{q - w}{r}, \quad \text{which equals tg } \delta. \tag{11}$$

When there are several techniques, as in Figure 1.2, profit maximization (which is assumed) ensures that at each wage rate that technique is chosen which forms the outer boundary or envelope WPF of all wpfs. So, if the economy goes through a sequence of values of r, starting from 0, there is a rate of profit (r_1) beyond which technique β is the profit maximizing technique instead of α. Beyond r_2 the profit maximizing production technique is γ. So, the previous statement becomes: When r rises, the economy switches from technique α to β to γ. For stylistic reasons I will continue to speak in terms of changes ('r rises', 'the economy switches'), although this is not justified. The model only compares stationary states and does not describe processes.

3   Characteristic propositions of neoclassical production theory

We now demonstrate a number of characteristic propositions of neoclassical production theory. They are:

1   When the rate of interest changes monotonically, a technique of production that had been profit maximizing never reappears after a switch to another technique has taken place. Figure 1.3(a) shows that technique α is followed by β which is followed by γ. Neither α nor β returns.
2   There is an inverse relation between the rate of interest r and the capital intensity of production in value terms pk. Figure 1.3(b) shows that as r rises, capital intensity decreases.
3   There is an inverse relation between the rate of interest r and output or net final product per head (see Figure 1.3(c)).
4   The production function relating the value of capital per head pk to the value of net output q is *well behaved*, i.e. to each value of pk corresponds only one value of q (in other words, $q = f(pk)$ is a function). Figure 1.3(d) shows the production function to be well behaved. The arrows indicate the rise in r.

4   Perversities and anomalies

In demonstrating the neoclassical case, it was assumed that both sectors of production have the same capital intensity (the ratio of their factor proportions is the same). If this is the case, the determinant of the coefficient matrix $D = 0$ and the wpf is linear (as may be seen from (10)). If there is a technique of production that does not operate with equal factor proportions, the wpf is no longer linear. I assume that in technique β production in the capital good sector is more capital intensive than production in the consumer good sector. This implies[3] a wpf for β as drawn in Figure 1.4(a). If the corresponding graphs are drawn for the pk–r, q–r and q–pk relations, we see that these are different from those showing the characteristic propositions of neoclassical production theory. This is why these relations were initially called anomalous and perverse: they are counterexamples to the typical neoclassical relations.

Figure 1.4(a) (where only two techniques are shown to maintain a clear picture) shows that as r rises from 0 to r_1 technique, α yields the maximum profit rate given

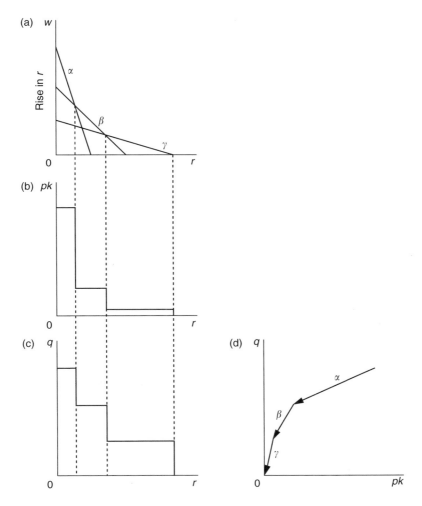

Figure 1.3(a)–(d) Switches of techniques and the well-behaved production function.

each wage rate. Beyond r_1, technique β is the profit maximizing technique. But for $r > r_2$ the production switches back to technique α: a case of reswitching.

The fall in capital intensity which takes place at r_1 in Figure 1.4(b) is what neoclassical production theory was expected to predict: with a rise in the interest rate, capital intensity decreases. But when r rises further from r_1 to r_2, capital intensity increases. This is called capital reversing or reverse capital deepening. For $r > r_2$, capital intensity returns to its former level, which shows that there is no unique relation between r and pk (in other words, there is no capital intensity uniqueness).

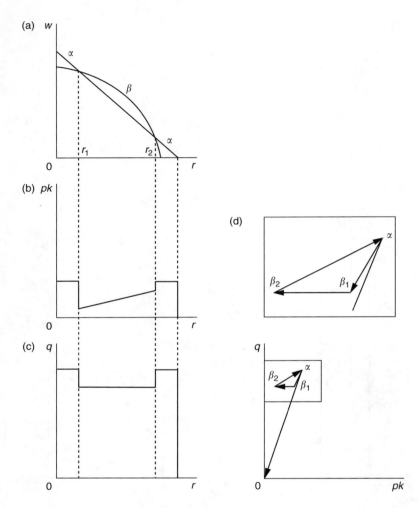

Figure 1.4(a)–(d) Switches of techniques and the naughty production function.

Figure 1.4(c) shows a 'dip' in the standard of living (net final product per head) as r rises above r_1, which is not in accordance with original neoclassical expectations. At r_2 net final product per head rises again.

Figure 1.4(d), finally, shows that the production function is multiple valued, which, again, is not in accordance with one of the characteristic propositions of neoclassical production theory. As r rises (indicated by the arrows) from 0, the values of the pair $\langle pk, q \rangle$ go through a sequence from α to β_1 to β_2 back to α and to the origin. Given the production techniques as drawn in Figure 1.4(a), the production function is not a function.

Notes

1 The basic model is as described in Ferguson (1969, Chapter 12). The graphs follow the elegant presentation of Compaijen (1981, Chapter 5), who follows the exposition of Bliss (1975). A similar exposition may be found in Harcourt (1972). Notice that in the next chapters, when discussing the various articles, I will take over the original notation. This makes it possible for the reader to refer quickly to the original publications, while it allows of a detailed discussion of what the authors are trying to do.

2 From (6) and the definition of $a_{LC} = L_C/C$ and $a_{KC} = K_C/C$, and $p_C = 1$.

3 For a proof, see Ferguson (1969: 262).

2 The background of the debate
Some history

> The more precise capital theory became, the more static it became; the study of equilibrium conditions only resulted in the study of stationary conditions.
> Hicks (1965: 47)

Either reswitching or capital reversing, or both, had been noticed earlier,[1] without, however, becoming the subject of a debate. It was not until the 1950s[2] that these phenomena began to be promoted to the prominent position they occupied in the discussions in capital theory in the 1960s and part of the 1970s. This was due to a change in the theoretical background in economics. This change in context was the renewed interest in economic growth. Keynes' *General Theory* had virtually dominated the stage ever since it was published in 1936. But Keynes' theory is a theory of the short period, i.e. it does not deal with the causes and consequences of changes in the capital stock. The neglect of the long run had been the focus of the criticism by Keynes' main opponent during the 1930s, F. A. Hayek. But the sweeping success of the *General Theory* pushed this criticism into the background.[3]

Nevertheless, Joan Robinson, who was very close to Keynes, made it her explicit goal to develop a theory of the long run which was to embed or encompass the short-run *General Theory* of Keynes.[4] What she envisaged was a theory of growth, though in a comparative static framework, with features that she derived from the work of Harrod. In view of her expressed intention to develop such a theory and the sequence of publications actually developing it, we may speak of a research programme.

1 Robinson's research programme

Robinson started work on her programme in the same year in which the *General Theory* was published. In one of her *Essays in the Theory of Employment* (1936), 'The Long-Period Theory of Employment', she writes:

> Mr. Keynes' General Theory of Employment has been developed mainly in terms of short-period analysis, and the background of equilibrium theory which corresponds to it is largely unexplored. The purpose of this essay is to

outline a method by which Mr. Keynes' system of analysis may be extended into the regions of the long period and by which it may become possible to examine the long-period influences which are at work at any moment of time.

(Robinson 1936: 75)

But if we are to go by Robinson's own later comment, this and other early essays were still in the 'wrong' methodological tradition: static analysis.[5] Though she kept using static analysis, she later observes that the publications between 1933 and 1946 'already expose . . . the weakness of the analysis' (Robinson 1975: viii).

'The Generalisation of the General Theory', of 1952, was, according to Robinson, her first attempt to break away from the static framework, though she later observes that 'it does not really belong to the new dynamics; it was only an attempt to expand a point – the meaning of liquidity preference – that Keynes had left in a primitive state.' (ibid.: iii). However, if we look at the article, we can see that it contains more than a discussion of liquidity preference. It is about the rate of profit in a growing economy, a growing stock of capital and growing technical knowledge.[6]

'The Production Function and the Theory of Capital' (Robinson 1953) was the preparation of Robinson's second attempt to formulate a non-static theory of capital accumulation: 'The defect of my "The Generalisation of the General Theory" was the lack of an adequate conception of the rate of profit and of its relation to the choice of technique . . . . To prepare for a second attempt . . . , I raised the question of the meaning of a quantity of capital as a fund of finance or as a stock of equipment.' (Robinson 1975: vi). That second attempt was *The Accumulation of Capital*, of 1956.[7]

All of these publications were very critical of neoclassical long-run capital theory, and more specifically of the way in which it dealt with capital. Robinson's main points of criticism concerned the neoclassical concept of equilibrium and the inability of marginal value theory to explain relative factor shares[8] and hence the functional distribution of income.

In 'The Production Function and the Theory of Capital' of 1953, Robinson noticed for the first time the possibility of reswitching and capital reversing. She even *explained* capital reversing as the result of differences in the time patterns of investment processes. But she did not draw the conclusion from this that the phenomena could better be dealt with in the framework of a dynamic theory. Instead, both in 1953 and 1956 she dismissed them as exceptions and curiosa.

Robinson was not the only author who failed to break out of a static framework and pursue a process-oriented line of analysis further; everyone else did so. The models used in capital and growth theory were comparative-static.[9] It is only with hindsight, long after the debate was over, that Robinson herself, and also Bliss, Solow and Burmeister, came to the conclusion that these were not suited for analysing processes, which, after all, are dynamic phenomena. Thus, Solow writes:

> Granted that the parable about high capital intensity and high steady-state consumption going along with a low rate of interest is only a parable, it

appears to be in the spirit of the underlying theory – what underlies the failure of the parable? The best answer I know is Bliss': The theory gives no warrant to compare steady states. Steady states that appear to be neighboring may come at the end of histories that are not neighboring at all.[10]

(Solow 1983: 184)

In an interview with the author,[11] Solow declined to acknowledge Robinson's role in pointing this out. Instead, he named Bliss as the first to make this clear. When confronted with the fact that Robinson mentions this criticism from a very early stage on, he replied that she had so many points of criticism that it was not even clear to herself that the dynamic–static criticism was the most important. So, Solow implicitly endorses the sleepwalker thesis.[12]

Let us turn to another source, Burmeister:

The relevant dynamic choices open to an economy . . . *cannot* be analyzed using the models discussed in this chapter, because the latter are all constructed assuming steady-state equilibria. This unrealistic and restrictive assumption is the basis for misunderstandings about certain 'paradoxical' results which . . . are no longer so surprising when we begin by asking the appropriate economic questions.

(Burmeister 1980: 154)

However, this was not perceived to be the major problem in the 1950s and 1960s, even though Robinson occasionally criticizes the use of comparative statics for analyzing processes in time. Nobody – and that includes Robinson herself – pursued work on diachronic or intertemporal models, even though these had been available since the 1930s, and despite the fact that these might have provided a scaffolding for the development of dynamic models. The best known of these is part of Hayek's theory of capital and the closely related theory of the business cycle. They were developed within a diachronic general equilibrium framework, and were explicitly meant to be extended to fully fledged dynamic theories. (Hayek 1941: 39–40).[13]

It is tempting to speculate that, if there had been a debate about reswitching and capital reversing in the 1950s at all, it would have taken a different course if Robinson's explanation and her criticism of comparative statics had been taken seriously, by others and also by herself, and a diachronic apparatus of analysis had been adopted. However, at the time the debate was not influenced by these considerations. Hindsight usually is very different from the perspective of sleepwalkers, and rational reconstruction is not the same as instant rationality.

2   Discontinuities in the recent history of economic thought

We can only conjecture why a diachronic framework was not introduced at this early stage. In the case of Robinson it may have been that she feared that choosing a diachronic framework might re-introduce the conception of saving as postponed consumption, which Keynes' *General Theory* criticized as one of the fundamental flaws of neoclassical theory. This would hardly have been in the spirit of her attempts to generalize the *General Theory*. Another possible reason for the neglect of dynamic theory was that the article by Samuelson (1962) which (as we shall see) was instrumental in getting the debate started, stated as one of its purposes the intention to provide a theoretical justification for the empirical growth models that were being developed and estimated in the 1950s and 1960s; these models were comparative-static, not dynamic.[14]

These are conjectures that have to do with the content of economic theories. But there are also methodological reasons. For one thing, it took some participants in the debate so long to come to their conclusion about the inadequacy of comparative statics because the capital theory debate in economics, like most debates in most sciences, evolved on the local level where formal puzzles are solved within the analytical framework that was introduced into the debate (partly as a matter of contingency). This apparatus of analysis dominated the discussion even to the extent that it dictated the questions that could be asked locally. These were not necessarily the same as the global questions that gave rise to the debate. While on the one hand local activities provide the momentum for the development of scientific disciplines, the very local character of the business of science may act as a restriction on global development.

That this is not unusual is illustrated by Solow's work. In the early 1950s he began to study economic growth both along theoretical and empirical lines. As was the case with Robinson, it was Harrod who was among those who inspired his work.[15] But Solow was not satisfied with Harrod's growth model, because it assumed that the rate of saving, the rate of growth of the labour force, and the capital–output ratio were constants, or at least exogenously determined: 'The saving rate was a fact about preferences; the growth rate of labor supply was a demographic-sociological fact; the capital–output ratio was a technological fact.' (Solow 1988: 307). Solow's feelings of uneasiness about these 'facts' might have led him straight back to the debates of the 1930s, more specifically to Hayek's theory of capital and the business cycle. Time preference and the variations of the capital–output ratio are key *variables* in this theory. Only the growth of the labour supply is abstracted from. However, there is no evidence in Solow's work that he looked to that period for inspiration. He was so busy solving local, largely technical and econometric problems, that he did not take time off to look back.[16]

A second reason for the long delay has to do with the relation between idealizing theories and associated models of a lower level of abstraction. One of the main conclusions of this book will be that this is a relation that as a matter of logic does not allow test results obtained with models of a lower level of abstraction (or a lower degree of idealization) to serve as refutations of models of higher levels of abstraction (degrees of idealization). This is because more highly idealized models are logically entailed by, but do not logically entail, less idealizing models. At this point I can no more than mention this. The arguments will be given in Chapter 12.

Notes

1 Ricardo (1821), 'On Machinery'; Wicksell (1923 and 1954). Also Hayek (1941, Chapters XXI and XXVII); Hayek (1942); cf. McManus (1963). According to Vellupillai (1975), also Fisher (1907).
2 In Robinson (1953 and 1956), and in Champernowne (1953).
3 For attempts to analyse the 1930's controversy between Keynes and Hayek, see Birner (1985) and (1997).
4 So, she shared Hayek's concern of the 1930s. But she did not share his diachronic general equilibrium framework. This seems to be the main point of difference between Robinson's theory of capital and Hayek's, which are otherwise very similar. The similarity extends to both authors' methodologies.
5 Cf. Robinson (1975). Sraffa made it clear that there was a 'profound inconsistency between the static base and the dynamic superstructure' in Marshall (p. vii). Robinson says: 'At this point, it seems to me now that I took the wrong turning.... Instead of abandoning the static analysis and trying to come to terms with Marshall's theory of development, I followed Pigou and worked out the *Economics of Imperfect Competition* [1930] on static assumptions.' (pp. vii–viii).
6 Liquidity preference (and the liquidity trap) are part of her criticism of the idea that a flexible wage rate is a remedy for unemployment. The article further contains a discussion of monetary policy and its limitations as a remedy for unemployment, and of the bottlenecks for growth, for the analysis of which Robinson introduces the concept of a golden age. She finds this a useful device for discovering the possible 'vicissitudes' to which the system may be subject. These comprise changes in thriftiness, the supply of labour, land or finance, the rate of interest, prices and tastes, and the most important source of disturbances: changes of technique. Other features of the article are the discussions of 'fossils': the past history of accumulation determines future development by influencing expectations; and of the idea that there are no built-in stabilizers. It is tempting to see in the former the influence of Hayek, and in the latter the influence of Harrod.
7 The next, third, step in the development of Robinson's thought did not take place until 1974. Cf. Robinson (1979: 4). I will return to this later.
8 Or the impossibility of reducing factor rewards to marginal factor productivities without residue.
9 This is one of the obstacles to a further development of growth theory that Hahn and Matthews mention in their 1964 survey.
10 Solow's unwillingness to acknowledge Robinson is all the stranger as he uses almost literally her words. Cf. for example Robinson (1971b: 103–4).
11 On 20 April 1989.
12 Cf. also Solow (1983: 180–5).
13 Hayek himself got stuck, too, in a special case of his own fully fledged production model. But that special case at least involved time, though in a way that is too limited. Cf. Birner (1999).
14 In the 1940s the Cowles Commission had succeeded in suppressing – temporarily at any rate – process analysis in econometrics. See Morgan (1989).
15 The others Solow mentions in his Nobel lecture are Evsey Domar and Arthur Lewis. See Solow (1988: 307).
16 In view of the prominent place the journals had given to the Hayek–Knight debate on the question of whether or not the quantity of capital is a technological datum, it is quite surprising to find Solow pronouncing: 'I cannot tell you why I thought first of replacing the constant capital–output (and labor–output) ratio by a richer and more realistic representation of the technology.' (Solow 1988: 308). There is, however, another explanation of Solow's neglect of Hayek's work, one that is more in line with Koestler's psychological approach. In an interview with the author (20 April 1989), Solow admitted that

he knew Hayek's *Prices and Production*: 'I did read Hayek as a student . . . I found it completely incomprehensible. I was assigned to read *Prices and Production* . . . [It was] not that I thought it was wrong so much as I did not understand it . . . I thought there's got to be something wrong with the man who could write that. And I never read any [other work of Hayek's], I simply found it incomprehensible.'

3 Clouds in the neoclassical sky

> We cannot abandon the production function without an effort to rescue the element of common-sense that has been entangled in it.
>
> Robinson (1953: 83)

In the process of developing her research programme, Robinson came across some results that led her to criticize the way in which neoclassical economics used the aggregate production function. It was this criticism that in the end led Samuelson to write the article that is generally considered to be instrumental in getting the debate started. Samuelson's role will be discussed later. This chapter concentrates on contributions by Robinson and Champernowne that preceded the actual debate. In the next chapter the case studies will be used for drawing up a first inventory of the methodological issues and means of analysis.

1 Robinson defines the problem

In 'The Production Function and the Theory of Capital' (Robinson 1953), Robinson argues that the relationships that are crucial for a theory of the long run are those among output, the supply of factors of production, and the state of technical knowledge. This is what neoclassical theory has to say about them:

1 The availability of capital determines the amount of it that is used in producing output.
2 For the analysis of these relations, some concept of equilibrium is needed.
3 In the long run, the rate of real wages tends to be such that all available labour is employed.
4 Technical progress may be incorporated in the equilibrium conditions.

Robinson says that as intuitions these ideas are sound. What she criticizes is the way in which neoclassics translate them into theory. In particular, the instruments they use for analyzing the relationships, namely the production function and a particular notion of equilibrium, are not only not up to their task, they are outright wrong. The production function makes use of capital as a factor of production, a particular quantity of which is employed as an input. Neoclassical theory does not indicate how capital is to be measured. This may not be a serious problem for analyzing the short term, when labour has to work with a given quantity of capital. But for long-term analysis the measurement, and more specifically the valuation, of capital poses serious problems. Yet these are not taken seriously by neoclassical economists. They go on using capital as an argument in their production functions as if no such problems existed.

There are three ways of measuring 'physical capital', in the sense of 'the specific list of all the goods in existence at any moment' (Robinson 1953: 81), that make it susceptible to economic analysis: in terms of future earnings, current purchasing power, and past costs. When we know the rate of output, future product prices, and the rate of interest, then we can value a capital good as the discounted future earnings which it will yield. This, however, is not in accordance with the production function approach, because 'we have to begin by taking the rate of interest as given, whereas the main purpose of the production function is to show how wages and the rate of interest . . . are determined by technical conditions and the factor ratio.' (ibid.). The alternative way of valuing capital as the labour cost expended on it in the past (in 'labour units') accords better with the spirit of the production function, 'for it corresponds to the essential nature of capital regarded as a factor of production' (ibid.: 82). But here we run into the difficulty that all labour in the past was assisted by some goods. So, the cost of capital includes the cost of capital goods, and interest enters into the value of capital. The same is true when capital is measured by its current purchasing power, as this is dependent on expected future earnings, hence on the rate of interest.

Still, if we want to analyze the effect that a change in the factor ratio has on output, we need to know the wage rate in terms of output, whether we measure capital in terms of its product or in labour units. But the wage rate changes with the factor ratio. So, even measuring capital in labour units does not give us an independent measure of capital. Despite these difficulties, the problem the tool of the production function was designed to solve is not a pseudo-problem. It is the relation between the availability of capital and the use that is made of it: Therefore, '[w]e cannot abandon the production function without an effort to rescue the element of common-sense that has been entangled in it.' (ibid.: 83). Robinson attempts to solve the problem as follows. In order to be able to handle the 'enormous who's who' (ibid.) of individual pieces of capital equipment, it has to be expressed as a quantity. But the different measures, real cost of production, purchasing power, and future productivity do not give the same value of capital unless the current rate of profit is the one that was expected to rule when the equipment was constructed and the one that will be ruling in the future. Only then are the past costs compounded and the future receipts discounted at the same rate of interest. The coinciding of expected with realized values is the definition of long-period equilibrium.

The assumption that the economy is in equilibrium is a useful device for examining the relations among the quantity of capital, the labour force, and technology.[1] But that is all the notion of equilibrium is: a theoretical construct that has definite limits to its use. Neoclassical theory oversteps these boundaries by thinking of equilibrium as a state towards which the economy is moving. Robinson consistently criticizes this concept of equilibrium and the consequences of its use. Thus, she refuses to think of *substitution* of capital for labour in a literal sense. All that we can do is to compare two states of the economy with different factor ratios.

Quantity of capital

Robinson measures the stock of capital goods, i.e. 'physical capital' in her terminology, in wage units. In equilibrium, the *value* of physical capital in terms of output, which Robinson designates simply by 'capital', equals the cost of the wage bill expended in the past compounded at the rate of interest. This capital measure in wage units is called 'real capital'.

It is useful to put these relations into formulas.[2] Output is assumed to be divided without residue between factors of production:

$$Q = wL_c + rK, \tag{1}$$

where Q is output, w is the wage rate, L_c is current labour, r is the rate of profit and K is capital. Thus, capital measured in terms of the rate of output, or 'capital' in Robinson's terms, is

$$K = (Q - wL_c)/r. \tag{2}$$

Capital in wage units, or 'real capital' (K_r), is

$$K_r = wL_p(1 + i)^t, \tag{3}$$

where L_p is the labour input t periods ago required to produce a unit of capital equipment and i is the rate of interest. In long-period equilibrium, which is assumed throughout Robinson's analysis, $i = r$, and[3]

$$K = K_r \cdot w \tag{4}$$

and

$$K_r = K/w = L_p(1 + i)^t. \tag{5}$$

Technique of production

Robinson examines the relations among the labour force, the amount of capital, and the state of technology. What the labour force is and how it is measured, is not considered to be problematic by her. For the quantity of capital she has devised the wage unit measure. The problem that remains is: 'How can we reduce the amorphous conception of "state of technical knowledge" to definite terms?' (ibid.: 90). This question is answered step by step, by making a number of assumptions. The first three steps concern technical assumptions.

First, it is supposed that a list is drawn up of the various techniques that produce different quantities of a particular commodity with a given quantity of labour currently employed and that are such that the capital equipment is maintained intact. It is assumed that 'a technique involving a longer production period (from clipping the sheep to selling the overcoat) requires a larger run-out of man hours embodied in work-in-progress. This is treated as part of the stock of capital goods required by this technique.' (ibid.). *Second*, it is assumed that the composition of the flow of output is constant and that for every volume of the flow of a given composition there exist subsets of the set of production techniques that produce it: 'We thus have a set of blue prints of techniques, each of which could be used to employ a given amount of labour to produce a flow of output.' (ibid.). The *third* step involves ordering the techniques according to the rate of output per man currently employed.

So far, only technical considerations are involved. In the *fourth* step the economic aspect is introduced by paying attention to the efficiency of techniques: 'The individual capitalist is assumed to choose between possible techniques in such a way as to maximise the surplus of output that a given amount of capital yields over wage cost in terms of his own product, and thus to obtain the highest rate of profit on capital that the available techniques make possible.' (ibid.: 92).[4] The cost of capital in wage units includes interest charges. The hierarchy of techniques is now reexamined to make sure that 'we are nowhere using more capital [in wage units] to produce less product.'(ibid.: 91). All techniques are ordered according to their capital costs in wage units *at the same rate of interest*. Robinson states without argument or proof that a high rate of output per man is associated with a greater quantity of real capital per man.

The result of the fourth step may be shown in Figure 3.1. Along the y-axis the techniques are ordered according to rate of output and indicated by A, B, C, D. The amount of real capital is measured along the x-axis.

In Robinson's notation the ordered triple of corresponding Greek and Latin letters $\langle \gamma, c, C \rangle$ indicates $\langle$production technique (also called 'plant'), amount of real capital, rate of output$\rangle$.

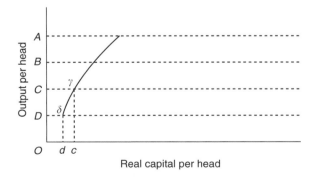

Figure 3.1 The productivity curve at a constant interest rate (source: Robinson 1956: 412).

Assuming the rate of interest to be constant and the labour force to be fully employed with an amount *Od* of real capital, output, which is at that point entirely produced by technique δ, can only be increased by replacing some δ-plants by more productive γ-plants. As the more productive γ-technique uses more capital by assumption, the substitution of γ- for δ-plants involves an increase in the amount of real capital. From *Od* to *Oc* output is produced by a mix of δ- and γ-plants. At *Oc*, output is entirely produced by γ-technique. The curve that relates output to real capital at the same rate of interest is the *productivity curve*. It indicates the set of equi-profitable techniques that yield different outputs.

In the *fifth* step the assumption of a constant rate of interest is released. Varying the interest rate means that the cost of all production techniques changes. It may even produce changes in the original ordering of techniques according to costs.[5] Thus, two techniques whose output–capital ratios differed by a small amount only at one rate of interest may be separated by a wide gap at a slightly higher interest rate. It is also possible that two techniques that were widely separated may find themselves close together for a slightly higher or lower interest rate. Such results may be caused by the different time profiles of the techniques involved. Techniques may even disappear altogether:

> For example, if the man hours required to construct a plant appropriate to Gamma technique are spread over a long time, or are heavily concentrated at the beginning of the gestation period, while those required to construct a Beta plant [which has a higher output per man than Gamma] are spread over a short time or are bunched near the moment of completion, or if a Gamma plant is more durable, so that the average age of the items making up a balanced outfit of plants is greater, a rise in the rate of interest may raise Gamma's cost above Beta's. But Gamma's rate of output is lower. Thus at this notional rate of interest Gamma falls out of the hierarchy.
>
> (Robinson 1953: 91–2)

One change in the hierarchy is explicitly excluded:

> Techniques may appear or disappear in the list as the notional rate of interest alters, but two techniques can never reverse their position, for they were listed in the first place in order of rates of output with a given amount of current labour, and this is a purely engineering fact.
>
> (Robinson 1953: 92)

For each interest rate we can draw the productivity curve. The productivity curves for lower interest rates lie further to the left in Figure 3.2, which shows a comparative-static picture of different productivity curves that obtain at different rates of interest.

Robinson now attempts to analyze the process of changes in techniques consequent on changes in the wage rate. A change in the wage rate is concomitant with a change in the opposite direction in the rate of profit, as may be seen from

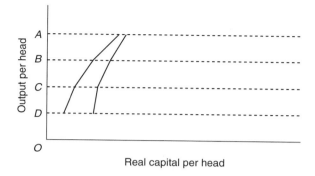

Figure 3.2 The productivity curves at different interest rates (adapted from Robinson 1953: 93).

(2): $dw/dr < 0$. In equilibrium, which is assumed, this affects the degree of mechanization or amount of real capital per head, as is shown in (4). The degree of mechanization is defined as the quantity of real capital per unit of labour currently employed (ibid.: 91), or K/wL_c. Thus, as the wage rate rises, the degree of mechanization is increased. The result of varying the wage rate is illustrated with a numerical example that is reproduced in Table 3.1.[6]

Table 3.1 Number of men per plant: 50

Plant	γ	β	α	γ	β	α
Wage rate	1	1	1	1.1	1.1	1.1
Capital	26	52	104	27.5	55	110
Product	55	60	65	55	60	65
Wage bill	50	50	50	55	55	55
Profit	5	10	15	0	5	10
Rate of profit (approximate)	19%	19%	14%	0	9%	9%

Wage rates and degrees of mechanization (reproduced from Robinson 1953: 93).

At a wage rate of 1, γ and β are equally profitable (at a profit rate of 19 per cent), so that output can only be increased by using ever more β-plants and fewer γ-plants. Capital is substituted for labour in the sense that the less mechanized[7] γ-plants are replaced by the more mechanized β-plants. Robinson warns against a false interpretation of this process if a constant labour force is assumed:

> This principle is usually described in a somewhat mystifying way in terms of a 'substitution of capital for labour' as the cost of labour rises. The essential point, however, is very simple. An Alpha plant involves a greater capital cost and yields a higher rate of output with a given amount of current labour than

a Beta plant. At a higher wage rate both plants yield a smaller profit per man employed than at a lower wage rate, but a given difference in the wage rate reduces the excess of output over wages (that is, profit) in a smaller proportion where output is higher.

(Robinson 1953: 92)

As the wage rate is gradually increased from 1 to 1.1, β remains the most profitable plant with rates of profit that vary from 19 to 9 per cent . At a wage rate of 1.1 and profit rate of 9 per cent, α becomes equally profitable with β, and producers are indifferent between using β and α.[8]

By extending calculations beyond the wage rate interval of 1 to 1.1 and by making the differences very small, we find pairs of values for w and r at which two subsequent techniques in the hierarchy yield the same, maximum rate of profit alternated by pairs of values at which only one technique yields the maximum profit rate. Lower rates of profit are associated with higher values of real capital. So, from $K_r = K/w = 52$ at a rate of profit of 19 per cent the value of real capital falls to $K_r = K/w = 55/1.1 = 50$ at a profit rate of 9 per cent.

On the basis of a table such as the above, a factor ratio curve can be drawn relating real capital per man currently employed to the rate of output per man (see Figure 3.3).

When we start from a production technique that yields the maximum profit rate at a given wage rate as represented by δ in Figure 3.3, output can only be increased by employing a certain number of γ-plants besides δ-plants. The amount of real capital and output rise, until we are at γ_1, where all output is produced by γ-technique. A further rise in the factor ratio and in output can now be obtained only by employing β-plants. This requires a rise in the wage rate. The rise in the wage rate lowers the rate of profit. We move to the left until we reach the rate of profit at which the producers are indifferent between using γ- and β-techniques. This is shown by the movement from γ_1 to γ_2. When we are at γ_2, output may be increased by substituting more productive β-plants for γ-plants.

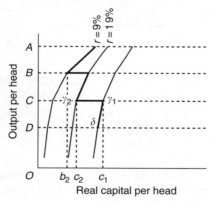

Figure 3.3 The factor ratio curve (based on Robinson 1953: 93).

At γ_2 the factor ratio is Oc_2 and the entire labour force is employed in γ-technique. The substitution of β-plants for γ-plants involves a rise in the factor ratio. At Ob_2 the entire labour force is employed in β.

> The relation between one curve and the next depends on the reaction of the cost of various outfits of equipment to differences in the rate of interest, and this depends, . . . in a complicated way, upon the gestation period and length of life of items of equipment. There is little to be said about it *a priori*, though *it is reasonable to suppose* that the most mechanized techniques are the most sensitive to the rate of interest . . . .
>
> (Robinson 1953: 94, emphasis added)

A note to this passage refers the reader to the Appendix for 'a "perverse" case which may occur when this is not true' (ibid.). The conclusion of the analysis is 'that the relation of capital to labour, in an equilibrium position, can be regarded as the resultant of the interaction of three distinct influences: the wage rate, the rate of interest and the degree of mechanisation.' (ibid.: 95).

Wicksell and interest effects

The influence that the wage rate and the rate of interest have on the capital–labour ratio is now examined in more detail. Two effects are distinguished. The *Wicksell effect* measures the influence of the wage rate on the value of capital in terms of output for the same technique. The higher the wage rate, the higher the value of capital in wage units (K_r) and the fewer the machines that can be bought with a given amount of product. As the Wicksell effect involves a higher wage rate and presupposes that there is no transition to a more mechanized technique (involving a lower labour–capital ratio), Robinson speaks of the workers benefiting from the Wicksell effect (ibid.: 96). The Wicksell effect is mitigated by the *interest effect*. A higher wage rate is associated not only with a higher value of capital but also with a lower rate of profit, and thus, in equilibrium, interest. But the interest rate enters into the cost of capital in wage units: $K/wL_c = L_p(1 + i)t/L_c$. So, the lower interest rate lowers the cost of capital.

Provided the Wicksell effect is not offset by the interest effect, a higher wage rate is in equilibrium associated with a more mechanized technique; this is named the 'Ricardesque effect', after Hayek's 'Ricardo effect'. As more of the product is going into investing in more mechanized techniques, less of it is left for the wage bill.[9] So, according to Robinson there is a conflict of interests: 'The more the capitalists have been able to take advantage of the Ricardesque effect, the less the workers have benefited from the Wicksell effect.' (ibid.).

We may show the two effects as follows. Taking logarithms of (3) and substituting r for i, we get

$$\ln K_r = \ln w + \ln L_p + t \ln(1 + r).$$

Totally differentiating this expression and remembering that L_p is constant and that $\ln(1 + r) = \ln r$ for small r, we get

$$\tilde{K}_r = \tilde{w} + t\tilde{r},$$

where $\sim$ denotes a relative change.

As w and r are positive and $dr/dw < 0$, $\tilde{w}$ and $\tilde{r}$ are inversely related. And this explains the possibilities of a perversity.

> It is evidently possible that the interest effect should also outweigh the Wicksell effect [i.e., $\tilde{w} < \tilde{r}$], so that the value of given physical capital in terms of product is smaller at a higher wage rate. This would occur if, first, the cost of capital goods in terms of wage units reacts strongly to changes in the rate of interest (their gestation period plus their working life is long), and second, the wage rate is already high relatively to output per man, so that a given rise in the wage rate produces a large proportionate fall in the share of profit in product, and so in the rate of profit on capital. . . . Where the interest effect more than offsets the Wicksell effect we see the apparently paradoxical result that a given amount of capital (in terms of product) provides a smaller amount of employment at a lower than at a higher wage rate.
>
> (Robinson 1953, emphasis added)

A footnote to this passage states: 'The rise in the wage rate entailed by the fall in the rate of interest must in most ordinary cases lead to a rise, on balance, in the cost of capital in terms of product, and cases in which the interest effect more than offsets the Wicksell effect *seem likely to be rather peculiar.*' (ibid.: n. 1, emphasis added). This is illustrated with a numerical example that shows that the relative fall in the cost of capital due to a relatively large change in the interest rate is quite small. When capital equipment is productive for a greater number of years, the interest effect is larger (the relative fall in the cost of equipment is greater), but its influence is likely to be reduced again when the greater cost of repair that is likely to be incurred with older equipment is taken into account.

In the Appendix the geometrical analysis is extended further. By assuming the productivity curves to be very close together (very small differences in the rate of profit), Robinson is able to draw a continuous factor ratio curve, which is shown in Figure 3.4. The tangents to the productivity curves at the points of intersection with the factor ratio curve intersect the y-axis in a point that measures the wage rate of the corresponding technique.[10]

In what seems like an attempt to downplay even further the importance of a non-normal relation between rate of output and factor ratio,[11] Robinson comments on this diagram: 'The geometry reveals a curious possibility.'[12] (ibid.: 106). This is not actually shown in a diagram, but Figure 3.5 is what she has in mind.

At higher wage rates, so at lower profit rates, the tangents to the productivity curves may get steeper and touch the productivity curves at lower levels of output. Then a lower rate of profit may be associated with a technique that has a lower

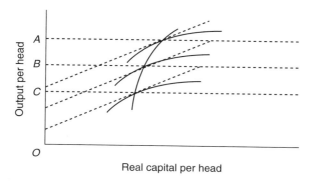

Figure 3.4 A continuous factor ratio curve (adapted from Wicksell 1954: 122).

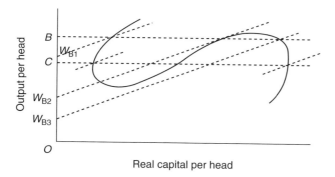

Figure 3.5 Robinson's ('Cohen's') curious curve (adapted from Robinson 1956: 93).

instead of a higher level of output (a lower degree of mechanization). This is the case when the wage rate in Figure 3.5 moves from W_{B2} to W_{B3}; the technique of production changes from the more mechanized β to the less mechanized γ (and then back to β again). This ' "perverse" behaviour of the factor ratio curve' is attributed to (i.e. explained by) a great interest sensitivity of the value of capital in wage units due to a long gestation period or working life of the equipment.

Robinson *proves* that the perverse behaviour ('where it occurs at all' (ibid.)) can only occur over a certain range of values of the interest rate:

> At very low values of the rate of interest the differential effect (as between techniques) must be small, so that there must be an upper range, on the way to Bliss, over which the factor ratio curve rises to the right as the rate of interest falls; and the degree of mechanisation must have reached a certain level before there is any scope for it to fall, so that there must be a lower range over which the factor ratio curve rises.

> (Robinson 1953: 106)

In other words, a 'perverse' trajectory of the factor ratio curve is always bounded from below and above by normal trajectories. Where the factor ratio curve falls to the left when the wage rate increases, there is a multiple equilibrium: three different wage rates, W_{B1}, W_{B2}, and W_{B3} in Figure 3.5, correspond to one technique, β.

Conclusion

Robinson considers the possibility of a multi-valued production function to be an anomaly. Yet, in her own model the association of a lower value of capital with a higher rate of interest is perfectly possible. It occurs when the interest effect outweighs the Wicksell effect. Robinson even *explains* this case *in straightforward economic terms*: it may be the consequence of a great interest sensitivity of the cost of capital. She observes that the interest sensitivity of the cost of capital may in its turn be explained by a long gestation period and a long working life, or to a high sensitivity of the rate of interest (or profit) to a change in the wage rate. The latter situation is likely to obtain at a very high wage rate. Moreover, Robinson *proves* that an anomalous stretch of the factor ratio curve is always bounded on both sides by a normal stretch. All this is consistent with her rather cautious judgment on the significance and consequences of the result. It is described in guarded terms such as 'apparently paradoxical' (ibid.: 96), 'a curious possibility'(ibid.: 106), and a scare-quoted 'perverse' (ibid.: 94). Robinson has such great doubts about the phenomenon that she fails to give a final judgment: 'A good deal of exploration of the possible magnitude and behaviour of the interest effect is needed before we can say whether the above is a mere theoretical rigmarole, or whether there is likely to be anything in reality corresponding to it.' (ibid.: 106).

2   Champernowne's solution

In 'The Production Function and the Theory of Capital: A Comment' (1953), Champernowne finds Robinson's proposal to measure the quantity of capital in wage units (he calls them 'labour units' or 'J.R. units') not 'convenient' (ibid.: 112). The disadvantage of this measure is that it cannot guarantee to preserve a 1–1 correspondence between output and the amount of capital. Apart from the fact that this prevents the factor rewards to be obtained generally by partially differentiating the production function with respect to the factor inputs, this gives rise to two anomalies. The first is that the same physical capital equipment may be measured as different amounts of capital in two equilibrium positions that differ only with respect to the wage and interest rates. The second anomaly is that output per head and the amount of capital per head may be negatively correlated. If comparative statics is used to analyze the process of accumulation, this may give rise to the 'paradoxical result' (ibid.) that in order to increase output per head the amount of capital per head would have to be reduced.

More specifically, Champernowne's criticism is that the labour unit measure introduces a negative bias which is due to the fall in the interest rate. It is what Robinson had called the 'interest effect'. Champernowne wants to eliminate this effect from the changes in the quantity of capital, as he conjectures the effect is purely a consequence of the measure used. This is a different opinion from Robinson's, who considered the interest effect to be a possible consequence of the economic theory which is used. Therefore, Champernowne constructs an alternative measure. It is a chain index measure that links the quantities of capital in all equilibria. The linking is done with the help of the following definition: 'The ratio of the quantities of capital in any two equipments which are both competitive at the same rate of interest ... is equal to the ratio of their costs calculated at that rate of interest ....' (ibid.: 116). If one takes the measure of the quantity of capital in one equilibrium as a basis, the quantities of capital in all equilibria are determined as multiples of this measure.

The article examines whether a model using this chain index measure of capital is indeed free of the anomalies it is designed to avoid. It turns out that it is not. Even if the amount of capital is specified in chain index units, the production function may still fail to be single valued. 'Contrary to intuitive expectations, our assumptions do not ensure that a graph of [the production function] is a single-valued curve sloping upwards to the right.' (ibid.: 118). A graph like the one in Figure 3.6 is not ruled out.

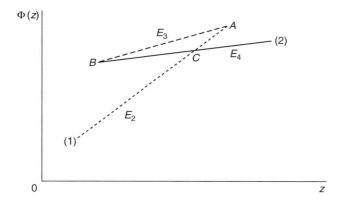

Figure 3.6 Champernowne's chain-index production function
(source: Champernowne 1956: 118).

If constant returns are assumed, the production function $y = f(x, z)$ may be written as $f(x, z) = x\Phi(z/x)$, and $\Phi(z) = f(1, z)$. So $\Phi(z)$ determines $f(x, z)$, where x is the amount of labour and z the amount of capital. E_2, E_3, and E_4 are single techniques which are drawn as - - -, – – –, and ——, respectively. At points A and B two techniques are used as they both yield the highest rate of profit. The graph shows that as the interest rate falls and the economy moves along the straight lines from E_1 to A to B to E_2, the same value of the factor ratio z (amount of capital per man) is realized more than once. This phenomenon has later become known under the names of capital reversal or absence of capital intensity uniqueness.

An additional assumption is needed to rule out multiple-valued production functions. The assumption is that of each pair of capital equipments that is the most profitable at a particular rate of interest, the one single equipment that is the most profitable at a lower range of interest rates has a higher labour productivity. Only then are a higher output and a greater amount of capital per man always associated with a lower interest rate. 'But although this may fit in well with our preconceived notions, there is no logical justification for the assumption.' (ibid.). Still, as long as the production function is used for comparing various possible stationary states, Champernowne does not consider a triple-valued production function to be a problem: 'This is no paradox, since the function merely tells about various possible stationary states.' (ibid.: 129). But as soon as the production function is interpreted as a description of a sequence of stationary states in time, 'formidable difficulties arise' (ibid.: 130). One such difficulty is that if the ordering of production techniques from low to high output does not coincide with their ordering from high to low rates of interest at which they are the most profitable; it may happen that a decrease in the interest rate makes competitive a technique with lower productivity and a lower factor ratio. So, adopting this technique would involve disinvestment. Positive net investment and rising productivity could only be maintained if the wage and interest rates were to skip the range of their values for which the production function is triple valued. As may be seen from Figure 3.6, this would eliminate E_3. Instead of going through the sequence of (mixed) techniques E_1E_2–E_2–E_2E_3–E_3–E_3E_4–E_4, a transition would have to be made from E_2 to E_4 by gradually replacing E_2-plants by E_4-plants. This mixed E_2E_4 technology is indicated in Figure 3.6 by C. 'But such a mixture is certainly not possible in a stationary state, since there is no real wage-rate and rate of interest at which E_2 and E_4 are both competitive.' (ibid.: 129–30). A related difficulty is that during the transition the factor rewards would not be equal to the values of the marginal factor products.

So, replacing Robinson's labour unit measure of capital by the chain index measure does not by itself, i.e. without assumptions additional to the ones made by Robinson, remove all the difficulties of the wage unit measure. But does it remove the main 'inconvenience' of Robinson's measure, namely that it may show two different measures for the same physical capital equipment in two stationary states that differ only with respect to the wage and interest rates? No, it does not do that either! The additional assumption that Champernowne makes[13] is really necessary. It 'rules out the possibility that an equipment may be competitive over two ranges of the rate of interest, although not competitive over an intermediate range.' (ibid.: 119). The excluded possibility has later become known as the reswitching of techniques.

> This assumption is necessary in order to get neat results, and intuition suggests that the excluded case is unrealistic, but it is shown . . . by simple numerical examples that there is no logical justification for the assumption: it is as easy to imagine a world featuring the excluded case as one free of it.
>
> (Champernowne 1953: 119)

Without the additional assumption, it is possible for two stationary states using the same equipment to have different pairs of values of the wage and interest rates.

> [B]ut the question of which [pair], and hence what income-distribution between labour and capital is fixed, is left in this model for political forces to decide. It is interesting to speculate whether more complex situations retaining this feature [a multiple-valued production function] are ever found in the real world.[14]

(Champernowne 1953: 130)

Conclusion

Champernowne originally conjectures that the anomalous prediction of Robinson's 1953 model is to be blamed on her choice of the technical or analytical device of measuring capital in wage units. But he rejects this conjecture after he has designed and applied a different measure, one explicitly chosen for avoiding the anomalous prediction. So, Champernowne has shown that the anomalous prediction is robust vis-à-vis the analytical choice of a measure of capital. He then traces the prediction to the violation of an assumption with economic content, namely about the relation between two techniques of production. Unlike Robinson, however, he does not advocate empirical research in order to discover whether the condition that has to be excluded in order to derive the prediction that is considered 'normal' can be found in reality. Instead, he stops at pointing out several difficulties that arise when one uses a comparison of two stationary states in order to describe the development of the relation among a few key economic variables in time.

3 Robinson returns to the problem

What in 1953 was a study criticizing the defects of the neoclassical production function as an analytical tool in capital theory was developed into a systematic and detailed theory of capital accumulation in *The Accumulation of Capital* (1956). In accordance with Robinson's research programme, the book is presented as an extension of Keynes' short-run analysis in the General Theory to a theory of the development of the capitalist economy in the long run. (ibid.: vi). The work is claimed to supply the theory of capital that was lacking in the *General Theory* (ibid.). Robinson concurs with Keynes that the deeper motives behind entrepreneurs' investment behaviour, which determines the rate of accumulation, largely elude economic explanation.[15] But enough scope is left for economics to analyse the proximate causes through which the deeper motives affect the rate of accumulation, and the consequences which differences and changes in the rate of accumulation may have.

Method

The organizing principle of the book is the method of decreasing abstraction. First, it presents a highly idealized basic model of the accumulation of capital.

Subsequently, layer after layer of complicating factors are incorporated into this model. However, the analysis is not carried forward to the level of empirical description for three reasons. First, empirical models are ruled out because of one basic idealization that is maintained throughout the book: relative prices are abstracted from in order to reduce the complexity of the subject matter and keep the analysis tractable:

> It is excessively difficult to conduct analysis of over-all movements of an economy through time, involving changes in population, capital accumulation and technical change, at the same time as an analysis of the detailed relations between output and price of particular commodities. Both sets of problems require to be solved, but each has to be tackled separately, ruling out the other by simplifying assumptions.
>
> (Robinson 1956: v)

Second, the book has the constructive purpose of organizing and disciplining our thinking about reality rather than generating precise predictions: 'The purpose of economic theory, of the generalised kind set out in the book, is to provide a framework within which . . . particular questions can be usefully discussed.' (ibid.: 63). Third and last, the analysis has a critical purpose. For example, the analysis of a change in the capital–labour ratio in a constant state of technical knowledge 'has been set out with so much elaboration not to provide a model for actual economies but in order to guard against a confusion of thought into which it is only too easy to fall.' (ibid.: 151). The confusion referred to is the interpretation of the directions of change of variables in comparative-static models with causal relationships.[16] It is the latter that we should go after, and not the former.

Theory

The central core (Robinson's own term[17]) of the theory of accumulation is expounded in Chapters 8 and 9. Chapter 8 describes the mechanism of accumulation in a two-sector model. The scarcity of labour determines money wages. Money wages determine the demand for the products of the consumers' goods sector. Output of consumers' goods determines the demand for machinery produced in the investment sector. And the demand for investment goods determines the level of employment, the rate of profit, and the rate of accumulation, which is equal to the rate of profit on the assumption that there is no consumption out of profits. On the assumptions that there is a single technique of production, that profits are not spent on consumption, and that the labour supply adapts itself to demand, the rate of accumulation is limited by the following factors, in order of importance:

1   The energy with which entrepreneurs accumulate.
2   The bargaining power of workers to enforce a particular level of real wages and hence profits.

3   The potential level of profits, which is the difference between the value of output and the level of subsistence wages.

When the growth of the labour force is autonomous, it is its rate of increase that sets a limit to the possible rate of accumulation. If accumulation cannot keep pace with it, unemployment increases.

The model of Chapter 8 that describes the mechanism of accumulation underlies all subsequent, more complicated models:

> Many of the conclusions will have to be extensively modified as the assumptions of one technique and no rentier consumption are relaxed, but we shall find that the argument holds good in all essential respects, and provides a picture of the basic characteristics of accumulation under the capitalist rules of the game.
>
> (Robinson 1956: 84)

Chapter 9 introduces technical progress and examines the conditions for stable economic growth. These are:

1   The level of real wages keeps pace with the growth of output per man so that the growing output of the growing stock of equipment is absorbed by demand.
2   For a stable level of employment to be maintained, a mismatch between the labour supply and existing capital equipment must be quickly redressed.

Four conditions under which the stability conditions break down are singled out for discussion in each of the subsequent layers of analysis:

1   An unexpected change in technical progress.
2   A failure of the mechanism of competition.
3   A discrepancy between accumulation and the rate of increase of productivity.
4   When technical progress affects one sector more than the other.

When these disturbances do not occur, there are no 'internal contradictions in the system' (ibid.: 99), and the economy enjoys a 'golden age'.[18] The positive contribution of Robinson's theory of accumulation as a whole is, to cite Asimakopoulos, that it makes clear 'the possible effects on the rates of accumulation of differences in the degree of thriftiness, the extent of competition, the organization and attitude of labour, rates of technical progress, and entrepreneurial energy, and thus [it] indicate[s] features of the possible growth paths.' (Asimakopoulos 1988: 204).[19]

We will now leave the general outline of Robinson's full theory of accumulation in all its richness and concentrate on the discussion of the special subjects of reswitching and capital reversing.

Anomalies

The first complication of the core model, in Chapter 10, is the relaxation of the assumption of a single technique in favour of a 'spectrum of techniques'. This introduces the problem of the choice of techniques. It is here that the anomalies that were discussed in Robinson (1953) re-emerge. But this time, they are situated in the broader context of a fully fledged theory of accumulation. Quite literally the anomalies are a complication of a complication of the core model, and Robinson goes out of her way to emphasize that the anomalies are unimportant exceptions to the general rule that a lower rate of profit is associated with a more mechanized technique of production. Thus, in Chapter 10, where the anomalies are discussed, the reader is warned off by the observation that the introduction of a spectrum of techniques 'very much complicates the foregoing analysis *without altering its broad implications*' (ibid.: 101, emphasis added), and involves a line of analysis which 'is difficult out of proportion to its importance' (ibid.: n. 1). Curiously enough, the anomalies are explained (so in point of fact cease to be anomalies) by the different time structures that production processes may have (ibid.: 109). It is stressed that the anomalies are 'rather unlikely' (ibid.: 110) or exceptional, and when a paragraph is devoted to 'The Perverse Case' the reader is told once more that the phenomenon described is of no relevance to the real world: 'This paragraph is recommended only to readers who take a perverse pleasure in *analytical* puzzles.' (ibid.: 147, n. 3, emphasis added). Apparently, the author is now strongly inclined to give a negative answer to her own, earlier question 'whether there is likely to be anything in reality corresponding to [the anomalies]' (Robinson 1953: 106).

4   Conclusion

Of the 1953 criticism of using comparative-static results for making predictions about the development of economic quantities in time, nothing much is left in Robinson (1956). Instead, the impression is given that the anomalies are only due to the analytical apparatus, and, if they can be encountered in the real world at all, are of no real interest. But Robinson does not go into this empirical matter. After all, the book had no empirical pretensions to start with, but has the purely theoretical purpose of developing an analytical framework which imposes some discipline on our thinking and provides it with a critical edge.

Notes

1 In fact, if the problem is posed thus, it is an indispensable device, for, as Robinson observes, out of equilibrium 'we are thrown back upon the who's who of goods in existence, and the "quantity of capital" ceases to have any other meaning' (Robinson 1953: 85).
2 Cf. Harcourt (1972: 24).
3 So, in the sequel the rate of interest and the rate of profit will be used interchangeably.
4 This assumption underlies equation (1).

5 As will become apparent in the next sentences, Robinson is thinking of measuring production techniques at least on an interval scale.
6 For a more complete example, see Harcourt (1972: 26).
7 Robinson uses 'degree of mechanisation' where Böhm-Bawerk and Wicksell would have said 'length of period of production'. Cf. Robinson (1953: 90, n. 1; 91; 92).
8 Because she does not consider pairs of w and r in between (1, 0.19) and (1.1, 0.09), Robinson speaks of a horizontal *jump* from one productivity curve to the next.
9 Robinson uses 'wage rate'. In the context of the relevant passage that is correct, as she assumed a 'given amount of accumulation'. Cf.: 'A rise up the hierarchy must be associated with a rise in the wage rate. But the more capital (in terms of accumulated product) has been absorbed by increasing the amount of machinery in existence, the lower the wage rate associated with a given amount of accumulation.' (p. 96). Leaving that assumption out and substituting 'wage bill' for 'wage rate' makes it less confusing.
10 This is to be found in Wicksell's *Value Capital and Rent*. Cf. Wicksell (1954 (1893): 121–3). Rewriting (1) in per caput terms, we obtain

$$q = w + rk, \quad \text{where } q = Q/L_c \text{ and } k = k/L_c. \tag{6}$$

$$r = \frac{q - w}{k}, \tag{7}$$

which in terms of Figure 3.7 can be written as $qw / Ok \cdot Ow$. That k is given in the figure by $Ok \cdot Ow$ can be seen from (5). In Figure 3.7, $Ow : ON = wq : Ok$. Rearranging yields

$$\frac{1}{ON} = \frac{wq}{Ok \cdot Ow},$$

which equals r. So, $ON = r^{-1}$. Now, (7) may be written in terms of Figure 3.7 as $Oq : Ow = kN : ON$. So, the wage rate is given by the intersection of the tangent to the productivity curve with the vertical axis.

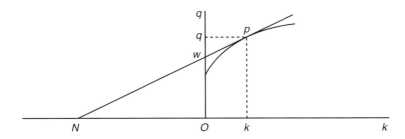

Figure 3.7 Determining the wage rate (adapted from Wicksell 1954: 122).

11 For a different reading of Robinson's remark, see Chapter 11.
12 In a note she adds: 'This was pointed out to me by Miss Ruth Cohen.' This is the 'private joke' that Robinson (1970: 309) refers to without telling us what the joke was. Here is the missing story as it was told to me by several people who were in Cambridge in the early 1950s. At that time, Robinson was often seen walking together with Sraffa busily arguing with him. That is, she did the arguing, and Sraffa commented only briefly, often by a mere nod. In these discussions, capital reversing came up. Robinson wanted to make use of this in her writings and also wanted to make an acknowledgment to Sraffa.

But Sraffa did not agree with the use she wanted to make of it and therefore refused to be implicated. When Robinson pressed the point, he, to put an end to the matter, is supposed to have said something like: 'Well, attribute it then to Ruth Cohen.' Robinson does make an oblique reference to Sraffa, however. She says she found the anomalies in Sraffa's introduction to Ricardo's collected works, 1951. Cf. Robinson 1979: 2: 'For me, the Sraffa revolution dates from 1951 . . ., not from 1960.'; and also Robinson 1970: 309–10: 'I had picked up the clue [of the Ruth Cohen Curiosum] from Piero Sraffa's Preface to Ricardo's *Principles* . . .' The reader is invited to point out to me the exact passage that contains the clue. The first convincing reaction will be rewarded by a bottle of my best wine. For comment on Sraffa's influence on the debate, see Chapter 5, para 1.

13 Assumption ix on p. 116 of Champernowne (1953).

14 Of the first sentence, about the political forces, Harcourt remarks: 'surely one of the most perceptive comments of the whole debate.' (Harcourt 1972: 171). But this conclusion follows in no way from Champernowne's model. All he has shown is that the model is too poor, or too idealized, to determine the rate of profit. Politics is only one among an indefinite number of exogenous factors.

15 Though she dissents from Keynes' appeal to 'animal spirits' as an 'explanation'. Instead, she wants economic analysis 'to be supplemented by a kind of comparative historical anthropology which is still in its infancy as a scientific study.' (Robinson 1956: 56).

16 The variables concerned are the rate of profit and the degree of mechanization. We shall come back to this later.

17 Cf. Robinson (1956: ix).

18 In summary, the golden age is characterized by neutral (in the sense of neither labour- nor capital-augmenting) and steady technical progress, a constant time pattern of production, perfect competition, steady growth of population, and a rate of accumulation that is fast enough to provide productive capacity to employ all available labour. In a golden age the rate of profit is constant and the level of real wages rises with output per man.

19 This article not only contains a useful discussion of Robinson's growth theory, but also of other aspects of her work.

4 Taking methodological stock (I)

> [The] strategy is to proceed step by step from the most severely simple assumptions towards greater complexity, squeezing out all that can be learned at each step before proceeding to the next.
>
> Robinson (1956: ix)

As was observed earlier, Robinson develops an idealized model containing what she considers to be the basic forces and mechanisms of accumulation and then systematically releases some of the idealizing assumptions, step by step. In economics, this method has been known, at least since Wieser (1914, para. 1), as the method of decreasing abstraction and has often been propounded as *the* method of economics: start with a highly idealized theory in which all but the forces that are considered to be most relevant are put on hold,[1] and subsequently introduce more and more complicating factors.

1 The Polish idealization model

In the literature of the philosophy of science, idealizations have not been studied very thoroughly until recently. This changed with the work of Wladyslaw Krajewski and Leszek Nowak, two Polish philosophers of science. Nowak (1980)[2] analyzes the idealizational structure of Marx' *Capital*. The focus of his analysis is on the way in which an abstract, highly idealized theory is gradually modified so as to include more and more complicating factors. Krajewski (1977) studies the use of idealizations in physics, and particularly the way in which physical theories succeed each other in time. His analysis focuses on the process in which particular theories, which were thought to offer a general and realistic description of certain phenomena, are replaced by more general theories, which show the previous theories to be special cases.

We may characterize Nowak's work, which describes the way in which an existing theory is adapted in order to be made applicable to reality, as a study of 'normal science'. Krajewski, on the other hand, deals with the situation in which one theory is overthrown by another; he studies 'revolutionary science'. Both authors, however, share the same basic model that describes the relationship between an idealizing theory on the one hand, and models with a higher factual content, or more general successor theories on the other hand. This model describes both the normal-scientific relation between theory and model and the revolutionary-scientific relation between two theories in the same logical terms. The model will be presented in more detail below.

Krajewski's theory has two features that make it eminently suitable for the purposes of the study that is undertaken here: it deals explicitly with the dynamic aspects of theories, and it is formulated clearly and succinctly. Therefore, Krajewski's theory will figure most prominently in my methodological apparatus, though it will be supplemented by elements of Nowak's analysis where these offer useful insights. I shall synthesize both analyses into one model, which I shall call the Polish idealization model, PIM for short.

According to PIM, a theory or a model[3] may be defined as a set of lawlike statements

$$(x)(C(x) \Rightarrow F(x)),$$

where $C(x)$ and $F(x)$ are statements about properties of x.[4] I shall assume that the properties of x can be fully described by mathematical functions assigning some numerical value to characteristic parameters of x. The antecedent $C(x)$ states the initial conditions or 'assumptions', the consequent $F(x)$ the predictions or 'theorems'.[5] The antecedent may contain factual or idealizing conditions or both. If it contains the latter, the model is an idealizing model. There is nothing in reality which corresponds to it; it is about ideal objects.

> x is an ideal object . . . when it is an ideal limit of a sequence of real objects with diminishing value of some characteristic parameter p_i (usually there is a set of parameters). In other words, some of its parameters are equal to zero ($p_i = 0$), however we know that in all real objects they are positive ($p_i > 0$).[6]
>
> (Krajewski 1977: 23)

Strategies of model development

PIM is not restricted to the description of the logical structure of idealizing theories; it can also be used to describe their development. Models may be developed in different ways, which we shall refer to as *strategies of model development*.[7] In PIM four strategies may be distinguished:

1. The strategy of *factualization or concretization*. This amounts to replacing the model's idealizing assumptions, $p_i(x) = 0$, by factual assumptions, $p_i(x) > 0$. PIM assumes that factualizations are intended to link idealizing models with empirical reality. This is shown by the adjustment of the consequent as the idealizing assumptions are factualized. Thus, starting from a purely idealizing model M_I, we obtain a sequence of models with decreasing degrees of idealization which ends, in principle, with the purely factual model M_F.

In a scheme:

$$M_I: \quad (x)(p_1(x) = 0 \,\&\, p_2(x) = 0 \,\&\, \cdots \,\&\, p_n(x) = 0 \Rightarrow F(x) = 0),$$

$$M_1: \quad (x)(p_1(x) > 0 \,\&\, p_2(x) = 0 \,\&\, \cdots \,\&\, p_n(x) = 0 \Rightarrow F_1(x) = 0),$$

$$M_{n-1}: \quad (x)(p_1(x) > 0 \,\&\, \cdots \,\&\, p_{n-1} > 0 \,\&\, p_n(x) = 0 \Rightarrow F_{n-1}(x) = 0),$$

$$M_F: \quad (x)(p_1(x) > 0 \,\&\, \cdots \,\&\, p_n(x) > 0 \Rightarrow F_n(x) = 0).$$

The scheme shows the last step in the chain of factualizations to be a factual model that contains no idealizing assumptions at all. It is doubtful whether any model in any scientific discipline ever reaches this fully empirical status.[8] Nevertheless, both Krajewski and Nowak seem to have the idea that this is quite commonly the case, even if the last step in the sequence is an approximation.[9] They share the idea that idealizing theories can be connected rather straightforwardly with empirical reality with much of the philosophical literature of the last decades, which concentrates on the role of testing scientific theories empirically. Testing in this sense means finding or creating a real-world situation which is a (full or approximate) instantiation of a model's initial conditions and checking whether the model's prediction is instantiated (fully or approximately) as well. Repeated negative test results may motivate the adaptation of the prediction, i.e. the consequent of the conditional statement which constitues a model; the initial conditions may or may not be adapted as well. Empirical tests are considered to be the only motivation for change, or at the very least the most important one. But there are other types of tests that may act as motors of change, such as thought experiments, or testing scientific theories for their consistency with other scientific theories or with metaphysical theories.[10] Therefore, the focus on empirical tests to the exclusion of other types of tests is unduly restrictive. I will refer to this exclusively empirical emphasis as the 'empiricist bias'. However, the empiricist bias is no essential part of PIM. The model is equally suitable for describing strategies of theory development in which empirical tests in the usual sense of the word have no role to play at all. This will now be demonstrated in the methodological analysis of the case studies we have seen so far.

The above scheme offers an accurate description of the structure of Robinson (1953) and (1956), even though neither publication contains even so much as a hint of how empirical tests of any of their predictions could in principle be carried out. Both publications lend themselves to an analysis in terms of PIM because of the fact that they are structured around a basic, simple and idealized model which is gradually made more complex, i.e. the influence of more and more factors is included, and it is examined in what way these factors alter the prediction.

Robinson (1953) gives a numerical example of the way in which the choice of technique is influenced by changes in factor prices. On the first level of analysis this example does not take into account the effect that a change in the interest rate has on the cost of capital; it is assumed that the cost of capital is insensitive to changes in the rate of interest (there is no interest effect). On the next level of her analysis Robinson releases the assumption that the interest effect is absent. The inclusion of the interest effect is a factualization,[11] and it gives rise to an adaptation of the prediction about the interest–capital intensity relationship.

Robinson (1956) is very systematically structured according to the methodological principle of gradual factualization. Chapters 8 and 9 describe the basic mechanism of accumulation. In the subsequent chapters the idealizing assumptions of the basic model are 'complicated', to use Robinson's term. Thus, the assumption of a single technique of production is replaced by the assumption of several techniques, and the assumption that rentiers do not consume part of the proceeds of their investment is released. This method of complication is identical to the method of factualization in PIM.

But the structure of Robinson (1956) is even more complex. On each level of factualization she systematically introduces a second set of complications. She examines the consequences of dropping the four conditions for stable growth with which she starts, one by one, on each level of factualization. Moreover, the whole of the analysis rests on the assumption that relative prices do not change. The scheme provided by PIM allows us to model this rather complex structure quite clearly. The basic model of accumulation[12] can be described as

$$M_B: \quad (x)(p_1(x) = 0 \,\&\, p_2(x) = 0 \,\&\, p_3(x) = 0 \,\&\, \cdots \,\&\, p_m(x) = 0$$
$$\&\, p_{m+1}(x) = 0 \,\&\, \cdots \,\&\, p_{m+4}(x) = 0 \Rightarrow F_1(x) = 0),$$

where p_1 is the characteristic parameter for the influence of changes in relative prices (its value is kept equal to 0 throughout the book);[13] $p_2 - p_m$ are the characteristic parameters of factors whose influence is abstracted from in the basic model M_B, i.e. $p_2(x)$ through $p_m(x) = 0$, but that are factualized 'irreversibly', i.e., once one of these parameters has been assigned a non-zero value, it never takes the value zero at a subsequent level of factualization (these parameters model the influence of the existence of several techniques of production, the saving behaviour of rentiers, etc.); $p_{m+1} - p_{m+4}$ are the 'revolving' characteristic parameters, i.e. the factors whose influence they characterize are factualized one by one on each of the levels of factualization of the 'irreversible' parameters. The 'revolving' parameters characterize the influence of (in order of factualization): (unexpected) changes in technical progress; the mechanism of competition; the ratio between the rate of accumulation and the rate of increase of productivity; and the relative influence technical progress has on either sector of production.

The first irreversible factualization introduces the effects of the choice of techniques ($p_2 = 0$ is replaced by $p_2 > 0$):

$$M_1: \quad (x)(p_1(x) = 0 \,\&\, p_2(x) > 0 \,\&\, p_3(x) = 0 \,\&\, \cdots \,\&\, p_m(x) = 0$$
$$\&\, p_{m+1}(x) = 0 \,\&\, \cdots \,\&\, p_{m+4}(x) = 0 \Rightarrow F_{1.0}(x) = 0),$$

which describes a golden-age economy. The subsequent analysis then proceeds thus:

$M_{1.1}$: $(x)p_1(x) = 0 \,\&\, p_2(x) > 0 \,\&\, p_3(x) = 0 \,\&\, \cdots \,\&\, p_m(x) > 0$
$\&\, p_{m+1}(x) = 0 \,\&\, \cdots \,\&\, p_{m+4}(x) = 0 \Rightarrow F_{1.1}(x) = 0)$,

$M_{1.2}$: $(x)p_1(x) = 0 \,\&\, p_2(x) > 0 \,\&\, p_3(x) = 0 \,\&\, \cdots \,\&\, p_m(x) > 0$
$\&\, p_{m+1}(x) > 0 \,\&\, \cdots \,\&\, p_{m+4}(x) = 0 \Rightarrow F_{1.2}(x) = 0)$, $\cdots$

When all four stable-growth idealizations have been factualized, the analysis proceeds to the next level of irreversible factualization, where the assumption that rentiers do not consume part of the proceeds of their investment is released. Again, this factualization is first examined as to its consequences for a golden-age accumulation path:

M_2: $(x)(p_1(x) = 0 \,\&\, p_2(x) > 0 \,\&\, p_3(x) > 0 \,\&\, \cdots \,\&\, p_m(x) = 0$
$\&\, p_{m+1}(x) = 0 \,\&\, \cdots \,\&\, p_{m+4}(x) = 0 \Rightarrow F_{2.0}(x) = 0)$,

and subsequently all four golden-age idealizations are released until the analysis arrives at a non-neutral-technical-progress, non-fully-competitive, non-steady-population-growth, profit-consuming-rentiers model:

$M_{2.4}$: $(x)(p_1(x) = 0 \,\&\, p_2(x) > 0 \,\&\, \cdots \,\&\, p_m(x) = 0 \,\&\, p_{m+1}(x) = 0$
$\&\, p_{m+2}(x) > 0 \,\&\, p_{m+3}(x) > 0 \,\&\, p_{m+4}(x) > 0 \Rightarrow F_{2.4}(x) = 0)$.

2. The second strategy distinguished by PIM is *idealization*, which operates usually in conjunction with *approximation*. This strategy works in the opposite direction of factualization, and can be shown in the above scheme as the transition from, for instance, M_F to M_{n-1}, where the prediction of M_{n-1}, $F_{n-1}(x) = 0$ may be an approximation of $F_n(x) = 0$, the prediction of M_F.

3. The third strategy in PIM is *the revealing of idealizing conditions*: at a particular moment it is discovered that the validity of a model which contains as a characteristic parameter Φ_1 and which was thought to be general is in fact conditional upon the assumption that a different factor, which was not included in the original model, influences the factor characterized by Φ_1. If we use Φ_2 for the characteristic parameter of this new factor, the discovery amounts to seeing that $\Phi_1 = f(\Phi_2)$, and that $\Phi_2 = 0$ in the reconstruction of the existing model.[14]

This is the result that Champernowne ultimately reaches. After a serious attempt to attribute the anomalies to the way in which capital is measured has failed, Champernowne concludes that the model generating the 'normal' prediction of the shape of the production function was enthymematic: its prediction is the result of the model *plus* a hidden premise about the ordering of production techniques according to labour productivity.

If, in addition to revealing idealizing conditions that had previously remained unnoticed, a more general model is constructed or discovered that contains the previous model as a special case, then we are dealing with a different strategy of model development.

4. This last strategy distinguished by PIM is the *correspondence strategy: finding a corresponding model*. The discovery that a particular theory, which was thought to contain realistic assumptions, i.e. initial conditions that are true descriptions of reality, is in fact not an adequate description as it contains one or more false assumptions and is in fact an idealizing model, is sometimes followed by the construction of a new theory which contains, or encompasses, the old model as a special case. In such a case we will say that there is a correspondence relation between the two theories if:[15]

1   The new theory is more general than the old one.
2   The new theory partly reconstructs the old one.
3   The new theory corrects the old one by replacing a parameter that was considered to be a constant by a variable.
4   The old theory is a limiting case of the new theory describing only what happens in a limited domain.
5   The new theory is logically incompatible with the old one.
6   The new theory explains why people holding the old theory thought their theory to be correct.
7   The new theory introduces a factor on which the value of the parameter that was considered a constant by the old theory depends.

An example of correspondence is given in Section 6 of this chapter. In more formal terms we can characterize the notion of correspondence as follows (I designate the old theory by T_i and the new one by T_j): T_j corresponds to T_i if:

1   T_i contains a parameter Φ_1 which is a constant.
2   T_j contains Φ_1 as a variable.
3   Φ_1 is dependent on a variable Φ_2, which in T_i is not relevant for Φ_1.
4   If Φ_2 approaches a certain limit value (e.g. 0 or ∞), Φ_1 in T_j approaches the constant value of Φ_1 in T_i.

If all of the above conditions are fulfilled, we will say, following Krajewski,[16] that the two theories are related by the *correspondence relation*.[17] The old theory is called the *corresponded* theory, the new one the *corresponding* theory.

Krajewski gives examples from physics of the revealing of idealizing assumptions and the construction of corresponding theories. But he does not say much about how the inadequacy of the old theory is discovered. The sequence of factual models which in PIM form the link between an idealizing theory and empirical reality may suggest that the incentive to look for hidden assumptions among a model's or theory's antecedent conditions is a falsification in an empirical test. But theorists may have other, not directly empirical, reasons for doubting a model's adequacy. One such reason is that a model's prediction violates certain theoretical or even (professionally educated) common-sense beliefs.[18] This, too, may prompt an investigation of the antecedent conditions of the model in order to locate the conditions that give rise to the offending prediction.

2   Back to the capital theory debate

Champernowne (1953) follows the strategy of revealing idealizing conditions. He observes that one of the predictions of Robinson's complicated model which includes the interest effect contradicts a firm theoretical belief of neoclassical economics. He examines which of the antecedent conditions is responsible for this, and he conjectures that it is the way in which capital is measured, namely in wage units. Therefore he develops a new measure. But as it turns out, this does not eliminate the anomalous prediction, so he concludes that it is not the measure of capital which is to blame. He then traces the anomalous prediction to the violation of the assumption that of each pair of production techniques that are equally profitable at a particular interest rate, the technique that is the more profitable at a lower interest rate also has the higher labour productivity. It is necessary to make this ordering assumption if one wants to rule out the possibility of an anomalous prediction. Conversely, Champernowne discovers that all models yielding the prediction that no previously eligible production technique returns as the rate of interest rises or falls further, contain a hidden premise. The premise is that the ordering of techniques according to labour productivity is inversely related to the rate of interest that makes them the most profitable technique.

Notice how carefully Champernowne arrives at his conclusion. He first examines whether a technical feature of Robinson's model, the measure of capital, is to be blamed for the anomalous prediction. This seems completely rational. If one holds a particular belief firmly and is confronted with a contradictory result, one first examines the way in which the model yielding the result is formulated. This includes formal and measurement features.

The discovery that the ordering assumption is necessary for the prediction to follow, is an instance of the revealing of a hidden assumption. Champernowne's intuition is 'that the excluded case is unrealistic, but it is shown ... by simple numerical examples that there is no logical justification for the assumption: it is as easy to imagine a world featuring the excluded case as one free of it.' (Champernowne 1953: 119). But though he remarks that '[i]t is interesting to speculate whether more complex situations retaining this feature [a multiple-valued production function] are ever found in the real world' (ibid.: 130), he does not examine this by means of empirical research. Instead, Champernowne factualizes the discrete-techniques, two-factor model to find out whether or not a multiple-valued production function can still be derived when a chain index of capital is used. It turns out that also in a model with a continuous sequence of techniques, and in a three-factor model the ordering assumption is necessary for avoiding a multiple-valued production function, even though capital is measured with the chain index method.

Champernowne does not go on from there to develop a corresponding model in which the existence or absence of an inverse relationship between labour productivity and interest rate is made dependent on some new factor (possibly one that has to do with certain dynamic features). Instead, he stops at observing that extending the conclusions of the comparative-static method to a dynamic context gives rise to 'formidable difficulties' (ibid.).

The correspondence strategy is a regular feature of Robinson's work. Thus, she makes it her explicit goal to develop a theory that is more general than Keynes' *General Theory* because she observes that the latter theory's predictions are derived under the assumption that no accumulation of capital and no growth take place. The objective of her research programme is to construct a theory that both generates the predictions of the *General Theory* and in addition shows what happens when the stock of capital changes. So, the theory of the long run that Robinson envisages is designed to be related to the *General Theory* by the correspondence relation. In terms that are perhaps more familiar to economists, Robinson's purpose may be described as making endogenous factors that were exogenous to Keynes' *General Theory* without coming up with a model that is *ad hoc*. In view of Robinson's purposeful purely theoretical approach, it seems reasonable here to think of '*ad hoc*' not in the sense of the requirement that the corresponding theory be independently testable though this in general would be a fair requirement for corresponding theories but rather in the sense of Robinson's corresponding theory being in the spirit of the Keynesian research programme.[19] That Robinson's *Accumulation of Capital* really was not programmatically *ad hoc* with respect to Keynes' research programme of the *General Theory* is, by the way, doubted by Asimakopoulos:

> *The Accumulation of Capital* . . . fails in its attempt to provide 'an extension of Keynes' short-period analysis to long-run development' (1956: vi), since the assumptions she makes in order to develop the theory represent a 'watering down' and even a denial, of what she considered to be essential elements of Keynes' theory.
>
> (Asimakopoulos 1988: 198)

Another example of Robinson following the correspondence strategy can be found in her discussion of the Wicksell effect. There she subsumes a model in which the interest rate and the time profile of investments were (tacitly) assumed to be of a very restricted form under a model in which the interest rate and the time profiles are variable.

3 Correspondence and factualization

One thing remains to be done in this chapter, and that is to examine the similarities and differences between correspondence and factualization. Perhaps the reader has by now got the feeling that, logically speaking, there is not much of a difference. If so, he is right. As Krajewski observes,[20] in the case of a factualization, the idealizing model or law L_1 is logically entailed by, or can be logically derived from the factualized model or law L_F plus an idealizing condition C_I:

$$L_F \,\&\, C_I \Rightarrow L_I \tag{1}$$

or, if, following Krajewski, we truncate the laws to their predictions and the relevant initial condition:

$$F_M(x) = 0 \,\&\, p_i(x) = 0 \Rightarrow F_I(x) = 0. \tag{2}$$

In the case of correspondence, when a corresponding model or law L_j has been found which contains as a variable the parameter that in the corresponded model or law L_i was falsely assumed to be a constant (and thus in the light of the corresponding model is an idealizing condition C_I), the corresponded model or law may be obtained in the same way from the corresponding one:

$$L_j \,\&\, C_I \Rightarrow L_i, \tag{3}$$

or again, if we consider the predictions:

$$F_j(x) = 0 \,\&\, p_i(x) = 0 \Rightarrow F_i(x) = 0. \tag{4}$$

Krajewski concludes:

> The scheme (2) is identical with the scheme (4). Indeed, the corresponded law is always idealizational and the corresponding law is more factual.
> (Krajewski 1977: 42)[21]

So, there is no difference in the logical structure of factualization and correspondence. The logical structure suggests that the relation is a reduction relation. This is indeed the conclusion that Krajewski draws, after discussing various types of reduction: 'A special kind of non-trivial homogeneous reduction is the reduction of an idealizational law to a factual one.' (ibid.: 38).[22] Krajewski raises a new problem:

> The reduction of L_I to L_F is obviously possible. It is not clear whether the opposite reduction of L_F to L_I is also possible. L. Nowak claims that it is, that L_F follows from L_I and some additional knowledge. Undoubtedly scientists in their theoretical reasoning usually start from L_I and pass to L_F, taking account of the factors disregarded earlier. But is it a deduction?
> (Krajewski 1977: 39)

Krajewski states that Nowak's claim is undecided. But what matters more is an important observation which he makes rather casually:

> We see, by the way, that the concepts of reduction and explanation of theories should not be identified. Maybe Nowak is right and reduction is possible in

both directions (of course, with different additional assumptions). Shall we then say that L_I explains L_F and L_F explains L_I? It would be a very strange conclusion.

In practice we do not say that L_F explains L_I .... Rather the opposite is true: in order to better understand a more complicated law L_F we start from a simpler law L_I and gradually add additional factors. We explain L_F by L_I though we are not sure whether there is a strict reduction here. We do not say that L_I is explained by L_F though there is an obvious strict reduction here.

(Krajewski 1977: 39)

There clearly seems to be a clash between the analysis of PIM and a rather widespread and commonly held intuition about the relations between idealizing and factualized laws and theories. Is PIM wrong, or is the intuition wrong, or both? I will propose a solution to this problem in Chapter 12, after we have studied some more case studies and developed the methodological apparatus further.

4   An excursion into the philosophy of science

Krajewski does not stand alone in his questioning of the nature of the logical relationship between idealizing and factualized laws, theories, or models. Thus, Rivett asks on what grounds theoretical and idealized hypotheses are applicable (Rivett 1970: 128). He rejects the answers given by Lionel Robbins ('because the assumptions of economic theory are (approximately) true') and by Milton Friedman ('because they are false'). He concludes:

One is thus forced to the unattractive conclusion that though economic theory must always be used along with empirical observations, it seldom *entails* explanatory hypotheses. In most situations it merely *suggests* them. In consequence, the proven hypotheses of economics are not linked deductively. Its theory is best stated as a set of analytical propositions which *are* deductively linked and which suggest hypotheses, while also giving them support.

(Rivett 1970: 128)

But he fails to make clear how the suggesting is to be analyzed. According to Körner, idealization leads to a deductive disconnection between theory and empirical basis, and further idealization may even lead to disconnection within theories (Körner 1963, 1966). Even John Maynard Keynes has something to say on the problem, in his *General Theory* (Keynes 1936: 371), where he discusses the difference between the method of Douglas, Malthus, Gesell and Hobson and that of the 'classics', 'who, following their intuitions, have preferred to see the truth obscurely and imperfectly rather than to maintain error, reached indeed with clearness and consistency and by easy logic but on hypotheses inappropriate to the facts.'

Laymon observes:

> Roughly, the choice is between true but vague descriptions or precise but false ones. But as Duhem already noted, if descriptions of natural phenomena are to logically attach to our theories, we must opt for the latter alternative.
>
> (Laymon 1980: 339)

Less roughly and more precisely, the problem of the relation between idealizing theories and empirical or factual models has been stated by Worrall. He poses the dilemma: either an idealizing theory is a true theory about ideal phenomena, or it is a false theory about real or empirical phenomena, but not both (Worrall 1982: 218).

Truth versus laws of nature

More recently, Nancy Cartwright has addressed the problem in *How the Laws of Physics Lie* and *Nature and its Capacities*.[23] She makes a clear choice for the option that idealizing laws are false descriptions of real phenomena. Their use lies in the fact that they organize and unify phenomenological laws, and '[t]here is no reason to think that the principles that best organize will be true, nor that the principles that are true will organize much.' (Cartwright 1983: 53). Against the view that the fundamental laws of physics state the facts, which she calls the facticity view, Cartwright maintains that

> nature is governed by a small number of simple, fundamental laws. The world is full of complex and varied phenomena, but these are not fundamental. They arise from the interplay of more simple processes obeying the basic laws of nature .... This picture of how nature operates to produce the subtle and complicated effects we see around us is reflected in the explanations that we give: we explain complex phenomena by reducing them to their more simple components .... [Following] Mill, ... [I] call *this explanation by composition of causes*.
>
> (Cartwright 1983: 58)

Simple laws do not state the facts, but they have explanatory power. On the other hand, phenomenological laws state the facts, but being low-level laws, they lack explanatory power.

> I think that the basic laws and equations of our fundamental theories organize and classify our knowledge in an elegant and efficient manner, a manner that allows us to make very precise calculations and predictions. The great explanatory and predictive power of our theories lies in their fundamental laws. Nevertheless the *content* of our scientific knowledge is expressed in the phenomenological laws.
>
> (Cartwright 1983: 104)

All this has consequences for the logical relations between idealizing, fundamental laws or theories and descriptive, phenomenological laws or models. What is her diagnosis? Speaking of the logical derivation between theory and model, she observes:

> Proponents of the D-N view tend to think that at least [when a model has been chosen] the generic-specific account holds good. But this view is patently mistaken when one looks at real derivations in physics or engineering. It is never strict deduction that takes you from the fundamental equations at the beginning to the phenomenological laws at the end.
>
> (Cartwright 1983: 104)

In a way, Cartwright is more audacious than Krajewski. She unhesitatingly draws the conclusion that the deductive-nomological account of explanation (or the generic-specific approach as Cartwright calls it) is wrong: 'The generic-specific account fails because the content of the phenomenological laws we derive is not contained in the fundamental laws which explain them.' (ibid.: 107). The point Cartwright is making is none other than the well-known logical principle that deductive inference cannot be ampliative, that is that 'one cannot deduce more from less'.[24] In Cartwright's second book, the diagnosis is repeated in different words: 'there is never any recipe for how to get from the abstract theory to any of the concrete systems it is supposed to treat.' (Cartwright 1989: 185). This is called the problem of material abstraction. The author discusses a number of kinds of abstraction. 'My central thesis is that modern science works by abstraction; and my central worry is that philosophers have no good account of how.' (ibid.).

Despite her position that fundamental laws are false descriptions of real phenomena, by introducing the mutual exclusiveness of truth and explanatory power Cartwright evades the dilemma stated by the scientific realist Worrall. Instead, she follows Duhem and chooses an intermediate position between realism and instrumentalism. That leaves her with the problem of explaining how fundamental laws are related to phenomenological laws. As part of her solution she introduces two different meanings of 'realism', thus restoring the link between truth and explanatory power that she had severed earlier. Both models and fundamental laws are realistic, be it in a different sense.

> The two senses act at different levels. The first bears on the relation between the model and the world. The model is realistic if it presents an accurate picture of the situation modelled: it describes the real constituents of the system – the substances and fields that make it up – and ascribes to them characteristics and relations that actually obtain. The second sense bears on the relation between the model and the mathematics. A fundamental theory must supply a criterion for what is to count as explanatory. Relative to that criterion the model is realistic if it explains the mathematical representation.
>
> (Cartwright 1983: 149–50)

Instead of the D-N model of explanation, Cartwright proposes a theory that she calls the simulacrum account.

> The simulacrum account is not a formal account. It says that we lay out a model, and within the model we 'derive' various laws which match more or less well with bits of phenomenological behaviour. But even inside the model, derivation is not what the D-N account would have it be, and I do not have any clear alternative. This is partly because I do not know how to treat causality.
>
> (Cartwright 1983: 161)

Instead of strict deduction as the relation between fundamental equations and phenomenological models, what is required is 'a variety of different approximations' (ibid.: 104).

In her second book the solution is introduced as follows: 'My basic idea is that the method of Galilean idealization, which is at the heart of all modern physics, is a method that presupposes tendencies or capacities in nature.' (Cartwright 1989: 188). The method is identified with 'the logic that uses what happens in ideal circumstances to explain what happens in real ones is the logic of tendencies or capacities' (ibid.: 190). But it is not clear what logic that is, and Cartwright gets stuck at this point. Later, I will go into the kind of logic that may enable us to model the relation between idealizing theories and factualized models. For the moment, I will let the quoted passage continue, as it elucidates what Cartwright means by 'ideal':

> What *is* an ideal situation for studying a particular factor? It is a situation in which all other 'disturbing' factors are missing. And what is special about that? *When all other disturbances are absent, the factor manifests its power explicitly in its behaviour.* When nothing else is going on, you can see what tendencies a factor has by looking at what it does. This tells you something about what will happen in very different, mixed circumstances – but only if you assume that the factor has a fixed capacity that it carries with it from situation to situation.
>
> (Cartwright 1989: 190–1, emphasis in the original)

5 Better roughly right than precisely wrong?[25]

As we have seen above, Menger holds the view that idealizing theories are true theories about ideal phenomena but then cannot solve the problem of how the 'exact' theories as he calls them are related to empirical reality. Against his will, he gets stuck between instrumentalism and realism. By separating truth from explanatory power, Cartwright chooses that position willingly. Krajewski, in his review of Cartwright's first book, argues that her position is very close to his own 'idealizational realism'. According to this position, an idealizing law describes one of the essences of a phenomenon. It does so in an ideal model, which

> takes into account only certain factors (main ones) and disregards others (side ones). Mathematically speaking, we assume that some magnitudes take on extreme values, usually zero, although in reality they take on other values. We state idealizational laws which are strictly fulfilled only in an ideal model but not in actual Nature. They are false in the simple classical sense (C-false) but they are true in a new, 'model' sense (M-true).
>
> (Krajewski 1987: 170)

Krajewski says that Cartwright's criticism of the facticity view of laws amounts to the idea that theoretical laws are C-false but M-true. According to Krajewski, the way in which Cartwright thinks fundamental laws are connected with phenomenological laws by being 'amended to be true' (Cartwright 1983: 45) is identical to the procedure of what he has called factualization, a fundamental notion in PIM. To this I add that Menger's idea of how exact laws may be related to empirical laws can be reconstructed in the same way with the scheme of PIM. The parallels between Menger and Cartwright do not stop here. They both believe in the existence of causes which have to be separated on a theoretical level before being reassembled so as to obtain an explanation by composition of causes. And both distinguish between, on the one hand, abstraction (Cartwright) or isolating abstraction (Menger) and, on the other hand, idealization (Cartwright) or emphasizing abstraction (Menger).

A major difference between Menger and Cartwright is the status they assign to idealizing laws. For Menger, these are true descriptions of ideal phenomena. For Cartwright, idealizing laws, if taken to be descriptive, are false. However, their real function is not to describe but to organize and unify phenomenological laws about surface phenomena and to allow scientists to calculate. Therefore, they must not be judged in terms of truth or falsehood, but rather by the extent to which they succeed in doing the job of organizing and unifying. Menger tries to maintain a consistent realism but fails to clarify the relation between idealizing theories and factualized models because of his justificationist epistemology. Cartwright identifies explanation with the subsumption of phenomenological laws under a fundamental, usually mathematical organizing scheme, yet at the same time she believes in the existence of causes which somehow or other are represented by the fundamental laws. The tension between the realism of the causes and the instrumentalism with respect to fundamental laws keeps her from formulating a satisfactory solution to the problem of the relation between idealizing laws and factualized models.

Mario Bunge points the way to the direction in which a solution may be found. In 'Concepts of Model' he discusses the problem that we have been concerned with here. His answer to the question in the title of the present paragraph is: It is better to be precisely wrong. That is because 'the failure of a precise idea is more instructive than the success of a muddled idea, for it may suggest the precise modifications producing more realistic (truer) models.' (Bunge 1973: 95). What this amounts to is a view of idealizing theories as part of a heuristic, a rational method of theory development.[26] Despite the fact that both Menger and Cartwright stand in the tradition of the method of analysis and synthesis, neither looks for the solution to the problem of the relation between idealizing theories and factualized models in the direction of a logic of discovery. In the case of Menger, not because he does not believe in a logic of discovery, but because of his justificationism. And in Cartwright is case, not because she is a justificationist, but because she concentrates on the static aspects of science rather than on its development.

In Chapter 11 I will argue that the function of idealizing theories and their relation with respect to factualized models may be better understood if one considers them as part of a logic of discovery. Suffice it to observe for the moment that in PIM the distinction between correspondence and factualization really boils down to the question of whether we are dealing with revolutionary or normal science.[27] This distinction may be interpreted in a syntactic manner: factualization is a strategy of normal science because the factor that is factualized is already part of the model; correspondence is a strategy of revolutionary science because a new discovery is made: a new relevant factor is discovered. The distinction may also be interpreted in an intentional or pragmatic way: it depends on what the researcher's aims are and which strategy of theory or model development he will follow. We will come back to this pragmatic dimension in Chapter 6.

6   An example of correspondence

By far the most influential example of correspondence in economics is John Hicks' 'Mr. Keynes and the "Classics"' of 1937. Before showing that what Hicks does there is an instance of correspondence, let me make a few observations. First, the IS-LM model that Hicks developed in 1937 became the cornerstone of modern macroeconomics. However, that was not his intention. All he wanted to do was to examine what the relations were between Keynes' *General Theory* on the one hand, and the class of theories to which Keynes had given the name 'classic'. They comprised the business cycle theory of Keynes' most important opponent during the 1930s, Hayek, and Pigou. Second, Hicks' article was not the only one to attempt a systematic comparison of these theories. Similar attempts were published by Reddaway (1936) and Lange (1938); history just happened to favour Hicks. Third, 'Mr. Keynes and the "Classics"' did not have the purpose of preparing an empirical confrontation between the two theories.[28] All the author wanted to do was to construct a framework that made it clear just what the differences were between Keynes' *General Theory* and the theories that Keynes criticized. In the terminology introduced above, Hicks examined the relations between the theories by *constructing* a corresponding theory. In fact, if we read Hicks, we find him saying that there is no such thing as a 'classical' theory of money (Pigou's theory runs in real terms) so that he has first to *construct* one before being able to compare the classical theory with Keynes'.

If we can construct such a theory, and show that it does give results which have in fact been commonly taken for granted, but which do not agree with Mr. Keynes' conclusions, then we shall at last have a satisfactory basis for comparison. We may hope to be able to isolate Mr. Keynes' innovations, and so to discover what are the real issues in dispute.

(Hicks 1937: 148)

Hicks presents the following theories[29] (M, quantity of money; Y, total income; I, investment; i, the rate of interest):

1	The classical theory:	$M = kY$,	$I = C(i)$,	$I = S(i, Y)$,
2	Keynes' 'special theory':	$M = L(i)$,	$I = C(i)$,	$I = S(Y)$,
3	Keynes' general theory:	$M = L(Y, i)$,	$I = C(i)$,	$I = S(Y)$.

In his reconstruction, Hicks relied on the formal structure of his own reformulations, and on what we might call a principle of symmetry: 'In order to elucidate the relation between Mr. Keynes and the "Classics", we have invented a little apparatus. It does not appear that we have exhausted the uses of that apparatus, so let us conclude to give it *a little run on its own*.' (Hicks 1937: 156, emphasis added). At this point Hicks introduces the unifying theory. He continues:

With that apparatus at our disposal, we are no longer obliged to make certain simplifications which Mr. Keynes makes in his exposition. We can reinsert the missing i in the third equation, and allow for any possible effect of the rate of interest upon saving; and, what is much more important, we can call in question the sole dependence of investment upon the rate of interest, which looks rather suspicious in the second equation. Mathematical elegance would suggest that we ought to have Y and i in all three equations, if the theory is to be really General.

(Hicks 1937: 56; I has been replaced by Y)

By this 'special-to-general' procedure he obtains

4	The 'generalized general theory':	$M = L(Y, i)$, $\quad I = C(Y, i)$, $\quad I = S(Y, i)$.

The new theory unifies in one framework (or encompasses) the three previous theories. The new theory has been arrived at by the correspondence procedure, and the others can be obtained from it by assigning extreme values (in this case 0) to some of its parameters. One such a special case is Wicksell's theory: the interest-elasticity of income equals zero, and the IS curve is horizontal. A crucial test among the elements of any subset of special-case theories could now be carried out, at least in principle, by measuring the empirical values of the parameters of the generalized general theory. In modern parlance: estimating the generalized general theory constitutes a test of the restrictions on the values of its parameters, and the restrictions tell us which of the special-case theories is data-admissible.[30]

Notes

1 Usually by the ceteris paribus incantation.
2 This book is a rather original attempt to defend Marx' method in a way that owes nothing positive to the slavish dialectic-materialistic tradition that used to dominate Eastern-European philosophical and scientific writing.
3 A note on terminology. Where Nowak and Krajewski (and also Musgrave, whose ideas are discussed later) speak of theories, I will usually speak of models. One reason is that this stays closer to the usage in economics. The word does not refer to models in the model-theoretic sense as is the case, for instance, in Sneed (1979). It is quite common to use 'theory' for a set of abstract propositions and 'model' for a set of propositions on a lower level of abstraction. As will be made clear in the text, according to PIM the question of whether or not something is called a theory or a model is mostly a matter of convention. What matters is how theories or models of different degrees of idealization are related, i.e. their relative levels of abstraction. Therefore, I will use 'theory' and 'model' interchangeably, although I will stick to the custom of speaking about idealizing theories and factualized models (that is models that are less idealized – see the sequel of the text).
4 As the relations among the various lawlike statements that may make up a model are not our main concern, a model will be identified with one lawlike statement.
5 Nothing much depends on these words. They are merely used here because they figure in some of the literature in these meanings. Sometimes, Friedman (1953) is blamed for giving rise to this or related confusing terminology. I will offer some suggestions for a rather consistent reading of Friedman's much-quoted article later.
6 Whereas in physics idealizations may quite straightforwardly be expressed by letting a parameter take or approach an extreme value of 0 or ∞, this may not always be the case in economics. It seems that the restriction of the parameter value to one constant occurs more often. Krajewski allows for this, too. Cf. Krajewski (1977: 29, n. 7). Restrictions may figure in an economic model itself, or be part of a methodological reconstruction.
7 Or strategies of theory development. These terms will be used interchangeably, in accordance with what was said in note 4. I speak of strategies in order to emphasize the dynamic aspect of the use of idealizations and factualizations. The term is not used by either Krajewski or Nowak.
8 Cf. Wieser (1914: 135): '[the theoretician] cannot rest content with these extreme abstractions; if he did, he would not have made reality completely understandable. Rather, he must make his assumptions more concrete and more numerous, step by step, through a system of decreasing abstraction.' (my translation). This is the way in which, according to Wieser, idealizing theories and more factualized models are related. But he recognizes that because both deal with typical phenomena, one can never arrive at the full empirical reality by this method. The way in which Carl Menger tried to solve the problem of the relation between idealizing theory and empirical model was briefly discussed in the Introduction. See also Birner (1990).
9 See, for instance, Krajewski (1977: 24) and Nowak (1980: 30).
10 Cf. Laudan (1977).
11 Perhaps it would be better to avoid Krajewski's term 'factualization' and use Nowak's 'concretization' instead so as to avoid unwarranted associations with factual or empirical applications and tests of models. But for aesthetic reasons I prefer the former term, which to a forewarned reader does not have to be burdenend with empirical associations.

12 Which also abstracts from the existence of money. Although this idealizing assumption could easily be included in the scheme that follows, it will be left out to keep the structure as simple as possible.

13 For expository reasons I diverge from the convention, followed both by Krajewski and Nowak, of providing the characteristic parameter that is factualized first with the index 1.

14 For the idea of a reconstructed model in the light of a revealed idealizing condition, cf. Krajewski (1977, para. 4.6).

15 'New' and 'old' do not necessarily have to be interpreted in the sense that the corresponding theory is a successor in time of the corresponded theory, as Krajewski does (cf. Krajewski 1977: 41). It may very well be the case that two theories which are related by correspondence exist side by side without anybody noticing that they correspond.

16 Cf. Krajewski (1977: 41–2). Krajewski borrows the word 'correspondence' from Popper. Cf. Popper (1972, Chapter 5).

17 We will see later that weaker correspondence relations exist other than the one described in the text and in Section 6; it is not necessary for *all* the conditions to obtain to still be able to usefully employ the concept of correspondence.

18 For an economist's views on the interaction between theory and professional common sense, cf. Solow (1985). Solow's views are very similar to those expressed by Robinson on pp. 63–4 of her 1956 work.

19 This has been called by Lakatos 'non heuristically *ad hoc*' (cf. Lakatos 1978: 182), though I prefer to use the term 'non programmatically *ad hoc*' for Lakatos' *ad hoc$_3$*. This is in the spirit of his methodology of scientific research programmes (cf. also Lakatos 1978: 112), and hence non programmatically *ad hoc*.

20 Cf. Krajewski (1977: 39).

21 On the same page, Krajewski goes into the logical relation between corresponding *theories* as well: 'In the case of theories . . . the CR [correspondence relation] between T_1 and T_2 takes place if it takes place between some of their basic laws. We must not speak about *all* laws.'

22 The reader is referred to pp. 30–8 of the same work for details of Krajewski's discussion of reduction. These details are of no consequence to the present discussion.

23 Cartwright (1983, 1989). Cartwright 1999 does not seem to me to add anything to the theory of the previous books.

24 Cf. Tietzel (1987: 319): 'An idealized explanans is logically too weak to state a concrete, singular explanandum.'

25 The paragraph title is suggested by Kamarck (1983: 2): 'too often in economics, the choice is between being roughly accurate or precisely wrong.' Of course, for applied science the answer is: we're satisfied when we're roughly accurate. The focus in this paper is on theoretical science, whose purpose it is to increase our understanding of reality.

26 Cf. also Tietzel (1987: 315): 'Idealized explanations are heuristic devices which, in the long run, ought to be transformed into adequate explanations.' They do so by simplifying the explanatory argument, in the way described by Nowak, to whom the author refers.

27 Cf. Krajewski (1977: 90): 'Revolutions in mature science lead to theories which are in CR [correspondence relation] with their predecessors. Each revelation of idealizing assumptions L_1 and formulation of L_2 being in CR with L_1 may be called a scientific revolution.'

28 As had been Colin Clark's purpose earlier. Cf. Birner (1993a) and 2002.

29 Notice that Hicks does not distinguish between definitional, behavioural and equilibrium equations, as is usual in more modern models. In his notation all three are conflated. Thus, the first equation in a modern model would be replaced by three separate ones, one specifying the demand for money, the other the money supply, the third equating supply and demand. The second and third Hicksian equations would be replaced by several equations: the definitional $Y = C + I$, the behavioural $C = C(\cdot)$ and $I = I(\cdot)$,

and the equilibrium equation $S = I$. If one keeps this in mind, Hicks' notation has the advantage of being succinct and concentrating on his aim, which is to bring out the differences among the various theories. Therefore I retain Hicks' original equations, except that I have replaced two of Hicks' symbols by their equivalents I and Y, which have become generally accepted.

30 For these aspects and more recent developments in crucial testing, cf. Birner (1993a) and (2002).

5 Triumph and crisis of the neoclassical production model

To understand a theorem you must understand its limitations.

Samuelson and Modigliani (1966: 275)

This chapter discusses the reaction of Samuelson to some of Robinson's criticism of the neoclassical approach to capital and production. The criticism issued from her earlier work, and was dealt with in the previous chapter. Initially, Samuelson (and others, apparently, too) thought that in his reaction he had developed an innovating and very successful idealizing model which was not only immune to the criticism but also had some additional desirable properties. This is the triumph referred to in this chapter's title. But then Samuelson's claims about the properties of his model were shown to be false by Garegnani. This is the sense in which there was a crisis for the neoclassical model.

Until the early 1960s, a point of criticism of neoclassical capital theory which emerged repeatedly, though with varying emphasis, was that neoclassical theory did not exclude the possibility of capital reversing. This possibility was considered to be an anomaly. It was not until sometime during or after the period of the altercation between Samuelson and Garegnani that another anomaly, the possibility of reswitching of techniques, came to occupy a prominent place in the discussion, together with capital reversing. But the history of how reswitching was introduced into the debate, and how reswitching and capital reversing moved to the centre of the stage, is by no means clear. I have three reasons for going into this in some detail.

First, an attempt to straighten some of the historical confusions is a valid enterprise in its own right. We simply want to know what happened, how, why, and in what order. Second, I will try to show that getting the historical picture right has consequences for the methodological analysis. Thus, the view or at least the suggestion that Sraffa gave the impulse to the debate because he discussed reswitching quite clearly in his book, implies a wrong picture of how this (and probably almost any) scientific debate evolves. The development and the direction of this debate in capital theory was not inspired by grand views of global results, but was rather the result of local analytical strategies and attempts by theorists to solve local puzzles and problems, usually of a formal kind. An indication for this is that the way in which capital reversing and reswitching are related was something which was only found out in the course of the debate. The fact that Sraffa saw all along the critical potential of his reswitching counterexample does not diminish the importance of this point. All other theorists behaved rather like sleepwalkers, groping their way around. A detailed study of the publications shows that there was no clash between two fully formed theories. It was even the case that the debate served to sort out which of the propositions considered to be characteristic of neoclassical production models belonged to the basic premises (or assumptions) of neoclassical production theory, and which to the set of its predictions. Finally, getting the historical picture right also helps us to form an opinion on the sort of strategies and arguments that served as moving forces of the debate. In particular, does empirical or factual criticism provide the fuel, or do purely formal arguments?

In what follows, the historical account and the discussion of the relevant articles in the form of case studies will alternate. The results of this exercise point to a need for extensions and improvements of the methodological analysis of the previous chapter. The improved analytical framework is presented in the next chapter.

1 Neoclassical triumph

In the literature dealing with the debate about reswitching and capital reversing, Robinson is quite generally depicted as the author who started it. But that can hardly mean that she performed the actual kick-off, as she had dismissed the phenomena at stake as mere exceptions. She later observes about her own 1953 and 1956 publications:

> I came across the phenomenon of 'reswitching', later so notorious, but I did not make much of it. At this stage, it seemed sufficiently startling to find that, of two techniques, the one that is more mechanised, in the sense of yielding a *higher* output per man employed may well have the *lower* value of capital at the rate of profit at which it is eligible.
>
> (Robinson 1975a: viii)

The first author to make the reswitching of techniques the explicit focus of his criticism of neoclassical capital theory was Sraffa in *Production of Commodities by Means of Commodities* (Sraffa 1960). So, it might seem obvious to assign the role of the direct initiator of the debate to him. That is exactly what a host of authors do. Spaventa says: 'The origin of the recent debate is to be found in P. Sraffa, *Production of Commodities by Means of Commodities....*' (Spaventa 1968: 16, n. 1). According to Dobb, Sraffa's book 'provoked a famous, if recondite, discussion of the mid-1960s, commonly referred to as the "multiple-switching of techniques" debate.' (Dobb 1973: 248). And '[i]n a sense its [the book's] rigorous demonstration of the possibility of what came to be called the "double-switching of techniques" with changes in the ratio of factor prices, came as an incidental corollary of that work. But it represented, perhaps, its most important single contribution to "a Critique of Economic Theory" and occasioned a debate that will one day, no doubt, become celebrated.' (ibid.: 252). Dobb is outright wrong. As

I will show in a moment, Sraffa did not think that reswitching was an incidental corollary of the rest of his book at all. Lachmann writes that the debate entered a new stage with the publication of Sraffa's book and that the analysis of Chapter XII 'gave rise to what became known as the "Reswitching Controversy".' (Lachmann 1973: 24). Brown has it that '[t]he reswitching controversy [was] initiated by Piero Sraffa' (Brown 1973: 937). In Harcourt we find: 'The 1965–7 debates were a direct result of the implications of the earlier examples of these phenomena in the literature – Sraffa (1960), Robinson (1953–4, 1956), Champernowne (1953–4) – beginning to sink in . . .' (1976: 29). Well, yes, perhaps at the level of Popper's World-3, but in the cases of Sraffa and Champernowne certainly not as a matter of history; the results they had obtained had to be *rediscovered*. According to Robinson, with the publication of Sraffa's book the discussion that Robinson herself had tried to get going took a new turn; Sraffa's demonstration that one technique may be profit maximizing at widely different profit rates made the 'mainstream economists' aware that their 'orthodoxy' was at stake and set off the debate. Cf. Robinson (1977: 173–4): 'Faisant des hypothèses très orthodoxes sur le caractère de la technologie, Sraffa a montré que la même technique peut être éligible à des taux largement différents de profit. *C'est cette conclusion qui a fait découvrir aux économistes du courant dominant que leur orthodoxie était mise en question*.' (emphasis added). Cf. also Robinson (1970: 309–10): 'When his own treatment of the subject was finally published [Sraffa 1960] . . . the "Ruth Cohen Case" (which I had treated as a curiosum) was seen to have great prominence; the striking proposition was established that it is perfectly normal . . . .' By failing to point out *by whom* this was seen, Robinson suggests that it was seen quite generally. But this was not the case, as will now be argued.

The widespread idea that Sraffa gave the kick-off for the debate is contradicted by a body of contemporary evidence that is hard to ignore. With one exception, not a single one of the numerous reviews of Sraffa's book so much as mentions Sraffa's discussion of reswitching, and these include two by Robinson (Robinson 1961, 1965). The exception is Harrod (1961). He refers to reswitching, and he discusses Sraffa's example that the system of production may switch back to the same technique that was used previously at a lower rate of interest. Harrod mentions that the example demonstrates that the quantity of capital is not independent of the rate of interest. However, he refers to it as 'one of Mr. Sraffa's subordinate propositions' (Harrod 1961: 786), and considers reswitching to be of little consequence: 'While it is important to bear it in mind, it does not seem that it damages the usefulness of, still less that it creates ambiguity in, the concept of the period of production.' (ibid.). Even Harrod did not attribute the crucial role to Sraffa's discovery of reswitching that others later ascribed to it.

So, all reviewers but Harrod missed reswitching, and everyone of them missed its consequences. However, they were given a second chance, so to speak. That is because Sraffa replied to Harrod, and his reply seems crystal clear on the matter: 'This example [of reswitching] is a *crucial test* for the ideas of a quantity of capital and of the period of production.' (Sraffa 1962: 478, emphasis added). Reswitching is called a crucial test because it demonstrates the impossibility of defining the quantity of capital and the period of production independently of the rate of interest.[1] Yet, all reviewers missed this opportunity as well. As one of them later admits: 'certainly the importance of part III [of Sraffa 1960] in which double-switching and capital-reversing are discussed did not get the prominence which we can now see it merited.' (Harcourt 1972: 178).[2] The conclusion must be that Sraffa's book cannot have been the direct impulse to the debate (and that the popular idea that it was is the result of wishful hindsight).

This conclusion might be taken to vindicate Blaug's statement that 'his [Sraffa's] contribution has absolutely nothing to do with the debate.' (Blaug 1975: 12). But things are not as simple as that, as a closer look at the chronology reveals. Nineteen sixty one is an important year in the events leading up to the debate. It was the year of Robinson's 'memorable visit' to MIT, as the event is called in the dedication of Samuelson (1962).[3] Let us look at one of the accounts that Robinson has given:

> The neo-neoclassicals took no notice [of reswitching],[4] they went on as usual drawing production functions in terms of 'capital' and labour and disseminating the marginal productivity theory of distribution. In 1961 I encountered Professor Samuelson on his home ground; in the course of an argument I happened to ask him: When you define the marginal product of labour, what do you keep constant? He seemed disconcerted, as though none of his pupils had ever asked that question, but next day he gave a clear answer. Either the physical inputs other than labour are kept constant, or the rate of profit on capital is kept constant.
>
> I found this satisfactory, for it destroys the doctrine that wages are regulated by marginal productivity . . . . The wage is determined by technical conditions and the rate of profit, as at a particular point on a pseudo-production function. The question then comes up, what determines the rate of profit?
>
> (Robinson 1970: 310)[5]

As we have seen, Robinson made no use of reswitching or capital reversing in her own criticism of the neoclassical production function approach, which she could have done had she understood the critical potential these phenomena had.[6] In what way and by whom *were* reswitching and capital reversing moved to the centre of the debate? Part of the answer to this historical question can be found in Samuelson's 1962 article, so let us proceed to discuss that.

Parable and realism

The parable according to Paul

Both in theoretical and in empirical work, the characteristic propositions of neoclassical capital theory have been used in a macroeconomic formulation, i.e. in terms of aggregates. As we have seen, Robinson in her 1953 article is very critical of this approach, and particularly of the use of an aggregate measure of capital. In response, Samuelson admits that it is possible to develop capital theory *without* conceiving capital as an aggregate or homogeneous good (as John Bates Clark and Frank Ramsey do) by making use of mathematical programming techniques. Yet, in his 'Parable and Realism' he undertakes to defend the neoclassical, macroeconomic approach to production and income distribution. For that purpose, he develops a model which assumes capital to be one homogeneous entity. Samuelson says this is an idealization because in reality capital, if considered to be the stock of capital goods, is not homogeneous but consists of a great variety of goods. He claims two virtues for an idealizing model with homogeneous capital ('homogeneous model' for short): It has 'considerable heuristic value in giving insights into the fundamentals of interest theory in all its complexities' (ibid.: 193). What Samuelson apparently means by this is that such a model may serve to determine both the factor prices and the relative factor shares. Second, it provides a theoretical justification for Solow's attempt to calculate the contribution of technical progress to economic growth by empirically estimating one macroeconomic production function, which contains homogeneous capital as an argument.

Samuelson emphasizes that his model is an idealizing model:

> I shall use the new tools of the surrogate production function [he adds in a note: 'One might call this the "as if" production function.'] and surrogate capital [read: 'homogeneous capital'] to show how we can sometimes predict exactly how certain quite complicated capital models will behave by treating them *as if* they had come from a simple generating production function (even when we know they did not *really* come from such a function).
>
> (Samuelson 1962: 194)

Samuelson is quite triumphant about the virtues of his idealized model, and he stresses its novel character. He emphatically and repeatedly presents the surrogate production function and surrogate capital as 'new concepts'.[7] The author leaves no doubt that he thinks he has made a new and important discovery, one that transcends the criticism. Though Samuelson admits that his idealized, homogeneous model is not valid under all circumstances, he claims that for particular purposes, such as the calculation of the relative factor shares, it predicts exactly[8] the same relations among some crucial capital theoretic variables as does a 'more realistic' heterogeneous model: 'mere *physical* heterogeneity need not lead to qualitatively new behaviour patterns.' (ibid.: 203).

The homogeneous model

A production function shows the relation between factors of production (the input in a production process, notably labour and capital) and the product that is being manufactured (the output, notably capital goods and consumption goods). This relation may be shown in terms of quantities (the technical relations: how much capital and labour go into the production of one unit of output) or, what is economically more interesting, in terms of values or prices: what value of the inputs goes into one dollar's worth of output. The usual neoclassical production function is assumed to be continuous. But Samuelson uses a discrete production model, instead. This is an occasion for another note of triumph: 'even in our discrete-activity fixed-coefficient model of heterogeneous physical capital goods, the factor prices (wages and interest rates) can still be given various long-run marginalism (i.e. partial derivative) interpretations.' (ibid.: 200).

Samuelson's model simplifies further by describing the production of only two goods: consumption goods and capital goods, each of which is produced in a separate industry or sector of production. If we assume that all capital goods are used up in producing consumption and capital goods within one production period, we may abstract from depreciation charges. I follow Samuelson in taking the price of the consumption good as the numéraire, i.e. the prices of all goods are expressed in terms of the consumption good. This eliminates one unknown from the set of equations without loss of generality. It is furthermore assumed that competition has driven prices down to the cost of production, and that a stationary equilibrium rules, so that the rate of profit equals the rate of interest. Then we may render Samuelson's model thus:[9]

$$1 = l_a w + c_a p_c r, \tag{1}$$

$$p_c = l_c w + c_c p_c r, \tag{2}$$

where l is the labour input coefficient (the quantity of labour per unit of output, L/Q, or q^{-1}), c is the capital input coefficient (the quantity of capital per unit of output, K/Q, or k^{-1}), w is real wage, r is the rate of profit, and p is price. Subscript a indicates the consumption good industry, c the capital good industry.

Equation (1) is the production function of the consumption good industry, (2) of the capital good industry. One such pair of production functions is called a *technique of production*. Different techniques of production are characterized by different input coefficients. So, a technique of production is described by the matrix of the input coefficients:

$$\begin{vmatrix} l_a & c_a \\ l_c & c_c \end{vmatrix}.$$

The production in the consumption goods industry is more, equally or less capital intensive as

$$c_a / l_a \gtreqless c_c / l_c.$$

This may be rewritten as

$$l_a c_c - l_c c_a = D \lesseqgtr 0,$$

where D is the determinant of the coefficient matrix.

For each technique of production we may derive the relation between the wage rate and the rate of profit from (1) and (2):

$$w = \frac{1 - c_c r}{l_a + (l_c c_a - l_a c_c)r} = \frac{1 - c_c r}{l_a - Dr}. \tag{3}$$

Equation (3) shows the maximum rate of profit which a particular technique under perfect competition allows to be paid given the wage rate (and conversely the maximum wage rate that can be paid given the rate of profit). When $r = 0$ the wage rate is maximal and equal to $1/l_a$, which equals the output of consumption goods per worker q (as l_a is the amount of labour per unit of the consumption good, L/Q).

Samuelson introduces homogeneous capital by means of the 'drastically simplifying assumption' (ibid.: 197) that the ratios of the input coefficients in both sectors are equal (both production techniques have the same capital intensity):

$$c_c/l_c = c_a/l_a. \tag{4}$$

He does so apparently in the belief that this assumption may later be released without altering the predictions of the model. This may be learned from an afterthought which Samuelson added to his article in reaction to Garegnani's criticism. He thanks Garegnani 'for saving me from asserting the false conjecture that my extreme assumption of equi-proportional inputs ... could be lightened and still leave one with many of the surrogate propositions.' (ibid.: 202, n. 1).

The assumption of equal factor proportion ratios, as expressed in (4), means that the determinant of the coefficient matrix equals 0. The determinant occurs in (3) as a factor of r, so (3) reduces to

$$w = \frac{1 - c_c r}{l_a}$$

$$= q - \frac{c_c}{l_a} r, \text{ the equation of a line.} \tag{5}$$

This is drawn in Figure 5.1.

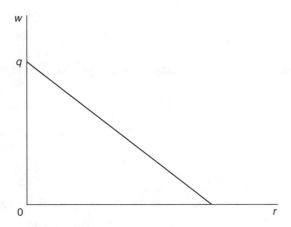

Figure 5.1 The individual factor price frontier (adapted from Samuelson, 1962: 195 and 197).

Samuelson baptizes the *w–r* relation the *factor-price frontier*, for reasons that will be made clear shortly. I have adopted throughout the more neutral name of *wage-profit frontier* (wpf).

Heterogeneous capital means that there are different possible techniques of production, each having its characteristic coefficient matrix and wpf. Which technique is chosen depends on the ruling wage rate, which is associated with a unique rate of profit if entrepreneurs maximize their profits. The economy-wide wage-interest frontier (denoted by WPF) is the north-east frontier or 'envelope' of all individual wpfs, as is shown in Figure 5.2.

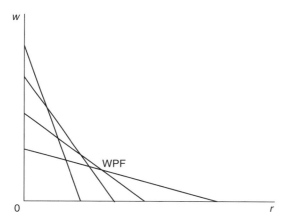

Figure 5.2 The economy-wide factor price frontier.

For Samuelson, the crux of his novel 'as-if' approach lies in the assertion:

> In the singular case where two economies have exactly the same factor-price frontier, however they may be different in the background, we can treat them as equivalent in so far as predictions about their long-run interest- and wage-rate properties are concerned. And, what may be more useful, if two economies have approximately the same frontiers within a given range, we can use either one to predict the long-run properties of the other in that range.
>
> (Samuelson 1962: 196)

So, the idealizing homogeneous model simulates the 'realistic' heterogeneous model provided it has the same, or approximately the same, WPF.

After drawing the WPF for a 'realistic' heterogeneous model, Samuelson constructs a homogeneous model with a WPF (named 'surrogate frontier') that mimics the shape of the heterogeneous WPF. In the homogeneous model, capital is homogeneous with itself and with the consumption good; it is a conceptually perfectly malleable 'jelly'. Instead of a great number of pairs of production functions (as in the heterogeneous model), we now have one economy-wide production function

$$Q = F(J, L), \tag{6}$$

where Q is output, J is homogeneous capital ('surrogate capital' or 'jelly'), and L is labour.

The following standard neoclassical assumptions are made about this macroeconomic production function: decreasing returns (see Figure 5.3a) and constant returns to scale. In mathematical terms this means that the production function (6) is homogeneous of the first degree, that is

$$Q = F(J, L) = LF(1, J/L) = LF(J/L),$$

and hence

$$Q/L = F(J/L).$$

Because capital is homogeneous with output, factor prices equal physical marginal factor productivities:

$$w = \delta Q/\delta L = F(J/L) - (J/L)F'(J/L), \tag{7}$$
$$r = \delta Q/\delta J = F'(J/L), \tag{8}$$

hence Samuelson's name 'factor price frontier'.

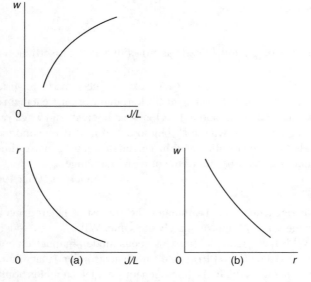

Figure 5.3 The homogeneous neoclassical production function and its surrogate frontier.

From (7) and (8) the wpf (which is here equivalent to the WPF) can be derived algebraically:

$$w = F(J/L) - (J/L)r, \quad \text{whose slope equals } \mathrm{d}w/\mathrm{d}r = -(J/L). \tag{9}$$

Graphically, this relation can be derived by combining the curves in Figure 5.3a, and is shown as Figure 5.3b. Samuelson claims that the properties of the heterogeneous WPF are rigorously equivalent to the homogeneous wpf, and do not merely approximate them (ibid.: 203),[10] and he comments:

> Note how generally similar are the frontiers of [Figure 5.2] and [Figure 5.3b], even though the former has been *rigorously* derived from a definitely *heterogeneous* capital-goods model and the latter from the neoclassical fairy tale. Indeed if we invent the right fairy tale, we can come as close as we like to duplicating the true blueprint reality [the heterogeneous model] in all its complexity.
>
> (Samuelson 1962: 201)

Samuelson's claim is that the homogeneous model simulates the 'realistic' heterogeneous one exactly; it yields the same predictions about relative factor shares and the relations among w, r, the capital–labour ratio and the capital–output ratio as does the heterogeneous model.

The story continues

In Robinson (1979) we are told that Samuelson (1962) is a reply to Sraffa. Had this indeed been the case, it would have been natural, if not inevitable, for Samuelson to discuss reswitching. But he did not. Samuelson (1962) does not react to Sraffa, but to Robinson. This may be concluded despite the absence of detailed references to her work, which is probably explained by the fact that the entire article is dedicated to Robinson and by the fact that it is a response to her 'memorable visit'. Now, Robinson is preoccupied with the distribution of income. Samuelson triumphantly extols the benefits of his approach, which uses an aggregate production function and an aggregate capital variable – the objects of Robinson's criticism in her 1953 article – for determining relative factor shares:

> If one believed the over-praised statement of Ricardo that 'Political Economy . . . should rather be called an inquiry into the laws which determine the division of the produce of industry amongst the classes who concur in its formation', the factor-price frontier would be among the most important concepts in this economic model. For, the frontier can (in the special diverse-goods model of the previous section) give us more information than merely what the wage and profit rates will be at any point. Improbable as it may first seem to be, it is a fact that the behavior of stationary equilibria *in the neighborhood* of a particular equilibrium point will completely determine the possible level(s) of relative factor shares in total output *at* that point itself.
>
> (Samuelson 1962: 199)[11]

From Samuelson's wording it is sometimes even possible to infer to what passages in Robinson's work he reacts. Thus, in note 4, Samuelson emphatically advertises his surrogate production function as superior to the construction of

> some modern economists [who] fall back in despair on wage units as a best approximation for measurement [of aggregate capital] . . . . The present model, in which we know rigorously exactly where we are at each stage illustrates how treacherous the use of wage units may be and how they create *unnecessary* complications to the problem.
>
> (Samuelson 1962: 203)

He shows this in a diagram which seems to be taken directly either from Robinson (1953) or (1956) and which shows a 'perversely' shaped factor ratio curve (and thus capital reversing without mentioning it by name). Next to this multi-valued production function Samuelson draws a construction in terms of his own surrogate model, which produces a single-valued function. According to Samuelson, the anomaly is due to measuring capital in labour units ('the gratuitous act of deflating [the jelly or surrogate measure of capital] by real wages'), and can be avoided by using his own surrogate production function.

Curiously enough, Samuelson does not refer to Champernowne (1953), which examines – and rejects – the hypothesis that the anomalies in Robinson's model are due to her measure of capital. Apparently, either Samuelson did not know Champernowne (1953), or he did not agree with its conclusion that capital reversing and a multi-valued production function could not be eliminated simply by offering an alternative measure of capital which does not use wage units.

Hence my conclusion that Samuelson in his 1962 article did not react to Sraffa's book, but to Robinson's criticism. Robinson's statement about Sraffa's influence (quoted above) is wrong. There is a reconstruction of the events, by Roncaglia, which seems to come to the same conclusion:

> It does not appear, however, that Samuelson had fully appreciated the importance of the results presented by Sraffa in his book. Indeed, it is more probable that his objective was, above all, to respond to the initial criticisms put forward by Joan Robinson. Sraffa's results, as might be guessed, were also destructive to Samuelson's efforts, as Garegnani [who, in 1961–2, was at MIT as visiting fellow[12]] immediately pointed out to him, even before Samuelson's article was published.
>
> (Roncaglia 1978: 100)

We have seen what Robinson's criticism was; she pointed out to Samuelson that neither wages nor profits are determined by marginal productivity, but she did not use the examples of reswitching or capital reversing as an argument. Samuelson defended his own position *vis-à-vis* Robinson's criticism by writing his 1962 article. He also defended the empirical work that was being done by Solow, which drew very much on the same set of ideas that Samuelson had.[13]

What Samuelson set out to do in his 1962 article is very well described by Solow: 'All theory depends on assumptions which are not quite true. That is what makes it theory. The art of successful theorizing is to make the inevitable simplifying assumptions in such a way that the final results are not very sensitive.' (Solow 1956: 161). Compare this to what Samuelson says: '[I] offer the surrogate production function only as a dramatic model to show that mere *physical* heterogeneity need not lead to qualitatively new behavior patterns.' (Samuelson 1962: 203).

Even before Samuelson's article was published, Garegnani, who was in 1961–2 visiting Rockefeller Fellow at MIT, pointed out to Samuelson (in a criticism that was not published until 1970 (Garegnani 1970)[14]) that his surrogate production model solved the problem it was designed to solve only under very restrictive conditions. Did reswitching play any part in his criticism? Reswitching is mentioned in one of the three paragraphs of Garegnani (1970) that were submitted to the *Review of Economic Studies* in April 1963 (ibid.: 407, n. 1), but further discussion of it is postponed to later paragraphs, which were not, apparently, written until later. Samuelson recalls that reswitching was not part of Garegnani's original criticism.[15] So, if it is the reswitching counterexample that Roncaglia means by 'Sraffa's results' that were 'destructive of Samuelson's efforts', it is doubtful that he is right in putting the introduction of reswitching into the debate at this early a date.

I have been able to resolve the matter through the kind help provided by Professor Garegnani, who sent me copies of the original papers both by Samuelson and himself. Samuelson's paper indeed does not mention reswitching. But in the copy of Garegnani's hand-written original criticism (dated, apparently after it had been written, 'MIT Winter 1961?'), reswitching is mentioned, in a footnote. It is there observed that 'The possibility of this seems sufficient to disprove any "Clark parable" '.[16] But the fact that Garegnani devotes almost all of the space of both his hand-written paper and the first three paragraphs of his 1970 article to criticizing Samuelson by means that do not involve reswitching, and the fact that reswitching is only mentioned in a footnote of the manuscript strongly suggest that it did not play a major part in Garegnani's criticism. A discussion of when reswitching did become important in the debate will be postponed until we have discussed Garegnani's criticism of Samuelson.

2   Crisis for the neoclassical model

Damning criticism from Rome

Garegnani's original criticism of Samuelson is contained in the first three paragraphs of his 'Heterogeneous Capital, the Production Function and the Theory of Distribution' (ibid.), which did not appear until 1970. The article is a greatly expanded version of the original paper, and the latter is largely a point-by-point reaction to Samuelson's paper. So, it is not easy to determine from this material alone by what theoretical interests Garegnani was driven to criticize Samuelson in the early 1960s. Fortunately, this information is provided by his dissertation, orig-inally written in English, and published in 1960, in Italian. The account it gives of the author's theoretical interests is consistent with what the later paragraphs of his 1970 article tell us. Garegnani's theoretical interest lay, as did Robinson's, in the analysis of the distribution of income. But according to himself, he was much more strongly and directly influenced by Sraffa[17] than she was. That prob-ably explains why his criticism of neoclassical economics is not mellowed by the words of sympathy that Robinson still had to spare in her 1953 article. But there is a basic similarity in both their approaches: both advocate a separation of the theory of accumulation from the theory of value,[18] be it for different reasons.[19] Garegnani wants to return to the pre-marginal revolution theory of distribution of Ricardo. According to him, the fundamental flaw of neoclassical distribution theory is that it considers capital as a factor of production like the others, one whose quantity is independent of the distribution of income. Neoclassical theory teaches that all factor prices are determined by supply and demand in the factor markets, including the market for 'capital' (or loanable funds). But Garegnani denies that this is the case. From this theoretical background, which is influenced by Dobb and Sraffa,[20] he criticizes Samuelson's defence of neoclassical distribution.

Garegnani disputes the generality of Samuelson's claim that the homogeneous model predicts the same relations as does the heterogeneous model. His method of criticism consists of examining the conditions under which the surrogate produc-tion function simulates the WPF of the heterogeneous model. As will be seen, he demonstrates that Samuelson's assumption of a linear WPF seriously restricts the domain of application of the model as the assumption cannot be released without affecting the general validity of the model's predictions.

Garegnani constructs a model with an infinite number of production techniques, each of which contributes one point to the WPF. He does not restrict his model to linear wpf's. This means that the WPF may very well have the shape of Figure 5.4.[21]

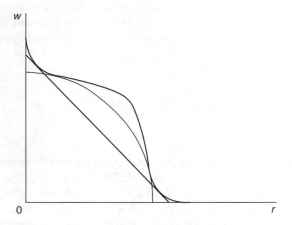

Figure 5.4 Garegnani's bulging envelope (adapted from Garegnani 1970: 413).

The equation of the heterogeneous WPF is

$$w = e(r), \tag{10}$$

and net physical product per head q in the heterogeneous model equals the wage rate when $r = 0$ and is written as

$$q = q(r). \tag{11}$$

What Samuelson's claim amounts to is that these relations obtain in an idealized model of an economy producing one consumption good from labour and capital which is assumed to be homogeneous with the consumption good, so that w and r are determined by marginal factor productivities. Alternatively, Samuelson's claim may be put thus: a production function

$$S = S(J, L) \tag{12}$$

can be defined that is homogeneous of the first degree and subject to the conditions

$$\delta S/\delta L = e(\delta S/\delta J), \tag{13}$$
$$S/L = q(\delta S/\delta J), \tag{14}$$

where $w = e(r)$ and $q = q(r)$ are the relations in the heterogeneous model. By Euler's theorem (12) yields

$$S/L = \delta S/\delta L + (\delta S/\delta J)(J/L). \tag{15}$$

In the homogeneous model the equilibrium rate of interest is $\delta S/\delta J$. Then, by virtue of (13),

$$S/L = e(r) + r(J/L), \tag{16}$$

from which the slope of the heterogeneous WPF can be obtained by differentiating with respect to $\delta S/\delta J$:

$$J/L = -d(\delta S/\delta L)/d(\delta S/\delta J), \tag{17}$$

and by (13),

$$J/L = -e'(r) \tag{18}$$

(e' is the derivative of the equation of the heterogeneous WPF).

In the case of a WPF of the shape of Figure 5.5, by virtue of (17) the ratio of capital to labour could rise as $\delta S/\delta J$ rises. This would be the case as we move

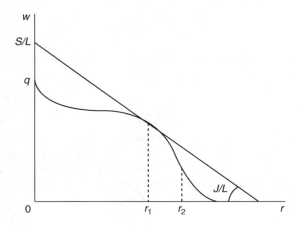

Figure 5.5 The end of Samuelson's parable.

from r_1 to r_2. But then 'the function $S(J, L)$ could not be a production function: equilibrium in the "imaginary" economy of the "Clark–Ramsey parable", requires that the marginal product of "capital" should *not* rise when the ratio of "capital" to labour J/L rises.' (ibid.: 415). So, Samuelson's parable is incompatible with a mixed concave–convex WPF.

Does that mean that the surrogate model simulates a heterogeneous model in the case where the latter has a linear WPF? No, it does not either, as 'we should then have to admit that the "marginal products" change, when the ratio of capital to labour does not.' (ibid.). May we then conclude that the convexity of the heterogeneous WPF is a sufficient condition for a successful simulation? No, we may not. A convex surrogate WPF would not fulfil condition (13) in the case where one of the WPFs was non-linear. So, the conditions are even stronger. Garegnani finds them as follows.

From (16) and (18),

$$S/L = e(r) + r(-e'(r)). \tag{19}$$

S/L is the intersection of the w-axis with the tangent to the WPF for a particular r, and q is the intersection of the w-axis with the wpf that is tangent to WPF for the same r. S/L and q coincide if and only if all wpf's are linear, because only then do the tangents to the WPF intersect the w-axis in the corresponding q.

In order to derive (19), condition (13) alone is sufficient. The production function cannot be chosen such that it also satisfies (14). We can only check whether (19) satisfies (14), so whether $S/L = q$. But as Figure 5.5 shows, this is not generally the case.[22] The production function $S = S(J, L)$ of the homogeneous model satisfies conditions (13) and (14) if and only if all WPFs of the heterogeneous model are linear. And a sufficient condition for this is that the factor proportions of each pair of production functions in the heterogeneous model be equal. However, Garegnani states that in Samuelson's two-sector model, 'but for the arbitrary choice of the capital-good unit, the input coefficients of the two industries are equal. The system is therefore *indistinguishable* from one where [commodity] A is produced by itself and labour.' (ibid.).[23] This is a strong condition. It is so strong as to reduce Samuelson's heterogeneous model exactly to his homogeneous model.

> Indeed, since 'heterogeneity' of commodities can here be properly defined only as a difference in their conditions of production, a straight-line wage-curve *means* that A is produced by itself and labour....
>
> When this is true for the whole family of systems, we have that A is produced with varying proportions of itself to labour.... It is then no surprise that the relations between r, w and q are compatible with the 'Clark–Ramsey parable'. The assumption of equal proportions of inputs has turned the 'real' economy with 'heterogeneous capital-goods' into the 'imaginary' economy of the 'Clark–Ramsey parable'....
>
> (Garegnani 1970: 415)

> In fact, 'surrogate capital' and 'capital' are one and the same thing: at any given level of r, J/L, the slope of the envelope, is also the slope of the wage-curve tangent to the envelope at that rate of interest, and measures the proportion of A to labour required to produce A with the system in use at that level of r. Samuelson's 'surrogate production function' is thus nothing more than the production function, whose existence in such an economy no critic has ever doubted.
>
> (Garegnani 1970: 416)

So, Garegnani proves that Samuelson's homogeneous model successfully simulates a heterogeneous model if and only if the heterogeneous model contains only one capital good, hence is not a heterogeneous model after all.

Notes

1 Sraffa had already said this explicitly in part I of his book. There he gives an example of reswitching, and he concludes from it: 'The [concomitant] reversals in the direction of the movement of relative prices ... cannot be reconciled with *any* notion of capital as a measurable quantity independent of distribution and prices.' (Sraffa 1960: 38).
2 But the failure to read on to part III cannot be the whole explanation of the oversight. Cf. the previous note.
3 See Samuelson (1962: 213, n. 1).
4 Nor did anyone else, as we have seen, not even Robinson.
5 The passage continues: 'But this was going too far. Professor Samuelson retreated behind what he called a surrogate production function [in Samuelson 1962]. It was a special case (as Piero Garegnani promptly pointed out) of a pseudo production function with labour-value prices.... Professor Samuelson believed that in this he had provided for the "neoclassical parables" of J. B. Clark.... At first the neo-neoclassicals were happy to accept this parable. (This was the period of Professor Solow's lectures and

of the first draft of Professor Ferguson's book in which, he tells us, he relied upon the surrogate production function to protect him from what he calls Cambridge Criticism.) For some years they remained cooped up in this position, repelling all attacks with blank misunderstanding. Then, growing bold, they descended to the plains and tried to prove Sraffa wrong.' (Robinson 1970: 311).

6 She did not use reswitching and capital reversing for criticizing neoclassical production and distribution theory until after the symposium papers were published in *Quarterly Journal of Economics* (1966). See Robinson and Naqvi (1967).

7 Besides in the passage quoted in the text, this can be found on pp. 194 and 201.

8 'Note: this is not an approximation, but a rigorous equivalence.' (p. 203).

9 In the notation of Garegnani (1970).

10 In this passage Samuelson sounds much more assertive than in others, such as the one quoted above (Samuelson 1962: 202, n. 1). For comment on this, see Chapter 6.

11 The relative factor shares are given by the point elasticity of the WPF in case the latter is smooth and without corners: $(dw/w)/(dr/r) = (dw/dr)/(r/w)$. In the case where the WPF has corners, 'the elasticity coefficient is defined within a limited range of values (corresponding to all the slopes between the limiting slopes to the left and right of the points in question). At such corner points, a limited range of relative shares must be possible, depending upon the relative proportions of labor and non-labor inputs that can coexist there.' (ibid.: 200).

12 See note 1 on p. 202 of Samuelson (1962).

13 Cf. Solow (1988: 313): 'Estimating an aggregate production function was hardly a new idea, but I did have a new wrinkle in mind: to use observed factor prices as indicators of current marginal productivities, so that each observation would give me not only an approximate point on the production function but also an approximate indication of its slopes. I am pretty sure that this idea was suggested to me by equilibrium growth theory. I want to emphasize that I did not have any notion that I was doing something intensely controversial.'

14 In a conversation with the author (13 June 1989), Garegnani mentioned as one of the reasons for the delay that he wanted to wait for Samuelson's revised version, in the light of Garegnani's criticism, of his 1962 article.

15 In an interview with the author on 20 April 1989.

16 In the same note of the manuscript, the possibility of reswitching is used to discuss the possibility of capital reversing (though this term is not used). Garegnani observes that he has 'been pointed out that this possibility is mentioned in J. Robinson, "The Accumulation of Capital" as a "curiosum" . . . .'

17 Interview with the author, 13 June 1989.

18 Cf. the Preface of Robinson (1956: v).

19 See the discussion in paragraph 9 of Chapter 12, 'Different models for different purposes? Three types of pluralism'.

20 The Preface of Garegnani (1960) acknowledges the influence of paragraphs IV and V of their Introduction to the first volume of Ricardo's collected works.

21 Notice that the figure shows reswitching. But though Garegnani mentioned reswitching in his original criticism of Samuelson, he makes no prominent use of it.

22 This can also be seen as follows. From the production function $S = S(J, L)$ Garegnani derives through (13) an expression for the maximum output per head (or labour productivity): $S/L = e(r) + r(-e'(r))$. According to (14) it must also be the case that $S/L = q(\delta S/\delta J) = q(r)$. Samuelson's claim that the relations among w, r and q in the heterogeneous model are simulated by the homogeneous model is only true if both these expressions are equal. Subsequently, Garegnani examines the conditions under which this is the case.

23 Cf. Harcourt (1976: 50), who distinguishes this from 'a more charitable view' (i.e. if Samuelson (1962) is considered to be a special case of Sraffa's production systems where

there *are* different capital goods as between the systems; this is the case in Robinson and Naqvi (1967); there, the WPF is also linear), where equal factor proportions do *not* have to be interpreted as implying homogeneous capital. But then *still*, in the case of a straight-line WPF, we only get, in the non-jelly world, a pseudo production function. I find Harcourt's argument hard to follow.

6   Taking methodological stock (II)

[A]bstract cases are always being constructed in economic theory, when they can simplify the complexities of the real world while retaining the relevant features which are being investigated.

Pasinetti (1969: 520)

1   The antipodean idealization model

While PIM analyses the syntactical structure of idealizing theories and models, Alan Musgrave pays attention to the pragmatic or intentional aspects of idealizations and strategies of model development. Thus, he is able to fill in some details which PIM does not describe, such as the role of criticism and the different functions which idealizing and factualizing strategies may have in the development of a model. Because Musgrave has lived and worked in New Zealand for a long time, I will refer to his analysis as the 'antipodean idealization model', or 'AIM'. According to this analysis, much of the confusion in discussions of false or unrealistic assumptions in economics is due to the fact that the analysis stays too much on the surface. Usually, idealizations[1] which are employed by economic theorists all have the same syntactical structure. But identical syntactical structures may conceal significant pragmatic differences. A feature that according to Musgrave further complicates the study of idealizations is that in the course of the life of a model they may change their meaning and function. And as different meanings and functions exert different influences on the model's further development, it is important to take this into account.

Following AIM, we may distinguish three strategies of model development:[2]

1   A *negligibility strategy* consists of introducing the assumption ('negligibility assumption') that particular factors G which are present in reality and which are expected to exert an influence may be omitted from the model's antecedent without altering its predictions at all, or without altering them in a way that is detectable (Musgrave 1981: 378).[3]

2   When a prediction by a model containing a negligibility assumption turns out to be false, one may decide to follow a *domain strategy*: maintain the

negligibility assumption but restrict the applicability of the model to just those cases in which the neglected factor is indeed negligible. The negligibility assumption is interpreted as a 'domain assumption'. Musgrave states that this transition may pass unnoticed, even though the status of the model undergoes a radical change; the transition

> replaces a stronger or more testable model with a weaker or less testable one. It is therefore an *ad hoc* modification in Popper's sense. But we cannot unreservedly condemn such modifications: we value strength but we also value truth, and the weaker theory might be true where its stronger ancestor was false.
>
> (Musgrave 1981: 381)[4]

3   When on further examination it turns out that there is no empirical domain in which the factor G can be neglected, a *heuristic strategy* may be initiated. The assumption that G is negligible is turned into a 'heuristic assumption' by examining what difference G makes to the prediction. According to AIM the rationale for this strategy is that the structure of some theories is too complex to directly derive empirical predictions from them. Instead, a method of successive approximation must be used. AIM's heuristic strategy coincides with the strategy of factualization which is distinguished by PIM.

The apparatus of PIM may be used to describe AIM's other strategies as well. The passage from Musgrave that was quoted above (ibid.: 378) suggests that we have to distinguish between two types of negligibility strategies. One, which for the moment I will call a type-one negligibility strategy, refers to a case in which the factor that is neglected does affect the prediction, but the effect is not detectable. This negligibility strategy may be shown as the transition from (1) to (1'):

$$(x)(p_1(x) > 0 \,\&\, p_2(x) > 0 \,\&\, \cdots \,\&\, p_n(x) = 0 \Rightarrow F(x) = 0), \qquad (1)$$

$$(x)(p_1(x) > 0 \,\&\, p_2(x) = 0 \,\&\, \cdots \,\&\, p_n(x) = 0 \Rightarrow F'(x) = 0), \qquad (1')$$

where F' is an approximation of F.[5]

The other type of negligibility strategy which is suggested by the quotation is the case where neglecting the influence of a particular factor does not lead to a different prediction. This might be called a type-two negligibility assumption, and it might be thought that this can be described in terms of PIM as the transition from (1) to

$$(x)(p_1(x) > 0 \,\&\, p_2(x) = 0 \,\&\, \cdots \,\&\, p_n(x) = 0 \Rightarrow F(x) = 0). \qquad (2)$$

Despite the assumption that $p_2(x) = 0$ (the factor whose influence is indicated by the characteristic parameter p_2 is ruled out), the consequent $F(x) = 0$ is claimed to remain unaffected. However, this would be a mistake. A so-called type-two negligibility assumption is no idealization at all. If a factor does not make a difference to the prediction of a model, its characteristic parameter (p_2) does not figure in the model at all. If we wanted to describe this situation in terms of PIM at all, it would look like

$$(x)(p_1(x) > 0 \,\&\, p_3(x) = 0 \,\&\, \cdots \,\&\, p_n(x) = 0 \Rightarrow F(x) = 0). \tag{2'}$$

Krajewski's examples from physics illustrate that a negligibility assumption often is not introduced by scientists with some express purpose, but that it is *discovered* that a particular theory or model implicitly makes one. That is why in PIM this move is described as the *revealing of idealizing conditions*.

The syntactical analysis of PIM is incapable of capturing the distinction between a negligibility strategy and a domain strategy; both are described by the transition from (3) to (4).

$$(x)(p_1(x) > 0 \,\&\, p_2(x) = 0 \,\&\, \cdots \,\&\, p_n(x) = 0 \Rightarrow F_3(x) = 0), \tag{3}$$

$$(x)(p_1(x) = 0 \,\&\, p_2(x) = 0 \,\&\, \cdots \,\&\, p_n(x) = 0 \Rightarrow F_4(x) = 0). \tag{4}$$

Their difference is pragmatic.

Musgrave stresses that the driving force behind the changing status of idealizations and the development of a model is *criticism*: 'criticism may change the status of an assumption. What in youth was a bold and adventurous negligibility assumption, may be reduced in middle-age to a sedate domain assumption, and decline in old-age into a mere heuristic assumption.' (ibid.: 385).[6]

And indeed, the discussion of the case studies in subsequent chapters will demonstrate that criticism gives the impulse for changes of strategy. However, Musgrave does not mention a possible strategy of criticism which a comparison of his own model with PIM might have suggested to him. It is the conscious search for hidden idealizations with the purpose of criticizing a particular model for being valid under restricted conditions only. Not only is this a possible strategy of criticism, it turns out to be an important strategy of criticism in the actual debate. This is also the case with the strategy which is often followed in response to this, namely the heuristic strategy, which attempts to demonstrate that the prediction continues to hold as the unrealistic assumptions are factualized. I will return to the comparison of PIM and AIM in paragraph 3 of Chapter 10.

2   Aiming at a complete model of idealizations

Now that both PIM and AIM have been discussed, I will examine how suitable they are for analyzing the Samuelson–Garegnani episode. It will turn out that they have to be amended.

1. Both AIM and PIM have to be supplemented so as to allow for the fact that idealizations are often made *for a specific purpose*. This is illustrated by what Samuelson does, or says he does, namely showing that *for the purpose of deriving the relative factor shares* the heterogeneity of capital may be abstracted from. Thus, he both introduces a negligibility assumption and an additional condition restricting

the domain of the idealized model to a particular application: the calculation of factor shares. In terms of PIM this may be shown as the transition from a model

$$(x)(p_1(x) > 0 \ \& \ p_2(x) = 0 \ \& \cdots \Rightarrow F_3(x) = 0) \tag{3'}$$

to

$$(x)(p_1(x) = 0 \ \& \ p_2(x) = 0 \ \& \cdots \ \& \ R(x) \Rightarrow F_4(x) = 0), \tag{4'}$$

where p_1 is a parameter which takes a value greater than zero for heterogeneous capital and zero for homogeneous capital; $R(x)$ indicates the restriction of the domain of x for which the assumption is valid. However, in this case assuming $p_1(x) = 0$ is not an idealization. If a negligibility assumption does not make a difference to the prediction at all, the factor that is neglected simply is not a relevant factor, and therefore assuming that it is negligible is not a false assumption nor is it an idealization. Musgrave wrongly fails to draw this conclusion. It is not very clear whether Musgrave considers negligibility assumptions to be idealizations or true assumptions about the irrelevance of factors: 'Negligibility assumptions are stated only for factors which might be *expected* to have some effect but which, we claim, will not.' (ibid.: 378, n. 2). But on what grounds would we expect them to have an influence? If they do have an influence, claiming that they do not and being satisfied with an approximation of the true prediction involves an idealization; if they do not have an influence, the claim or assumption that they do not is true. Musgrave's wording in a related passage suggests that he does not distinguish between negligibility assumptions which are true and those which are idealizations. Compare ibid.: 378, where a negligibility assumption is said to be a 'hypothesis that some factor F which might be expected to affect that phenomenon actually has no effect upon it, or at least no detectable effect.' The first half of the sentence refers to a true assumption, the second to an idealization.

That this ambiguity is not the exclusive trademark of a philosopher of science is shown by the fact that a similar ambiguity or confused intuition can be found in Samuelson's article.[7] He offers the assumption of the homogeneity of capital as an idealization. If we grant, for a moment, that it is, it is not quite clear for what purpose it is introduced. The afterthought added at the last moment, and which was quoted in the previous chapter,[8] leads one to believe that Samuelson thought he was following a heuristic strategy. If we assume that the homogeneity assumption is an idealization, it may be observed that the article contains several more ambiguities as to the nature of the homogeneity assumption: a type-two negligibility assumption, a type-one negligibility assumption, or a heuristic assumption. The ambiguity is due to attempts by Samuelson to incorporate as much of Garegnani's criticism as he could.[9]

But Samuelson's confusion goes even deeper. Because he fails to distinguish between what we have called type-two and type-one idealizations, Samuelson is confused as to whether or not a particular assumption is an idealization at all. Stating that the homogeneous model can also generate reliable predictions about a world with heterogeneous capital, would be a (legitimate) idealization if the predictions were approximately true. But Samuelson has claimed rigorous truth for them, in which case the homo- or heterogeneity is not relevant. If it does not matter whether or not capital is heterogeneous, abstracting from heterogeneity is not an idealization. The fact that the proposition that capital is homogeneous is a false descriptive statement about reality does not for that reason make it an idealization. Garegnani shows that it does matter whether capital is homogeneous or not, and that Samuelson's homogeneity assumption restricts the domain of application of Samuelson's model to a world with homogeneous capital. So, what Garegnani shows is that the homogeneity assumption is an idealization *relative to* the claim that a model containing it can simulate a more complex, heterogeneous model and, moreover, that the claim cannot be upheld. Thus, we have the paradoxical situation that although Samuelson *says* he idealizes by assuming capital to be homogeneous, this is not true until Garegnani *proves* that he does. But this is no paradox according to PIM: an old theory (or model) is only discovered to be idealizational *in the light of* a new theory (or model). This is explicitly recognized by Krajewski.[10]

2. There seems to be an even more fundamental methodological confusion underlying Samuelson's article, one that precedes the ones discussed above. Have another look at the crux of Samuelson's allegedly novel approach:

> In the singular case where two economies have exactly the same factor-price frontier, however they may be different in the background, we can treat them as equivalent in so far as predictions about their long-run interest- and wage-rate properties are concerned. And, what may be more useful, if two economies have approximately the same frontiers within a given range, we can use either one to predict the long-run properties of the other in that range.
>
> (Samuelson 1962: 196)

There is nothing idealizational about this, at least not according to PIM, where idealizations are special cases of more general models, which are related by the correspondence relation or by factualization.[11] What is claimed here by Samuelson is that as long as models generate identical (or approximately identical) predictions, they are equivalent. Now, where have we heard that before? Of course, in Friedman's much-discussed 'The Methodology of Positive Economics' (Friedman 1953)! Friedman stresses time and again that the most important, if not the only, criterion for choosing between alternative theories or models ('hypotheses' or 'sets of assumptions' in Friedman's terminology) is the accuracy of the predictions they help to generate. Thus, we find him saying: 'The choice among alternative hypotheses equally consistent with the available evidence must to some extent be arbitrary, though there is general agreement that relevant considerations are suggested by the criteria "simplicity" and "fruitfulness", themselves notions that defy completely objective specification.' (ibid.: 10).[12] And about the law of falling bodies of classical mechanics, $s = 1/2gt^2$, which is used to predict the distance a falling body travels and which assumes the existence of a vacuum: 'For all I know there may be other sets of assumptions that would yield the same formula. The formula is accepted because it works, not because we live in an approximate vacuum – whatever that means.' (ibid.: 18). We could phrase this differently by saying that – considerations of simplicity and fruitfulness apart – different models are equivalent as long as they generate the same predictions. It is not the theory or theories describing the underlying mechanism that Friedman is interested in; he is only interested in the question: does it work? This is instrumentalism. But if it is, then so is Samuelson's approach. Only, in Samuelson's case the instrumentalism travels under the false guise of an idealizing approach. It is not until Garegnani's demonstration that Samuelson's model is a special case of a more general model that Samuelson's approach is revealed to be an idealizing one. Until that moment Samuelson, because he does not present his model as a limit case, nor tells us why his surrogate model works, is no more than an instrumentalist. An instrumentalist, moreover, who is much less sophisticated than Friedman, whose name is quite generally associated with instrumentalism. For Samuelson states that his simplified 'as if' model simulates or mimics a more complex model without going into the details of the relation between both models. Friedman, on the other hand, does discuss the relation between hypotheses and more general theories, a relation that is relevant to the problem of the choice of hypotheses:

> [One] hypothesis is more attractive than [another] not because its 'assumptions' are more 'realistic' but rather because it is part of a more general theory that applies to a wide variety of phenomena, of which the position of leaves around a tree is a special case, has more implications capable of being contradicted, and has failed to be contradicted under a wider variety of circumstances.
>
> (Friedman 1953: 20)

Friedman describes a case of preference for a particular hypothesis (or theory) on the basis of the fact that it is a special case of a corresponding theory which not only has more explanatory power but is also corroborated.[13] The interpretation of Friedman's methodology as an attempt to come to grips with the nature of idealizations in economics finds confirmation in Musgrave's analysis, which, from a background that is entirely different from PIM, reconstructs Friedman's methodology as a theory about idealizing models. Indeed, the combination of PIM and AIM may very well serve to yield by far the most consistent and interesting interpretation of Friedman's methodology. This project will not be carried out here.[14] But we may observe as a general point that a correspondence strategy may turn a model that was introduced and judged to be satisfactory on instrumentalist grounds, i.e. because it obtained 'better' predictions, into a 'deeper' explanation. More will be said about this in the last chapter.

In the light of Garegnani's criticism, which involves a reconstruction of Samuelson's argument in terms of the relation between a more general model and a special case, and in the light of PIM, Samuelson's model is indeed an idealizing one. So we need not be bothered here by considerations of instrumentalism, and we can continue to analyze Samuelson's article with the help of AIM. But not without some further qualifications.

3. Unlike Musgrave's suggestion to the contrary, the transition between a negligibility or a heuristic assumption and a domain assumption does not always pass unnoticed. For instance, it is the crux of Garegnani's approach. This has to do with the purpose for which he utilizes a domain strategy, as will be elucidated in the next paragraphs.

4. AIM's core proposition is corroborated by the Samuelson–Garegnani episode: criticism changes the status of assumptions. What to Samuelson's mind was a negligibility or a heuristic assumption, is shown by Garegnani to be a domain assumption. Garegnani demonstrates that Samuelson's intended strategy fails, and he concludes that Samuelson's homogeneous model is true for a domain in which capital is in fact homogeneous. It looks as if Garegnani's result is accurately described by Musgrave's observation that a domain strategy may lead to the abandonment of a stronger, more testable yet false model in favour of a weaker but truer one. This would be in keeping with the methodological virtues Garegnani claims for separating the theory of value from the theory of production and accumulation:

> [T]he separation of the pure theory of value from the study of the circumstances governing changes in the outputs of commodities, does not seem to meet any essential difficulty. On the contrary, it may open the way for a more satisfactory treatment of the relations between outputs and the technical conditions of production. Moreover, by freeing the theory of value from the assumption of consumers' tastes given from outside the economic system, this separation may favour a better understanding of consumption, and its dependence on the rest of the system.
>
> With this, the theory of value will lose the all-embracing quality it assumed with the marginal method. *But what will be lost in scope will certainly be gained in consistency and, we may hope, in fruitfulness.*
>
> (Garegnani 1970: 428, emphasis added)[15]

This is strongly reminiscent of the reason Musgrave gives for following a domain strategy:

> [W]e value strength but we also value truth, and the weaker theory might be true where its stronger ancestor was false.
>
> (Musgrave 1981: 381)[16]

However, there is a major difference. We have to bear in mind that Garegnani's domain strategy was not meant to demonstrate the strength or truth in a limited domain of Samuelson's homogeneous model. Instead, he follows the strategy of showing Samuelson's negligibility assumption to be a domain assumption because he wants to demonstrate that marginal value theory cannot explain changes in the output of commodities. According to Garegnani a different theory is needed for that.

Though AIM improves on PIM by paying attention to intentional aspects of idealizing strategies, it does not do so to a sufficient extent. Musgrave tacitly assumes that critics have constructive purposes only. With Garegnani this is clearly not the case; his criticism is intended to be critical of neoclassical theory. This oversight of Musgrave derives from AIM's empiricist bias: AIM presupposes that the impulse for a transition to a different strategy is given by empirical criticism only.[17] It is in that sense that we have to interpret Musgrave's observation: in AIM's book strength and truth are empirical (or factual) strength and empirical (or factual) truth. But in the episode described above no empirical arguments are employed to directly criticize or refute predictions. What happens instead is that theorems are put forward, and the formal, mathematical conditions are stated from which they can be proved (the sufficient conditions), or that can be proved from them (the necessary conditions). Does this mean that AIM is not suitable for describing the development of the debate after all? What role is played by formal arguments? And do empirical arguments have no role to play at all in the debate? I will return to these questions in Chapter 9, after several more case studies have been discussed.

Notes

1 Musgrave speaks of 'assumptions that seem to be quite obviously false' (Musgrave 1981: 377).
2 Musgrave distinguishes types of assumptions, not strategies. But I think it better to speak of strategies, for both conceptual and stylistic reasons. On a number of issues I attempt to give a more precise formulation than can be found in Musgrave's article.
3 As will be argued below, there is a fundamental difference between the case when a factor does not affect the prediction at all, and the case where neglecting a factor's influence still allows a good approximation.
4 The word 'theory' has been replaced by 'model'.
5 Cf. Nowak (1980: 30).
6 The calm and dullness of the changes suggested by Musgrave is belied by the tone and vigour of the capital debate, which one commentator called 'one of the fiercest battles ever fought in theoretical economics' (Pen 1971: 417). For further comments on Musgrave, see below.
7 So we may conclude that Musgrave is a good philosopher of science in the sense that his methodology closely reflects the features of his empirical material.
8 'the false conjecture that my extreme assumption of equi-proportional inputs ... could be *lightened* and still leave one with many of the surrogate propositions' (Samuelson 1962: 225, n. 7, emphasis added).
9 This is confirmed both by Samuelson himself (conversation of 20 April 1989), who says that he also added criticism of his own, and by Garegnani (conversation of 12 June 1989).
10 Cf., for instance, Krajewski (1977: 37): 'the first Kepler law is, in the light of CM [classical mechanics], idealizational.'
11 Or, what amounts to the same, idealization. The only difference between factualization and idealization is the 'direction' of the relation.
12 Logical completeness and consistency are mentioned as further, though subsidiary, criteria.
13 Not only is Samuelson's approach more instrumentalist and less sophisticated than Friedman's, Samuelson also seems to bear some responsibility for the quite generally accepted reputation of Friedman as an instrumentalist. Cf. Samuelson (1963), where he both describes and dismisses Friedman's approach as instrumentalist under the name of F-twist.

14 The author intends to carry out such a reconstruction at a later date.
15 The close similarity with Robinson's approach in her 1956 article has already been pointed out above, in the text dealing with Garegnani's criticism of Samuelson.
16 The word 'theory' has been replaced by 'model'.
17 In a letter to the author (20 November 1988), Musgrave insists on this: 'But on my main critical point I remain unrepentant. I insist that only *empirical* considerations can turn a negligibility assumption into a domain assumption. More precisely, it is only because we regard a prediction or consequence *P* of some model containing negligibility assumptions *as false* that we will turn those assumptions into domain assumptions. Now on what sort of grounds will we regard this *P* as false? The possible grounds range from hard-headed empirical ones (gathering data), to matters of common economic knowledge, to independent theoretical considerations (e.g. we know from production theory that different factor coefficients yield different production functions from a homogeneous capital model). Let us call these *factual* considerations rather than *empirical* ones, since the former suggests that *only* the gathering of empirical data can turn the trick. The contrast remains clear: purely logical (as opposed to factual) considerations cannot turn the trick.' The distinction between factual and empirical is useful, and will be taken over. But I will argue later that the insistence on empirical or factual as opposed to formal counterexamples unnecessarily restricts AIM's domain of application.

7   From curiosum to issue

[R]eswitching became an issue instead of a curiosum.

Solow (1983: 184, emphasis deleted)

In criticizing Samuelson (1962), Garegnani repeated what was essentially the argument of his own 1960 book in Italian (Garegnani 1960),[1] namely that the amount of capital cannot be determined independently of the rate of profit. But this time, drawing upon Sraffa (1960), he put his criticism in terms of the wpf, which he had not done in his book, and he mentioned reswitching, without, however, assigning any central role to it in his criticism.

I suggest that the subsequent course of events was as follows: Garegnani's criticism referred to Sraffa (1960) and mentioned reswitching. This prompted Samuelson to read Sraffa's book, or study it more closely,[2] and it was not until then that he realized reswitching was a counterexample to some of the predictions of neoclassical models which he had believed to be true. One of these was 'Samuelson's theorem'.[3] So it was only via Garegnani's criticism and through Sraffa's book that at least one 'mainstream economist', namely Samuelson, realized that his 'orthodoxy' was at stake, as Robinson relates.[4] I think that we have to take Robinson's observation quite literally: the *only* other economist who realized the importance of the reswitching result was mainstream, orthodox Samuelson.

One more proviso seems in order. Solow in his 1955 article had written his own criticism of the aggregate production function, which had nothing to do with reswitching. He stated the conditions under which it is legitimate to use an aggregate production function, and concluded that these are so restrictive as to make the aggregate production function of very limited usefulness. It is he who expressly coined the term 'pseudo production function'[5] in order to emphasize that this instrument of static analysis was not up to the task of describing the *process* of production and accumulation in time.[6] But neither he nor anyone else pursued this line of criticism at the time. Solow even continued to use the production function in his own subsequent empirical work. Solow the econometrician was not inhibited by the results of Solow the theoretician.[7] But with the exception of these authors it was apparently generally believed that Samuelson (1962) provided a satisfactory account of the neoclassical, idealizing approach to distribution theory: 'For several years everyone (except Garegnani) was somewhat baffled by the surrogate production function.' (Robinson 1975c: 36).[8]

In the meantime, Samuelson had become convinced that the possibility of reswitching was a serious criticism, and he tried to find a way of saving his 1962 model. But he did not reply to Garegnani's main criticism, which, as we have seen, did not make use of reswitching. Instead, Samuelson focused on the *different* question of how reswitching might be avoided. He thought that the reswitching counterexample, which he had encountered in Sraffa's book, was not so strong as to render his surrogate production function model inapplicable in general. So, Samuelson changed the problem. And he sought the solution in the conjecture that indecomposable models are not affected by reswitching. Then 'sometime in 1964' (Solow 1983: 184) Samuelson told David Levhari, who was writing his Ph.D. thesis under Samuelson's supervision, about his conjecture. In 1965 Levhari published his proof of Samuelson's conjecture that reswitching cannot occur in an indecomposable production system.[9] Pasinetti was the first to come up with what he claimed was a counterexample to this result. During the 1965 Econometric Society Conference in Rome a symposium was organized to discuss Levhari's proof. The symposium papers were published in *Quarterly Journal of Economics*, 1966. They demonstrated in various ways the falsity of Levhari's proof: 'Counterexamples were soon produced and reswitching became an issue instead of a *curiosum*.' (ibid.). The 'Cambridge debate' had gained momentum. How this came about will be shown in more detail with the aid of the following case studies.

1   A little theorem with big consequences

Levhari sets out to prove Samuelson's conjecture (or theorem) that reswitching cannot take place: 'in an "indecomposable" or "irreducible" technology (which means a situation in which *every single* output requires, directly or indirectly as input for its production, something *positive* of *every single* other output).' (Levhari and Samuelson 1966: 518–19).[10] The idea behind this conjecture was apparently that in an indecomposable model the production of any good involves as inputs the goods produced by all other production processes, including the ones in which diminishing returns prevail. And with diminishing returns reswitching could not occur.[11] Levhari admits that reswitching

> may indeed be observed in the production of a single good. This would have the unfortunate consequence that we could no longer say that the lowering of the interest rate brings about a process of 'deepening' and each process is more capital-intensive than its predecessors.
>
> (Levhari 1965: 99)

But he expects his proof to 'show that it [reswitching] is impossible with the whole base of production. . . . [E]ven though we cannot order the activities according to "degree of mechanisation", we can do so with the matrices.' (ibid.).

There are k_1 activities that can be used for producing good 1: $a^{11}, a^{12}, \ldots, a^{1k_1}$; k_2 activities for good 2: $a^{21}, a^{22}, \ldots, a^{2k_2}$; and k_n for good n. Each activity is characterized by a column vector with $n + 1$ elements: the first element, denoted by 0, represents the labour input requirement, and the remaining $1, \ldots, n$ elements represent the inputs of goods that are required to produce one unit of output of the commodity concerned. All capital is assumed to be written off in one period, so there is only circulating capital. There are $\prod k_i$ $(i = 1, \ldots, n)$ Leontief input–output matrices, which are denoted by a, b, c, etc. The matrices are assumed to be non-negative and indecomposable. The latter assumption is made because indecomposability is considered to be crucial, both by Samuelson and Levhari. Only stationary states are considered.

So, there are $\prod k_i$ $(i = 1, \ldots, n)$ books of blueprints or *production techniques*

$$\begin{bmatrix} a_0 \\ a \end{bmatrix}, \quad \begin{bmatrix} b_0 \\ b \end{bmatrix}, \ldots$$

for producing the output mix in the economy that differ by one activity.

Levhari's proof is in terms of wage units, i.e. he puts $w = 1$. So, in his analysis the w/p–r relationships or wpf's take on the special form of relationships between $1/p$ and r. Furthermore, he chooses to analyse the choice of technique not in terms of maximizing the real wage but in the dual terms of minimizing the output price given the rate of discount $\lambda = 1/(1 + r)$. So his wpf is the relationship between p and λ.

For a pair of input–output matrices a and b representing two different techniques of production, the condition for a to be chosen is that $p_a \leq p_b$.

$$p_a = a_0(\lambda I - a)^{-1} \quad \text{and} \quad p_b = b_0(\lambda I - a)^{-1},$$

so

$$a_0(\lambda I - a)^{-1} \leq b_0(\lambda I - b)^{-1}.$$

Hence,

$$a_0(\lambda I - a)^{-1}(\lambda I - b) \leq b_0$$

and

$$a_0(\lambda I - a)^{-1}(\lambda I - a + a - b) \leq b_0.$$

Multiplying out yields

$$a_0 + a_0(\lambda I - a)^{-1}(a - b) \leq b_0$$

or

$$a_0(\lambda I - a)^{-1}(a - b) \leq b_0 - a_0. \tag{1}$$

Beyond the switch from technique a to technique b,

$$p_b < p_a \quad \text{or} \quad a_0(\lambda I - a)^{-1}(a - b) > b_0 - a_0,$$

and this inequality continues to hold if a is not to return. The inequality continues to hold if $a_0(\lambda I - a)^{-1}(a - b)$ is a monotone non-decreasing function of λ. In that case, as λ increases, the price inequality between the outputs of techniques a and b will not be reversed, so that technique a will not become eligible again. In other words, a sufficient condition for non-reswitching is that $a_0(\lambda I - a)^{-1}(a - b)$ is a monotone non-decreasing function of λ. Levhari now proceeds to find the conditions for this function to be monotone non-decreasing.

He has already proved that all the elements of $a_0(\lambda I - a)^{-1}$ are monotone decreasing functions of λ, i.e. $-a_0(\lambda I - a)^{-1} < 0$. So, whether $a_0(\lambda I - a)^{-1}(a - b)$ is a monotone non-decreasing function of λ depends on the sign of $(a - b)$. As a and b are matrices, so is their difference d. And if it is assumed that a and b differ by only one technique of production, i.e. by one column, d is a matrix with all zeroes and one column of elements that are not all zero. If the column by which a and b differ contains both positive and negative numbers, we cannot establish whether or not a switch between the two production matrices has occurred. For $a_0(\lambda I - a)^{-1}(a - b)$ to be monotone non-decreasing, the difference $(a - b)$ has to be seminegative, i.e. the elements of d have to be smaller than or equal to zero.

Levhari introduces a mathematical device that obtains this result in the following lemma:

> For two positive indecomposable matrices a and b there exists a semipositive vector x such that either $(a - b)x \geq 0$, or $(a - b)x \leq 0$.[12]

This mathematical lemma is given 'some economic meaning' (ibid.: 105) in the following way:

> there exists some activity level x such that we need more circular capital of all goods either with a or with b, or we are indifferent.
>
> (Levhari 1965: 105)

As a next step, both sides of (1) are multiplied by the semipositive column vector x^* that has the properties described in the lemma:

$$a_0(\lambda I - a)^{-1}(a - b)x^* \leq (b_0 - a_0)x^*.$$

The function on the left-hand side is called $\psi(l)$. The first-order condition for this function to be monotone non-increasing is

$$\psi'(l) = -a_0(\lambda I - a)^{-2}(a - b)x^* \leq 0.$$

As $a_0(\lambda I - a)^{-2} > 0$, the direction of the inequality is determined by the sign of $(a - b)x^*$. If $(a - b)x^* \geq 0$, then $\psi'(\lambda) \leq 0$ and $\psi(\lambda)$ is monotone non-increasing.

When technique a has been used and the system switches to a different technique b at a higher λ, $\psi'(\lambda) < 0$ at the switch point. The monotonicity of the function guarantees that $\psi'(\lambda) < 0$ for all λ. And the monotonicity of the function is guaranteed by the lemma that either $(a - b)x^* \geq 0$ or $(a - b)x^* \leq 0$.

2 The symposium

In 1965 a symposium was devoted to the matter. A number of authors criticized Levhari's results. Their papers were published in 1966 in *The Quarterly Journal of Economics*.

Strengthen and destroy

Bruno, Burmeister and Sheshinski (BBS) (1966) give Solow credit for pointing out that no semipositive vector x exists such that for any two matrices either $(a - b) \geq 0$ or $(a - b) \leq 0$. So, Levhari's lemma is false. This would have sufficed as a criticism. But still, BBS prove that Levhari's theorem is true if it is made conditional upon the *assumption* that a vector x with the above properties exists. Subsequently, they analyze the economic interpretation of this condition, and of an alternative condition for non-reswitching. Then they argue that both of these conditions are very restrictive in the sense that the class of cases for which Levhari's non-reswitching theorem would remain valid is 'restricted quite heavily' (ibid.: 527).

Before criticizing Levhari's theorem, BBS show that Levhari's circulating-capital model can be generalized. First, they take μ_j to be the rate of depreciation of the tth capital good; r is the rate of interest. Then, assuming wages to be paid at the end of the production period,

$$P_j = wa_{0j} + \sum_{i}^{n}(\mu_i + r)P_i a_{ij}, \quad j = 1, \ldots, n$$

or in vector notation

$$p = a_0(I - \rho a)^{-1}, \tag{2}$$

where $p = P_i/w$, and $\rho = (\mu + r)$, a diagonal matrix with $\rho_{i=j} = \mu_i + r$.

BBS conduct their further analysis in terms of (2), which is more general than Levhari's equation, and differs from it by the assumption about wage payments. This may be seen as follows: put wages equal to unity, assume capital goods to be written off in one period ($\mu_i = 1$), and assume wages to be paid at the beginning of the period; then

$$p = (1 + r)a_0(I - (1 + r)a)^{-1},$$

from which Levhari's price equation $p = a_0(\lambda I - a)^{-1}$ follows if we take $\lambda = 1/(1 + r)$.

The model is also generalized so as to incorporate capital inputs in earlier periods, and intermediate capital goods. It is indicated (but not proved) that whether or not the technique matrices are indecomposable is irrelevant for reswitching.

The structure of the rest of BBS's argument is as follows. First, they find conditions that rule out reswitching in the habitual two-sector model. Then they examine what conditions rule out reswitching in an n-sector model where $n > 2$. It is at this stage of their analysis that Levhari's theorem is introduced, not as a generally valid statement, but rather as a hypothetical statement. It is concluded that if a vector with the properties described by Levhari exists, then his theorem would be correct. But the assumption of the existence of the vector implies very restrictive economic conditions. Third, non-reswitching is proved to follow from the model and an alternative sufficiency condition, which, if interpreted in economic terms, is less restrictive than the previous condition, but is still very restrictive.

So far, the analysis has dealt with the nature of reswitching. BBS then examine the consequences that reswitching has for the pattern of steady-state consumption.

Conditions for non-reswitching in a two-sector model

For a technique a producing a capital good and a consumption good, the price equations are

$$P_K = a_{01}w + a_{11}(r + \mu_a)P_K,$$

where P_K is the price of capital goods and w is the wage rate, both in terms of the consumption good and

$$1 = a_{02}w + a_{12}(r + \mu_a)P_K,$$

where a_{ij}: fixed input coefficients ($i = 0$: labour; $i = 1$: capital; $j = 1$: capital good; $j = 2$: consumption good). From these, the equation for the wpf may be derived:

$$w = \frac{1 - (\mu_a + r)a_{11}}{a_{02} + (\mu_a + r)G_a},$$

$$G_a = \det \begin{vmatrix} a_{01} & a_{02} \\ a_{11} & a_{12} \end{vmatrix},$$

the determinant of the coefficient matrix.

The wpf is convex or concave to the origin according as $G_a > 0$, respectively $G_a < 0$. $G_a > 0$ if $a_{01} \cdot a_{12} - a_{11} \cdot a_{02} > 0$, so if

$$\frac{a_{01}}{a_{11}} > \frac{a_{02}}{a_{12}}.$$

In economic terms this means that the consumption goods industry is more capital intensive than the capital goods industry. The converse holds if $G_a < 0$. In an analogous way the wpf for a technique b, which uses a different capital good with a different depreciation rate μ_b, but which produces the same consumption good,

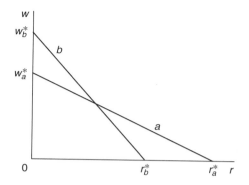

Figure 7.1 'Linear' production techniques (adapted from Bruno, Burmeister and Sheshinski 1966: 532).

may be derived. Reswitching does not occur if the production techniques are as in Figure 7.1.

$$r_a^* = r_a^{\max} = \frac{1}{a_{11}} - \mu_a \qquad \text{(the net productivity in the capital good sector)},$$

$$w_a^* = w_a^{\max} = \frac{1 - \mu_a\, a_{11}}{a_0 + \mu_a\, G_a} \qquad \begin{array}{l}\text{(the net labour productivity in the} \\ \text{consumption good sector)}.\end{array}$$

But in this model it is not generally the case that reswitching is excluded, as may be seen from Figure 7.2.

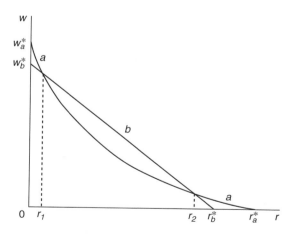

Figure 7.2 A 'non-linear' technique and reswitching.

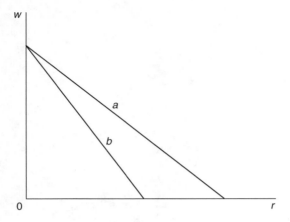

Figure 7.3 Technique dominance.

At r_2 the economy switches back to technique a, which was used when r was smaller than r_1. The conditions for non-reswitching are formulated in the following *theorem*: 'It is sufficient for no reswitching that the ordering of techniques by r^* is exactly the reverse of the ordering by w^*.' (ibid.: 535). In economic terms, this means that 'whenever the technique which has a higher capital/output ratio in the capital good industry is also more labor-productive in the consumer good industry, then these techniques can be ordered in an unambiguous manner.' (ibid.: 534).

The authors point out that this condition is weaker than the one given by Hicks (1965: 154), which is that the ratio of the factor intensities must be the same for all techniques in order for reswitching to be excluded. Hicks' condition 'is overly strong since it also includes cases of complete dominance which are irrelevant.' (BBS 1966: 535, n. 5). Such a case of dominance is illustrated in Figure 7.3. More generally, if the factor intensity ratios are the same in all activities (so, $G_i = 0$ for all $i = a, b, \ldots$), the wpf's are straight lines, and 'the system degenerates to Samuelson's [1962] simple surrogate capital model in which reswitching obviously cannot occur.' (ibid.: 535).

The fact that in a two-sector economy with many alternative independent techniques no reswitching occurs provided there is only one capital good in the system, is stated as a theorem. The proof consists of demonstrating that with one capital good the system reduces to Samuelson's 1962 surrogate model. The theorem is said to hold more generally for a multi-sector economy with many consumer goods but still one capital good.

BBS show that their sufficiency condition is not a necessary condition for non-reswitching. In Figure 7.4 each pair of techniques satisfies the sufficiency condition, but technique b is irrelevant as it is dominated by the WPF formed by techniques a and c.

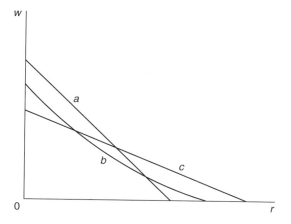

Figure 7.4 A consequence of technique dominance (adapted from Bruno, Burmeister and Sheshinski 1966: 535).

In the model used so far, the consumer good industry uses capital goods, but no consumer goods enter the capital good industry as inputs. So the systems are decomposable and thus fail to meet Levhari on his own ground. However, BBS deny that indecomposability is relevant for the occurrence or absence of switches of techniques. Nonetheless, they give a numerical counterexample to Levhari's theorem as presented because this is 'pedagogically preferable and logically crucial' (ibid.: 537).

Generalization: non-reswitching in a model with more than two sectors

After the preliminaries of the two-sector model, BBS deal with reswitching in a more general, n-sector model. They state that, *if* a vector x exists such that for any pair of matrices a and b either $(a - b)x \geq 0$ or $(a - b)x \leq 0$, '[s]trangely enough, *then* Levhari's theorem would be correct.' (ibid.: 543, emphasis in original).[13]

So, BBS make the truth of Levhari's theorem conditional upon the *assumption* that a vector with the required properties exists. Then, they analyse the condition's economic interpretation, and argue that 'it is a *very* restrictive assumption: it rules out (at least) all switches which involve only one activity and which we considered the "normal" case.' (ibid.). Note 5 to this passage provides further elucidation:

> If $(a - b)$ has one column of mixed positive and negative elements and $(n - 1)$ zero columns, then there does not exist *any* vector x such that either $(a - b)x \geq 0$ or $(a - b)x \leq 0$. This sufficiency condition can apply only when there are at least two nonzero columns in $(a - b)$, which in the present model, as we have seen, is not in general the case.

This may be illustrated with an example adapted from Garegnani (1966: 561). Take $(a - b)$ to be

$$\begin{vmatrix} 0.1 & 0 \\ -0.1 & 0 \end{vmatrix}, \quad \text{and} \quad x = (x_1, x_2).$$

Then $(a-b)x = (0.1x_1, -0.1x_2)$, a vector whose components have opposite signs. There exists one vector which fulfils the requirements, but it does so trivially; it is one with all elements equal to zero. The problem which this vector poses in economic terms is discussed in Pasinetti (1966).

An alternative sufficiency condition

At a switch point, two wpfs intersect at one rate of interest r or, assuming that all capital goods depreciate at the same rate μ and defining the scalar $r = \mu + r$, at one rate $r = r_1$. Thus the price vectors for the two techniques concerned are equal: $p_a(r_1) = p_b(r_1)$, or

$$p_a(\rho_1) - p_b(\rho_1) = a_0(I - \rho_1 a)^{-1} - b_0(I - \rho_1 b)^{-1} = 0. \tag{3}$$

For just one switch point to exist, the polynomial (3) must have one positive root. Descartes' rule of signs gives a condition for the existence of one positive root: the number of positive real roots is equal to the number of variations in sign of the coefficients of the polynomial or is less than this number by a positive even integer. So, the condition for non-reswitching in mathematical terms is that the polynomial (3) has one, three, etc. changes in sign.

BBS clothe the mathematical skeleton of this condition with economic flesh via the mathematical device of expanding $p_a(r_1)$ and $p_b(r_1)$ in a vector power series:

$$p_a(\rho r_1) = \alpha_0 + \alpha_1 \rho_1 + \alpha_2 \rho_1^2 + \cdots,$$

where $\alpha_0 = a_0$, $\alpha_1 = a_0 a$, $\alpha_2 = a_0 a^2$, etc. Then (3) is transformed into

$$p_a(\rho_1) - p_b(\rho_1) = (\alpha_0 - \beta_0) + (\alpha_1 - \beta_1)\rho_1 + (\alpha_2 - \beta_2)\rho_1^2 + \cdots = 0, \tag{4}$$

where α_0 is the vector of direct labour inputs; α_1 is the input of direct labour in the second round of production or, what amounts to the same thing, the indirect labour inputs in the first round of production; α_2 is the second-round indirect labour input, etc.

Next, BBS assume that the right-hand side of (4) has only one sign variation and take the example that the first term of (4) is negative for the ith good ($\alpha_{0i} \leq \beta_{0i}$), while all other coefficients are positive ($\alpha_{ji} \geq \beta_{ji}$ for $j = 1, 2, \ldots, n$). Then the first derivative of $p_a(\rho_1) - p_b(\rho_1)$ is positive for $\rho > 0$, so (4) has at most one root.[14]

If 'indirect labour' is replaced by 'capital', the economic interpretation of this example is that activity a_i uses less labour but more capital than b_i, so a_i is more capital intensive. BBS conclude from this 'that if for any pair of relevant techniques *a* and *b* all pairs of corresponding activities a_i and b_i can be ranked in terms of "capital intensity" (in the above sense, which is independent of the rate of interest), then reswitching cannot occur.' (BBS 1966: 543). This condition is a generalization of the two-sector case, and it is 'somewhat less restrictive' as it 'allows changes of single activities while the former does not'. (ibid.). But though weaker, the condition is still 'highly restrictive' (ibid.) as

> except for highly exceptional circumstances, techniques cannot be ranked in order of capital intensity. We thus conclude that reswitching is, at least theoretically, a perfectly acceptable case in the discrete capital model.
> (Bruno, Burmeister and Sheshinski 1966: 545)

Whether reswitching may be observed in the real world is an empirical matter. This is relegated to a footnote: 'there is an open empirical question as to whether or not reswitching is likely to be observed in an actual open economy for reasonable changes in the interest rate.' (ibid.: n. 2).

The condition for non-reswitching concerns only *pairs* of techniques. If reswitching is ruled out for any two techniques, it is certainly excluded for the WPF of many techniques. Indeed, 'assuming that *any two wpfs* can intersect only once is almost certainly an overly strong sufficient condition for nonswitching.' (ibid.: 542).[15] But there is a reason for maintaining the stronger condition: it preserves a negative relationship between the rate of interest and the steady-state level of consumption. This is dealt with in the part of the article that discusses some of the implications of reswitching.

Steady-state consumption

Following Morishima (1964: 126), BBS show that reswitching indicates a 'perverse' relationship between steady-state consumption and the rate of interest. This is shown in the following model. It is assumed that capital is replaced every period; thus, the part of this period's output which is not consumed is equal to the input of the next period:

$$X(t) - C(t) = aX(t+1),$$

where $X = (X_1, \ldots, X_n)$ is the output vector and $C = (C_1, \ldots, C_n)$ is the consumption vector. The labour supply is assumed to be constant, and fully employed.

A steady-state solution $X(t) = X(t+1) = X$ must satisfy:

(a) $X = aX + C$,   or

(b) $X = (I - a)^{-1}$ subject to the labour constraint:

(c) $L = a_0 X.$

The price vector is

(d) $P(r) = (1+r)wa_0(I - (1+r)a)^{-1}$ (*w*: wage rate).

Then[16] consumption (or net national product) is

(e) $P(r)C = wL + r(wL + P(r)aX)$.

For $r = 0$ this becomes

$P(0)C = wL$.

Setting $w = L = 1$ and rearranging yields

$C = 1/P(0)$.

The relationship between reswitching and steady-state consumption can now be shown. For simplicity set $C_2 = \cdots = C_n = 0$, and examine C_1 in different steady states. There is a set of alternative techniques

$$\begin{bmatrix} a_0 \\ a \end{bmatrix}, \begin{bmatrix} b_0 \\ b \end{bmatrix}, \cdots$$

A high steady-state consumption pattern that corresponds to a low rate of interest recurs at a higher interest rate, after a lower level of consumption has been maintained. $C(r)$ is not a monotone function. As may be seen from Figure 7.5, the

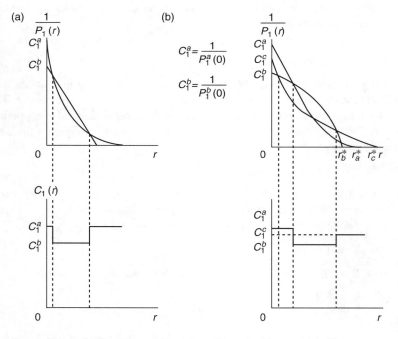

Figure 7.5(a)–(b) Perverse consumption with and without reswitching.

'perverse' behaviour of consumption may exist without reswitching. There may be non-monotonicity of $C(r)$ without reswitching, but there is no reswitching without non-monotonicity of $C(r)$. So, reswitching is a sufficient but not a necessary condition for $C(r)$ to behave 'perversely'. As was observed above, the sufficiency condition for non-reswitching found by BBS (any pair of wpfs can intersect only once) is stronger than required. But it is maintained because the condition 'may be necessary if the monotonicity of $C(r)$ is to be preserved.' (BBS 1966: 549, italics deleted).

What a pleasant surprise!

Pasinetti initiated the entire discussion of the symposium with his claim that he had found a counterexample to Levhari's theorem. However, as the coefficient matrices he uses are not indecomposable, it is not, strictly speaking, a counterexample. Pasinetti states without proof that indecomposability is not crucial. We will here only examine Pasinetti's criticism of Levhari's proof and the consequences he draws from the falsity of Levhari's theorem.

Levhari's lemma

When discussing BBS we noticed that there is one trivial case in which a vector x exists such that the inequality required for non-reswitching holds. Pasinetti observes that this is the case in which the element of the vector x that multiplies the non-zero column of the difference matrix $d = a - b$ of technical coefficients equals zero.[17]

Only in that case can a vector x be found for which it is generally the case that $(a - b)x \geq 0$, $(a - b)x \leq 0$, or $(a - b)x = 0$. Pasinetti comments:

> But this will simply eliminate the column. And if precisely that column is eliminated which contains all the differences between the two matrices, it will become impossible to tell which of the two is more profitable .... Levhari's device would then lead us to the straight equality $(a - b) = 0$, and to the false conclusion that matrix a and matrix b are indifferent for all levels of the rate of profit.
>
> (Pasinetti 1966: 512)

Pasinetti starts from Levhari's lemma, and examines the condition, in purely mathematical terms, under which it is true. After having established the condition, he proceeds to interpret it in economic terms, and to argue that it leads to a contradiction of one of the economic premises.

The rate of profit and the quantity of capital

What is the relationship between the profit rate and the quantity of capital? Traditionally it was thought that the physical quantity of capital per man bears an inverse monotone relationship to the rate of profit, so that as the profit rate is lower, the quantity of capital is higher, and vice versa: 'This belief is, in fact, crucial to the notion of a neoclassical production function ....' (ibid.: 513). However, the belief is not warranted, as Pasinetti makes clear with the following counterexample. Consider the case in which the wpfs of two techniques intersect twice. The net final products of a and b differ. They may be read off the w-axis as the points of intersection of the wpf's, where $r = 0$. At those points the net final products equal the maximum wage rate. In Figure 7.6 the net final product of a is higher than the net final product of b, and this is so in terms of any standard of value.[18]

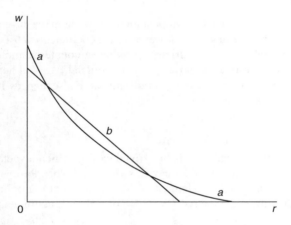

Figure 7.6 Pasinetti's counterexample.

What happens is that

at all switching points, the wage rate is the same for both technologies, in terms of any standard of value. Therefore, the amount of profit per man (in terms of any standard of value) is higher for technology a than for technology b. Since the rate of profit is the same, it follows that at all switching points the total value of capital per man (in terms of any standard of value) is higher for technology a than for technology b.

This is a remarkable result. It means that at the first switching point, an increase of the rate of profit entails a switch to a technology with a lower total value of capital per man, and at the second switching point, an increase in the rate of profit entails a switch to a technology with a higher total value of capital per man ....

(Pasinetti 1966: 516)

The two-techniques case may be generalized, even to the extreme case 'in which all switching points, except the first, represent switches to a higher total value of capital per man, as the rate of profit is increased ....' (ibid.). Pasinetti concludes that 'switches of techniques due to changes in the rate of profit do not allow us to make any general statement on changes in the "quantity of capital" per unit of labor.' (ibid.: 514). As for the consequences:

> The theoretical implications . . . are rather far-reaching, particularly with reference to one of the most vexed questions in capital theory: the question of whether – at any given state of technical knowledge – there is any relationship between changes in the rate of profit and changes in the 'quantity of capital' per unit of labor.
>
> (Pasinetti 1966: 512–13)

Whereas it has 'long since'[19] been discovered that a change in the rate of profit which is not accompanied by a change in the physical capital goods may change the value of the capital goods in ways that differ greatly amongst the different capital goods,

> [i]t has always been taken for granted . . ., simply by analogy from other fields of traditional economic theory, that when a change in the physical capital goods themselves takes place, as an effect of a change in the rate of profit (i.e., at switching points), the 'quantity of capital' per man required by the new method of production will change in an inverse monotonic relationship to the rate of profit.
>
> (Pasinetti 1966: 513)

But the reswitching examples have shown that this need not be the case. This result is far reaching as it affects the neoclassical production function, to which this traditional belief is crucial: 'The most astonishing aspect of these results is, perhaps, that they go so much against the way in which we have been accustomed to think that even the most careful economists have been unable to grasp their implications.' (ibid.: 514–15). This is why Robinson and Champernowne, and also Morishima and Hicks, though they observed the possibility of reswitching, considered it to be an exceptional case and did not study what consequences it might have: 'The implications have clearly not been seen, and have remained entirely unsuspected.' (ibid.: 515).

Notes

1 In the book, reswitching is not discussed.
2 Garegnani mentioned to me (16 January 1990) that at the time of his stay at MIT (in 1961–2) Samuelson taught a course on Sraffa's book (though in Garegnani's memory it was more on matrices and Samuelson's own 'non-substitution theorem'). So Samuelson must have read the book, or at least part of it. When asked (on 20 April 1989) whether he had read Sraffa's book, Samuelson replied that he did not want to say that (at that time) he understood all the things that were in this cryptically written book. But he was rather emphatic in his recollection that reswitching had not come up in Garegnani's oral criticism.

3 Samuelson (1976) mentions 'Samuelson's false theorem', 'discovered' (and, of course, thought to be true) about 1952 (on the plane home from a visit to Cambridge, UK; cf. Samuelson 1976: 13) but not published, that the level of steady-state consumption (or net national product, NNP) and the rate of interest are negatively related. Though reswitching is not necessary for a positive relation, it is sufficient and so could have shown the falsity. Cf. Samuelson (1966: 577, n. 6): 'The reversal of direction of the (i, NNP) relation was, I must confess, the single most surprising revelation from the reswitching discussion.' This expression of surprise suggests that Samuelson, too, had not realized the critical potential of Robinson (1953), Champernowne (1953) (if he knew this article at all; this was discussed in the previous chapter), Robinson (1956), or Sraffa (1960) (until he studied that book more closely), thus reinforcing the argument in the text above.
     It is more than a little confusing that Samuelson seems to give a contrary account in his 1989 article. There (p. 139) he strongly suggests that Robinson 1956 opened his eyes to the possibility of a different relation between the rate of interest and net national product than an inverse and monotone one. But if that had really been the case, would Samuelson not have reacted sooner? However, in a letter to the author of 25 August 1989 Samuelson again mentions 1956. This may not be a typo, in which case Samuelson did get the idea, from Robinson 1956, that his theorem might not be generally valid. In that case he apparently shared Robinson's belief that reswitching was an exception, and did not realize that this might not be true until after the *Quarterly Journal of Economics* symposium.
     During the interview already referred to, Samuelson made the comment which was quoted in the Introduction and which reinforces the idea that he, like other participants in the debate, behaved as a sleepwalker: 'until you know a subject perfectly, you always are in a state where you believe in A and you also believe in non-A.'

4 Cf. Robinson (1977: 174).

5 Cf. Robinson (1975c: 38): 'Professor Solow seems to have forgotten that it was he who first called it by that name . . .' Robinson refers to Solow (1963a).

6 Interview with the author on 20 April 1989.

7 Nor was the Nobel committee. About his own lack of inhibition (or schizophrenia as we may call it), Solow said in the interview of 20 April 1989: 'I did the aggregates, because I wanted to do practical work.'

8 I suggest that we read 'everyone' rather comprehensively so as to include Joan Robinson herself.

9 This must be the 'descent to the plains' referred to by Robinson; see Chapter 5, note 5.

10 Actually, Levhari gives proofs of two theorems by Samuelson. The other one is the 'non-substitution theorem' of Samuelson (1961) and (1962), which will not be dealt with here.

11 Cf. Solow (1983: 184): 'Samuelson had the notion that universal diminishing returns, together with the assumption that every line of production involves every commodity directly or indirectly [so, the assumption of a non-decomposable production system] would rule out the paradoxes of reswitching even in models with many capital goods. The role of the supplementary assumption is presumably to guarantee that diminishing returns permeate everywhere and to disallow multiple solutions.' Samuelson seems to have held the opinion that his original conjecture that indecomposability ruled out reswitching might still be true, be it 'by approximation'. Cf. Bruno, Burmeister and Sheshinski (1966: 531, n. 2): 'Samuelson has suggested [no reference is given] an alternative argument using the fact that any decomposable capital matrix can be turned into an indecomposable one by adding some arbitrarily small elements in the right places thereby causing only an infinitesimal change in the FPF.' As Samuelson admitted later, if decomposable and indecomposable matrices can be converted one into the other that easily, indecomposability cannot be fundamental.

Whether or not Samuelson got the idea that indecomposability mattered from Sraffa (1960) is not known, but it is likely. In a letter to the author of 25 August, Samuelson comments on his mistaken belief that an indecomposable system should be incapable of reswitching: '*I mistakenly* thought (before 1956) that this convexity [diminishing returns in a convex technology] carried over to imply convexity (more exactly, monotonicity) of steady-state plateaus' relations (C^i, r^i). Any deviation from this (*quite-mistaken*) truth I thought had to be due to some singularity – such as decomposability.' It is not certain whether 1956 should not be 1965. But cf. n. 3 above. Cf. also n. 7 of Samuelson (1966).

12 Levhari's correction reported in Pasinetti (1966) has been incorporated.

13 It is hard to share their feelings of amazement, as their proof consists of a slightly involved way of saying that if a function is monotone increasing or decreasing, it is, indeed, monotone increasing or decreasing. For the part played by $(a - b)x$ in this, we refer to the discussion of Levhari's original theorem above.

14 As the function is monotone increasing.

15 'WPF' has been substituted for FPC – factor price curve – in the original.

16 From:

$$a_0 = L/X,$$

$$C = [I - a]X,$$

$$P(r)C = (1 + r)x(L/X)[I - (1 + r)a]^{-1}[I - a]X$$
$$= (1 + r)wL[I - a][I - (1 + r)a]^{-1}$$
$$= [I - a]P(r)X,$$

as $P(r)X = (1 + r)wa_0[I - (1 + r)a]^{-1}X = (1 + r)wL[I - (1 + r)a]^{-1}$.

17 It is assumed here that d has only one non-zero column. But as Pasinetti points out, if 'by a fluke' (p. 511, n. 7) more than one activity were switched at a switch point, so that d had more than one non-zero column, x would have to contain more than one zero element corresponding to the non-zero columns of d.

18 By Samuelson's non-substitution theorem.

19 p. 513; the reference is obviously to Ricardo.

8   Neoclassical reactions

The reswitching phenomenon brought to light...that the central proposition in neoclassical production theory, namely the monotonic relation between the round-aboutness of production and the interest rate, need not always hold. There are two ways to cope with this situation. One is to accept what is true, however cumbersome it may be. The other is to look for conditions which rule out 'perverse' phenomena in the hope that such conditions are empirically acceptable.

Sato (1976: 428)

The *Quarterly Journal of Economics* symposium had shown that the possibility of reswitching and capital reversing could not be ruled out. Levhari and Samuelson admitted the correctness of the criticism: 'The Non-Switching Theorem is False' (Levhari and Samuelson 1966). And 'Pasinetti, Morishima, Bruno–Burmeister–Sheshinski, Garegnani deserve our gratitude for demonstrating that reswitching is a logical possibility in any technology, indecomposable or decomposable.' (Samuelson 1966: 582). Samuelson also admits that reswitching shows the possibility of capital reversal, and a positive relation between changes in the interest rate and changes in the steady-state consumption level and the capital–output ratio. And he concludes: 'If all this causes headaches for those nostalgic for the old time parables of neoclassical writing, we must remind ourselves that scholars are not born to live an easy existence. We must respect, and appraise, the facts of life.' (ibid.: 583).

Now, if to respect means to leave alone, we may observe that several neoclassical scholars appraised rather than respected the fact that reswitching had been proved to be a possible consequence of the two-sector fixed-coefficient production model. They took Samuelson's remark about the scholar's predicament literally and started looking for ways of saving as much of the original neoclassical predictions as they could. But their defence did not concentrate on refuting the results of the critics, but rather on the question of how perverse, inconvenient and worrying reswitching and capital reversing are. We shall discuss two reactions: one by Brown, who develops an idea of Hicks, the other by Ferguson and Allen.

Brown examines the conditions under which the relation between the rate of profit and capital intensity is 'perverse'. He extends the analysis of Hicks (1965).

Hicks[1] had constructed a model in which the rate of profit operates on the choice of technique via two intermediate mechanisms. One is a change of the production coefficients *within* a sector of production, which Hicks baptizes the *substitution effect*. The other is a change in the relative capital intensity *between* production sectors. The latter effect is later called[2] the *composition effect*.

In what follows we will first see how Hicks dealt with the relation between the rate of profit and the choice of a technique with a particular capital intensity. Then it will be shown how Brown uses Hicks' analysis to try and make some progress in finding the conditions that ensure that there is a unique relationship between the rate of profit and the capital intensity of the technique of production that is chosen. This batch of case studies will be concluded by a discussion of an article by Ferguson and Allen, who go a step further than Brown did in finding conditions that rule out reswitching and the possibility that one particular capital intensity may be associated with more than one rate of profit. But now first Hicks.

1 Hicks hunts the snark

In the chapter on the choice of production technique in his *Capital and Growth*, Hicks goes after

> the snark which economists have been hunting ever since Ricardo: 'Is there any general way in which we can specify the direction of the change in technique which will be likely to correspond to a lowering of the rate of profit (or to a raising of the level of real wages)?'.

> (Hicks 1965: 153)

He uses the following two-sector linear production model to analyze the question.[3]

$$1 = q\alpha + w\beta,$$

$$p = qa + wb,$$

where 1 is the numéraire; p is the price of the capital good; w is the wage rate; r is the rate of profit; $q \equiv rp$ are the earnings of the capital good; α, β is the capital resp. labour production coefficient in the consumer good industry; a, b is capital resp. labour production coefficient in the capital good industry.

The wpf, or 'wage equation' as Hicks calls it, is then

$$\frac{1}{w} = \beta + \frac{r\alpha b}{1 - ra}. \tag{1}$$

Using $m \equiv (\alpha/\beta)/(a/b) \equiv \alpha b/a\beta$ for the composition ratio, this yields

$$(m - 1)\beta war + \beta w + ar = 1, \tag{2}$$

or[4]

$$w = \frac{1 - ar}{\beta(1 + ar)(m - 1)}. \tag{3}$$

If $m = 1$, so if the two sectors have the same capital intensity, the wpf is a straight line in the w–r plane, joining $w = 1/\beta$ and $r = 1/a$. If $m > 1$ (the consumer good sector is more capital intensive), the wpf is convex towards the origin, and if $m < 1$ (the machinery sector is more capital intensive), the wpf is concave. Given the intercepts of the wpf with the axes, in order for w and r to be positive, $w < (1/\beta)$ and $r < (1/a)$, or $(1 - ar) > 0$ and $(1 - \beta w) > 0$.[5]

Hicks distinguishes two cases: a linear wpf ($m = 1$) and a non-linear wpf ($m \neq 1$).

1   In the linear case Hicks proves graphically that a fall in the rate of profit leads to the adoption of a more capital-intensive technique of production.[6] A lower r means that a shift takes place from wpf₁ to wpf₂ with their corresponding intersections with the axes, $(1/a, 1/\beta)$ resp. $(1/a', 1/\beta')$ (see Figure 8.1). The production technique becomes more capital intensive in the sense that a, the capital coefficient in the capital good industry, is now higher and β, the labour coefficient in the consumer good industry, is lower. These are the only 'two firm rules' (ibid.) for an inverse relation to exist between capital intensity and rate of profit when $m = 1$. There are no comparable rules for α and b.

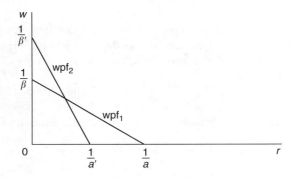

Figure 8.1 Hicks' linear case (adapted from Hicks 1965: 152).

2   In the non-linear case these rules are complied with provided that m is constant along the two wpfs, no matter if $m > 1$ or $m < 1$.

These two cases lead Hicks to the following distinction:

> The effect on technique of a change in the rate of profit (or real wage) can thus be divided into two parts: (1) a straightforward 'substitution effect' due to a change in a and β (with constant m) for which the rules that we have been enunciating will hold quite strictly; and (2) an effect from the change in m (if there is one) which breeds exceptions. Not a very satisfactory situation, but one that has parallels in other parts of economic theory.
>
> (Hicks 1965: 154)

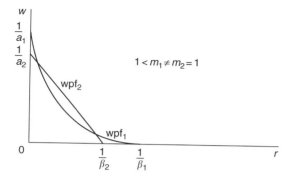

Figure 8.2 Hicks' non-linear case (adapted from Hicks 1965: 155).

The result of a change in m which accompanies a fall in the rate of profit may be that the two wpfs intersect twice, as is illustrated in Figure 8.2. In this case a lower r goes together with a higher a but not with a lower β. So, the capital good sector becomes more capital intensive (the capital–capital coefficient rises), but the consumer good sector does not (the labour–consumption coefficient rises instead of falling). There is no unequivocal way of saying anything about the capital intensity in the economy.

> All that can be said in such cases is that at least one of the rules must hold. That is not much help; but . . . we do not seem to be entitled to regard such cases as exceptional.
>
> (Hicks 1965)

Though cases in which the rate of interest is not inversely related to the overall capital intensity of the economy may not be exceptional, they do not seem to be very likely. The reason for this is

> that variability of technique does work in the direction of making it more likely that the wage curve that will actually be followed will be inward-bending. Though the possibility that the envelope curve will be outward-bending is not removed, it looks less likely that it did in the case where there was only one technique that could be used.
>
> (Hicks 1965: 153)

Underlying this likelihood judgment is a distinction of three possible shapes of the wpfs and the resulting shapes of the WPF. If $m = 1$ (linear wpfs) and $m > 1$ (the wpfs are convex towards the origin), the WPF that results when there is a great number of different techniques is convex towards the origin. In the case of concave wpfs ($m < 1$), 'cases can be constructed . . . where the possibility of

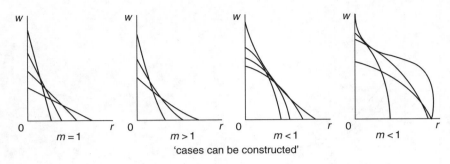

Figure 8.3 Which Wage Profit Frontier is more likely? (adapted from Hicks 1965: 150).

shifting from one technique to another is not sufficient to prevent the envelope curve (based upon outward-bending individual curves) from itself being outward bending.' (ibid.: 151–2). And if the WPF is concave, or outward bending, it is not the case that a lower r goes together with a higher capital intensity. The cases are shown in Figure 8.3.

Hicks' two 'firm rules' do not allow him to say more about the effect of a change in factor prices on the choice of technique and the possibility of capital reversing.

2   Brown pursues the trail

But Brown is not satisfied to let the matter rest at that. He extends Hicks' analysis in order to indicate in more detail when reswitching and capital reversing can and cannot occur. First of all he introduces the assumption of continuously variable production coefficients. This allows him to apply the apparatus of the calculus.[7] Furthermore, as we shall see, he makes constructive use of dimension analysis so that more may be said about all four production coefficients, and not just about two as in Hicks' case. Whereas Hicks had to limit himself to analyzing the substitution and composition effects *separately* (by distinguishing cases, according to whether $m \gtreqless 1$), Brown analyzes the *relations* between changes in the composition ratio and the substitution effect with the purpose of assessing the effects of various relative strengths of both effects.

The structure of Brown's argument is as follows. He starts with Hicks' two rules for an inverse relation between the rate of profit and capital intensity, or 'capital intensity uniqueness' (CIU) for short. Then he constructs a single condition for these two conditions, one in terms of the relative changes in the two relevant production coefficients. Then he states a further condition for the one he already had, this time in terms of both the composition and the substitution parameters jointly. So, Hicks' two conditions are made conditional upon one composite condition comprising both the substitution and the composition effect. Subsequently, this condition is given an economic interpretation, and the argument is concluded with a judgment on the perversity or otherwise of the absence of CIU.

Now, let us look at the analysis and the chain of conditions in more detail. Brown utilizes Hicks' two-sector model, and he takes over the two conditions for CIU:

1   with a rise in the real wage rate w, the capital–capital coefficient a must rise;
2   with a rise in the real wage rate, the labour coefficient in the consumer good sector, β, must fall.

A change in the technique of production is tantamount to a change in the production coefficients. But only a and β can be ordered between techniques, as may be seen from Figure 8.1. As Hicks had observed, nothing further can be said about the ordering of the remaining coefficients α and b.

Now Brown argues that whereas the *separate* coefficients α and b cannot be compared with either of the others, their *product* $y = \alpha b$ can be compared, as it has the same dimension as β. Parameter b has the dimension labour–capital good, and α the dimension capital–consumer good. So, y has the dimensions labour–consumer good, as does β. This enables Brown to compare the sets of production parameters (a, β, y) of different techniques.

Brown offers three different economic interpretations for the 'composite production coefficient' (ibid.: 337):

1   An 'indirect labour–capital coefficient': the amount of labour required to produce the machinery which produces a unit of the consumer good.
2   What by analogy to 1 we may call an indirect capital–labour coefficient: 'the amount of capital required to produce the consumption good, which in turn remunerates labour for producing a unit of capital.' (ibid.: n. 1).
3   A coefficient affecting the demand mix between the sectors, which has, however, no unambiguous effect on capital intensity: 'A rise in y increases the capital intensity of the consumption-good sector *relative* to that of the capital-good sector . . . .' (ibid.). Brown assumes that the book of blueprints of the techniques has a sufficient number t of pages, each page representing a technique, which is characterized by a particular set of values for a, β and y. He takes t to be continuously variable, writes $a = a(t)$, $\beta = \beta(t)$, and $y = y(t)$, and assumes that these functions are continuous and twice differentiable with respect to t.

A particular technique of production is selected if it maximizes the rate of profit. From the equation of the wpf

$$\frac{1}{w} = \frac{\beta + r\alpha b}{(1 - ar)},$$

(4)

we obtain

$$r = \frac{1 - \beta w}{w(\alpha b - a\beta) + a}$$

(5)

or

$$r = \frac{1 - \beta w}{(yw - a\beta w + a)}. \tag{6}$$

By assumption of perfect competition, this r is the same for both sectors. Remembering that $a = a(t)$, $\beta = \beta(t)$ and $y = y(t)$, the first-order condition for maximizing r, $dr = 0$, yields

$$-\beta' \frac{w}{r} - (wy' - a\beta' w - a'\beta w + a) = 0, \quad \text{where } \beta' = \frac{\partial \beta}{\partial t}, \dots \tag{7}$$

or

$$-\beta' \frac{w}{r}(1 - ar) - wy' - a'(1 - \beta w) = 0. \tag{8}$$

The second-order condition, $d^2 r < 0$, yields

$$-\beta'' - wy' + a'\beta' w + a\beta'' w + a''\beta w + a'\beta' w - a'' < 0, \tag{9}$$

or

$$-\left(\beta'' \frac{w}{r} + wy'' - 2a'\beta' w - a\beta'' w - a''\beta w + a''\right) < 0. \tag{10}$$

One of Hicks' rules is in terms of the relation between (a change in) the capital–capital coefficient and the real wage rate. In order to obtain this relation, (8) is differentiated with respect to w:

$$-\left(\beta'' \frac{w}{r} + wy'' - 2a'\beta' w - a\beta'' w - a''\beta w + a''\right)\frac{\partial t}{\partial w} - \beta' \frac{1}{r} - y' + a\beta'$$

$$+ a'\beta - \beta' \frac{w}{1 - \beta w}\left(y + \frac{(1 - ar)\beta}{r}\right) = 0. \tag{11}$$

From (8) it follows that

$$-\beta' \frac{1}{r} - y' + a\beta' + a'\beta = \frac{a'}{w} \quad \text{and} \quad (1 - \beta w) > 0.$$

As $(1 - \beta w) > 0$, $(1 - \beta w)/w > 0$. Then, using C for the factor of $\partial t/\partial w$, (11) can be written as

$$\frac{a'}{w} - \beta' \frac{w}{1 - \beta w}\left(y + \frac{(1 - ar)\beta}{r}\right) = -C\frac{\partial t}{\partial w}. \tag{12}$$

$C < 0$, as C is smaller than the left-hand side of (10) (by a term $2a'\beta' - 2a'\beta' w - a\beta'' w$), and the left-hand side of (10) is smaller than zero.

If $a' = \delta a / \delta t = 0$, we get

$$\frac{(a')^2}{-C} \left(\frac{1}{w} - \frac{\beta'}{a'} \frac{w}{1 - \beta w} \left(y + \frac{(1 - ar)\beta}{r} \right) \right) = \frac{\partial t}{\partial w} \frac{\partial a}{\partial t}. \tag{13}$$

The first requirement for CIU is that a rise in the wage rate raises the capital–capital coefficient a, so $\delta a / \delta w > 0$. Given that $-C > 0$, $\delta a / \delta w > 0$ for all admissible values of all other parameters only if $\beta'/a' < 0$, i.e. only if the labour–consumption coefficient varies inversely with the capital–capital coefficient. But if w varies directly with a, and a varies inversely with β, β varies inversely with w. And this is precisely the second of Hicks' conditions for CIU. So both conditions for CIU as stated by Hicks are satisfied if one single condition is, namely if $\beta'/a' < 0$. The conditions for $\beta'/a' > 0$ can be examined by expressing the first-order condition (7) in terms of β'/a':

$$\frac{\beta'}{a'} = \frac{r}{(1 - ar)w} \left(\frac{y'w}{a'} + (1 - \beta w) \right). \tag{14}$$

Multiplying both sides by a/β we get the elasticities:

$$\frac{\tilde{\beta}}{\tilde{a}} = -\frac{aryw}{\beta w(1 - ar)} \frac{1}{a} \left(\frac{\tilde{y}}{\tilde{a}} + \frac{(1 - \beta w)a}{yw} \right). \tag{14'}$$

From (4) we have $yw = (1/r)(1 - \beta w)(1 - r)$; so

$$\frac{\tilde{\beta}}{\tilde{a}} = \frac{-(1 - \beta w)}{\beta w} \left(\frac{\tilde{y}}{\tilde{a}} + \frac{ar}{1 - ar} \right). \tag{15}$$

For the composition effect to be introduced, $m = \alpha b / a \beta = y / a \beta$ is differentiated with respect to t, and the result is expressed in relative changes,

$$\tilde{m} = \tilde{y} - \tilde{\beta} - \tilde{a},$$

and substituted in (15). This yields

$$\frac{\tilde{\beta}}{\tilde{a}} = -(1 - \beta w) \left(\frac{\tilde{m}}{\tilde{a}} + \frac{1}{1 - ar} \right). \tag{16}$$

Now, $\beta'/a' < 0$ if $\beta/a < 0$, and this is the condition for CIU. As $(1 - \beta w) > 0$ and $1/(1 - ar) > 0$,[8] the sign of $\tilde{\beta}/\tilde{a}$ depends on $\tilde{m}/\tilde{a}$.

Brown distinguishes four cases:

1   $m/a = 0$. This is Hicks' condition of the constancy of m between techniques. Even if there is substitution, the composition ratio and thus the curvature of the wpf remain the same, so that if a moves along the r-axis, β moves in the opposite direction along the w-axis, and CIU prevails (see Figure 8.4).

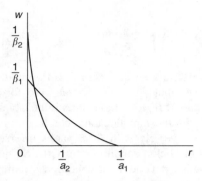

Figure 8.4 A constant composition ratio (adapted from Brown 1969: 340).

Cases 2 and 3 go beyond the condition found by Hicks.

2   $m/a > 0$. Substitution and composition effects work together. If a changes, the curvature of the wpf changes even more in the same direction. So, if a increases, the wpf becomes more convex towards the origin, so that its point of intersection with the w-axis, $1/\beta$, moves upward. So β decreases when a increases and, again, CIU is preserved (see Figure 8.5).

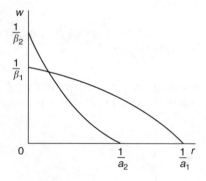

Figure 8.5 Substitution and composition effects work together (adapted from Brown 1969: 341).

We might compare the way in which m and a work together with the move-ments of a caterpillar.[9] It moves forward by moving its hindmost legs (a change in a) and by curving its back (a change in m). Knowledge of the relative mag-nitudes of the two changes enables one to calculate where the caterpillar's head ends up.

3   $m/a < 0$, but $1/(1 - ar) > |m/a|$. The relative change in m is less than a fraction of the relative change in a. So, the composition effect is more

than compensated by the substitution effect: 'In sum, if there is sufficient substitution in one sector CIU is assured.' (ibid.: 341) (see Figure 8.6).

4   There is, however, no CIU when $m/a > 0$ but $|m/a| > 1/(1 - ar)$. The curving of the caterpillar's back overreacts to the moving of the forelegs so that its hindmost legs end up a step backward (see Figure 8.7). The intersection with either axis could have been taken as the point of departure (the pivotal 'hind feet'). Therefore, 'the analysis could have been conducted in terms of the substitution effect in either sector, a or β, [so] we can say that sufficient substitution ensures CIU.' (ibid.: 342).

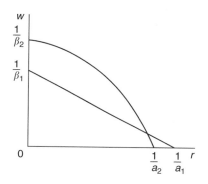

Figure 8.6 The composition effect opposes but does not outweigh the substitution effect (adapted from Brown 1969: 341).

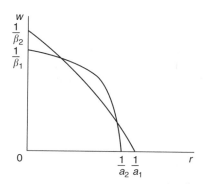

Figure 8.7 a and β move in the same direction, so there is no CIU (adapted from Brown 1969: 341).

Why y?

Brown argues that y is a more crucial parameter than m. Contrary to what Hicks says, it is not the constancy of m that is necessary for CIU, but the constancy of y. This is shown in Brown's cases 2 and 3, where m need not be constant for CIU to prevail. His arguments for the more crucial character of y are the following two. Equation (15) 'clearly states that it is the y component of the composition ratio that is ultimately responsible for CIU.' (ibid.). And second, 'the exposure of the role of the indirect labour–capital coefficient may be empirically valuable.' (ibid.). These arguments will be commented on in Chapter 9.

3   More neoclassical resources are mobilized

So far, all the authors who had analysed the conditions for capital reversing concentrated on the switch points between techniques. Samuelson's non-substitution theorem asserts that at the points where the wpfs intersect, relative commodity prices are constant. The conditions for reswitching and capital reversing have been formulated for the switch points themselves.

Ferguson and Allen (F&A) argue that too little is made of the neoclassical case if the debate is left at that. They analyze what remains of the reswitching results if changes in relative prices are taken into account. So, they concentrate on what happens before and after the switch points: '[R]elative commodity prices change beyond the switch point; we examine the likely effects of this change on the aggregate capital–labour ratio and, therefore, upon the likely validity of the "Cambridge Criticism".' (ibid.: 96).

The structure of their argument is as follows. F&A take for the aggregate capital–labour ratio the value-weighted mean of the sectoral capital–labour ratios. They rewrite the customary two-sector model in terms of relative changes so as to make it amenable to an analysis of changes in relative prices. From this adapted model they derive a wpf. But instead of analyzing the relation between the ratio of the factor prices and the capital–labour ratio directly, as was done in all the models discussed so far, they link these two ratios via a term that takes account of relative commodity prices. Commodity prices do not necessarily remain constant outside switch points, and changes in commodity prices may affect the relation between factor prices and capital intensity. This, according to F&A, has far-reaching consequences for the criticism of the neoclassical predictions:

> We show that it is virtually impossible to invalidate the neoclassical relation between relative factor price and relative factor usage (a) when reswitching occurs at rates of interest higher than a certain critical rate, and (b) when relative commodity price falls as entrepreneurs readopt some previously used technique.
>
> (Ferguson and Allen 1970: 97)

The model in relative changes

There are two sectors. Constant returns to scale prevail. Demand equals supply in the factor markets, so that

$$a_{LC}C + a_{LM}M = L,$$ (17)

$$a_{KC}C + a_{KM}M = K,$$ (18)

where C, M, L, K are consumer goods, machinery, labour, and capital, respectively.

Under perfect competition prices equal cost per unit:

$$a_{LM}w + a_{KM}rp = p,$$ (19)

$$a_{LC}w + a_{KC}rp = 1,$$ (20)

where w, r, p are wage rate, rate of interest, and price of capital goods, respectively.

The relative capital intensity of the sectors can be read off the determinant of the technology matrix:

$$A = \det \begin{vmatrix} a_{LM} & a_{KM} \\ a_{LC} & a_{KC} \end{vmatrix} = a_{LM}/a_{KM} - a_{LC}/a_{KC}.$$ (21)

Production in the machinery sector is more, equally or less capital intensive as compared to the consumption good sector as $A < 0$, $A = 0$, $A > 0$, respectively.

The relative price of commodities is determined by relative demand:

$$C/M = p.$$ (22)

As F&A want to examine the effects of changes in relative commodity and factor prices, the model in quantities is written in relative changes:[10]

$$\lambda_{LM}M^* + \lambda_{LC}C^* = L^*,$$ (23)

$$\lambda_{KM}M^* + \lambda_{KC}C^* = K^*.$$ (24)

λ_{ij} is the proportion of factor i used in sector j. The same is done with the model in prices:[11]

$$\theta_{LM}w^* + \theta_{KM}r^* = p^*(1 - \theta_{KM}),$$ (25)

$$\theta_{LC}w^* + \theta_{KM}r^* = -\theta_{KC}p^*.$$ (26)

θ_{ij} is the proportion of factor i used in sector j.

$[\lambda_{ij}]$ and $[\theta_{ij}]$ are matrices. As $\lambda_{i1} + \lambda_{i2} = 1$ and $\theta_{i1} + \theta_{i2} = 1$ for $i = 1, 2$, $\lambda_{i1} = 1 - \lambda_{i2}$ and $\theta_{i1} = 1 - \theta_{i2}$. So, the determinants of the matrices are

$$\lambda_{LM} - \lambda_{KM} = \lambda_{KC} - \lambda_{LC} = \lambda$$ (27)

and

$$\theta_{LM} - \theta_{LC} = \theta_{KC} - \theta_{KM} = \theta. \tag{28}$$

λ and θ^{T} now take the place of A and A^{T} (where T indicates the transpose of a matrix) and the machine sector is more, equally or less capital intensive as either λ or $\theta \gtreqless 0$.

Equation (22) written in relative changes yields the elasticity of substitution between commodities demanded:

$$\sigma_D = -(M^* - C^*)/p^*. \tag{29}$$

The relation between relative commodity price and the ratio w/r for one technique (and for one wpf) is obtained from (25) and (26) using (28):

$$p^* = \theta/(1 + \theta)(w^* - r^*). \tag{30}$$

The next step is the construction of a relation between the change in the capital–labour ratio and the relative price change:

$$K^* - L^* = (\lambda_{KM} - \lambda_{LM})M^* + (\lambda_{KC} - \lambda_{LC})C^* \qquad \text{from (23) and (24)},$$
$$K^* - L^* = -\lambda M^* + \lambda C^* \qquad \text{from (27)},$$
$$K^* - L^* = \lambda \sigma_D p^* \qquad \text{from (29).} \tag{31}$$

By substituting (30) in (31) the final link is made with the relative changes in factor prices:

$$K^* - L^* = \theta\lambda/(1 + \theta)\sigma_D(w^* - r^*). \tag{32}$$

What happens to the capital–labour ratio *along the same* wpf may be seen from (32). If $w^* > r^*$ we move up the wpf. As $\sigma_D \geq 0$, $\theta\lambda > 0$ because θ and λ have the same sign, and $|\theta| < 1$, $(K^* - L^*)$ rises for movements up the wpf as r falls.

But (32) does not say how relative commodity price behaves if the economy switches from one technique to another, as the wpf has a kink at the switch point.

> The kink is important. It means that after the switch occurs, relative commodity price may 'jump'; and if it does, there is no reason why it cannot jump downward ($\sigma_D < 0$ at the switch).
>
> (Ferguson and Allen 1970: 101)

On the wpf for technique α relative commodity price is

$$p = a_{LM}/(a_{LC} + Ar). \tag{33}$$

Whether p is higher, lower, or the same after the switch from α to β takes place depends on whether $a_{LM}(b_{LC} + Br) \gtreqless b_{LM}(a_{LC} + Ar)$.

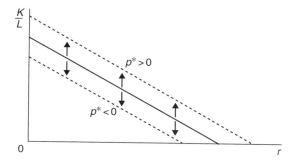

Figure 8.8 Changes in relative commodity price and shifts in the capital–labour ratio.

When we allow for different factor intensities in the sectors, this condition is difficult to interpret . . . . [O]ne cannot say a priori anything about the behavior of relative commodity price beyond the switch point. . . . [The direction of change of the capital–labour ratio] all depends upon the behavior of s_D at this point.

(Ferguson and Allen)

By (32), $K^* - L^*$ rises continuously for movements up the same wpf. This is tantamount to the ratio K/L falling, for the same technique, as r rises.

In (32) σ_D is a shift parameter which shows the effect of a change in relative price. The direction of change consequent on a change in σ_D is the same in (32) as in the simpler relation $K/L = f(r, \sigma_D)$. If p^* rises, K/L increases for all values of r, as $\sigma_D = -(M^* - C^*)/p^*$, and as it is assumed that the M-sector is labour intensive relative to the C-sector (the wpf is convex towards the origin).

Figure 8.8 shows the relation between K/L and r.

The effect of changes in relative commodity price on capital intensity

The analysis starts with Figure 8.9. There are two techniques: α with a linear wpf (identical factor proportions in both sectors), and β with a non-linear wpf.

F&A state that from examples such as these the 'Cambridge conclusion' (ibid.: 102) is drawn that there is no monotone relation between the rate of interest and the aggregate capital–labour ratio; as r rises the less capital–intensive technique α is adopted, but as r rises still further the more capital-intensive technique β returns. But this is not always the case. Equation (32) shows that the capital–labour ratio and the commodity price at $s_{\alpha\beta}$ is lower than at $s_{\beta\alpha}$. 'Hence it is clear that when the Beta technique comes back, it does not represent the same technique of production, or *aggregate capital–labour ratio*, as it did when it went out of use.' (ibid.). This means that a return to β after the less capital-intensive α has been used need not mean a reversal in capital intensity. Whether it does or not depends on relative

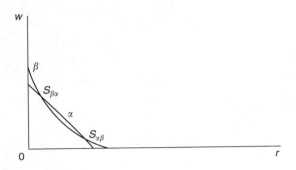

Figure 8.9 Mixed techniques.

commodity price, which may increase, decrease or remain the same. The rest of the article examines these three cases. But first the idea of a critical rate of interest is introduced, which is to play a crucial role in the analysis of the effect of changes in relative price. The critical rate of interest serves to differentiate cases in which reswitching implies capital reversing from those where it does not. This is made clear as follows.

When there is one linear and one non-linear wpf, there is according to F&A one rate of interest r_c for which the capital–labour ratios of both techniques are equal. That this 'critical rate of interest' exists is argued as follows:

1   From the intercepts with the w-axis we know that $(K/L)_\beta > (K/L)_\alpha$ at $r = 0$.
2   $(K/L)_\beta$ falls when r rises. This is what (32) tells us.
3   If all individual entrepreneurs adopt less capital-intensive techniques when going over from technique β to technique α at $s_{\beta\alpha}$, the aggregate capital–labour ratio falls. This is so because under α the two sectors have the same factor proportions.
4   As the wpf of α is linear, the capital–labour ratio for α is constant.

These relations are illustrated in Figure 8.10. If reswitching takes place at a rate of interest smaller than r_c, capital reversal occurs, as the K/L ratio falls from A to B at the first switch point ($s_{\beta\alpha}$), and remains constant for the range of interest rates for which α is used, rises again from C to D at the second switch point ($s_{\alpha\beta}$), and falls again for the range of interest rates at which β is used. So, provided reswitching does not occur at a rate of interest lower than the critical rate, there is no capital reversing. This is the only condition for non-capital reversing when relative commodity price is constant at the switch point.

Changes in relative price shift the $(K/L)_\beta$ curve. F&A distinguish three cases.

1   When relative price falls as the economy returns to the β-technique, $(K/L)_\beta$ shifts downward (see Figure 8.11). So, even if reswitching takes place at a

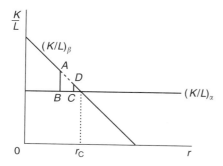

Figure 8.10 The critical interest rate.

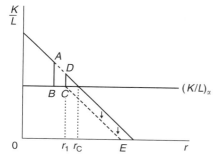

Figure 8.11 Reswitching, but a fall in price makes capital reversing unlikely.

rate of interest smaller than r_c, the shift may be sufficient to prevent capital reversing.

2 With unchanged relative price the K/L ratio would go from A to B (at the switch point), from B to C (for as long as α is in use), and back up again from C to D. If the downward shift of $(K/L)_\beta$ is of sufficient magnitude (the distance CD in the diagram), the K/L ratio falls from C to E after the switch back to β.

> Of course, one cannot be certain that the aggregate capital–labor ratio will never rise in this case. The possibility is greatly reduced, however, when the switch itself reduces relative commodity price.
>
> (Ferguson and Allen 1970: 105)

3 Finally, what happens when relative commodity price rises at the point of reswitching?

> Of the three possible alternatives, this offers the greatest probability that a return to Beta technique will be accompanied by an increase in the capital–labor ratio.
>
> (Ferguson and Allen 1970: 105)

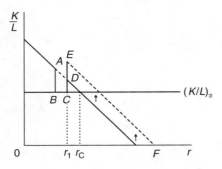

Figure 8.12 Reswitching together with a price increase: the likeliest case of capital
reversing.

As the wpf for β is drawn, a rise in relative commodity price increases the
relative weight in demand of the more capital-intensive good when the economy
returns to β. This is illustrated in Figure 8.12.

F&A observe that when relative commodity price rises, no capital reversing
need take place. This is so if the switch back to technique β occurs at an interest
rate equal to or higher than the rate at which the shifted β-wpf intersects the α-wpf.
'Thus it is clear that even under the most unfavorable conditions, the neoclassical
relation between factor intensity and relative factor price may hold.' (ibid.: 106).

Do these results hold only for the specific wpfs which F&A have used? The
result is generalized and the conditions for the exclusion of capital reversing in the
case in which *both* wpfs are non-linear are given, too:

> When the sector factor intensities differ under both techniques, it is necessary
> for the technique that represents the larger aggregate capital–labor ratio at
> zero interest rate to react more strongly to changes in the rate of interest than
> the technique with the smaller aggregate capital–labor ratio at zero interest.
>
> (Ferguson and Allen 1970: 107, n. 34)

Compare this to Hicks' conclusion, which does not take into account the effect
of changes in relative price:

> When there is a rise in the rate of real wages (or a fall in the rate of profit)
> there will always be a tendency to shift to a technique with a wage curve [wpf]
> which is . . ., at that level of wages, a curve with a slope that is [greater]. [I]t
> is . . . a technique in which wages are more affected by a given rise in profits.
> In that sense, and only in that sense, we can safely say that the new technique
> is one of greater capital intensity.
>
> (Hicks 1965: 166–7)[12]

Conclusion

What do F&A see as the consequence of their results for neoclassical theory?

> [R]eswitching and related phenomena do not necessarily imply a reversal of
> the aggregate capital–labor ratio. Given any two techniques, there will gen-
> erally be a critical rate of interest at which the aggregate capital–labor ratio
> is the same for both techniques. Thus, whether reswitching involves a 'per-
> verse' change in the aggregate capital–labor ratio depends, first of all, on
> whether the economy has passed the critical rate before reswitching occurs.
> Once the critical rate has been passed, it is virtually impossible for the aggre-
> gate capital–labor ratio to rise as the wage–rate of interest ratio falls. When
> reswitching occurs before the economy has passed the critical rate, but when
> relative commodity price falls as a result of reswitching, it is equally unlikely
> that the capital–labor ratio will rise.
>
> (Ferguson and Allen 1970: 107)

They grant that the critics of neoclassical capital theory have demonstrated that
the relation between the aggregate capital–labour ratio depends crucially on the
rate of interest: 'This is an incontestable and unalterable fact . . .' (ibid.: 108) which
was revealed by the reswitching examples. In a fixed-proportions heterogeneous
model '[t]here is a possibility that at some wage–rate of interest configuration, the
neoclassical relation will not hold. However, when one considers the interrelations
among factor endowments, factor prices, and commodity prices, the probability
does not appear to be so great as some of the Cambridge critics would imply.'
(ibid.). The authors concede, however, that their results are based on a model
that has neoclassical features which may not be acceptable to critics, such as the
absence of intermediate goods (ibid.: 96, 108).[13]

Notes

1 Both Hicks and Brown do not distinguish between reswitching and capital reversing.
2 By Murray Brown. See below.
3 Hicks' general framework is growth theory, as is Brown's. But no dynamic models are
  used. The growth aspect shall be left out of the discussion that follows. For the purpose
  of analyzing reswitching and capital reversing, a steady-state growth environment is
  equivalent to a stationary equilibrium.
4 Alternatively,

$$w = \frac{1 - ar}{\beta + ar(\alpha b - \beta a)}.$$

  This last transformation is not to be found in Hicks, but is given here in order to facilitate
  comparison with previous models, where the determinant of the coefficient matrix was
  used to determine the shape of the wpf.
5 The inequality sign in Brown (1969, p. 336) must be corrected in order for his formula
  to be consistent with Hicks'.

6 I have interchanged the axes of the diagrams in Hicks (1965) and Brown (1969) for ease of comparison with the other publications.
7 He anticipates the potential criticism that the continuity assumption is empirically untenable by arguing that assuming 'sectionally continuous' variations in the relevant parameters would indeed, mean a 'gain in realism'. But this would be 'accomplished at the price of a considerable increase in complexity.' (Brown 1969: 338, n. 1)
8 And not <0, as printed in Brown (1969: 336).
9 Brown does not use this entomological metaphor.
10 The derivation, which may also be found in Ferguson (1969, para. 12.8.1), is as follows:

$$L_M + L_C = L, \text{ so } L_M/L + L_C/L = 1, \text{ which is written as } \lambda_{LM} + \lambda_{LC} = 1.$$

$$(L_M/M)M + (L_C/C)C = L, \text{ or } a_{LM}M + a_{LC}C = L.$$

Taking total differentials yields $(L_M/M)\mathrm{d}M + (L_C/C)\mathrm{d}C = \mathrm{d}L$, as the production coefficients are constant.

$$(L_M/L)(\mathrm{d}M/M) + (L_C/L)(\mathrm{d}C/C) = \mathrm{d}L/L,$$

$$\lambda_{LM}M^* + \lambda_{LC}C^* = L^*.$$

11 The derivation is

$$a_{LM}w + a_{KM}rp = p.$$

The coefficients of production are constant, so taking the total differential yields $a_{LM}\,\mathrm{d}w + a_{KM}r\,\mathrm{d}p + a_{KM}p\,\mathrm{d}r = \mathrm{d}p$.

$$\frac{a_{LM}w}{p}\frac{\mathrm{d}w}{w} + \frac{a_{KM}rp}{p}\frac{\mathrm{d}p}{p} + \frac{a_{KM}rp}{p}\frac{\mathrm{d}r}{r} = \frac{\mathrm{d}p}{p},$$

$$\theta_{LM}w^* + \theta_{KM}r^* = (1 - \theta_{KM})p^*.$$

12 The quotation has been adapted for the way in which the wpf diagram is drawn here.
13 This has been emphasized by Harcourt (1972: 173).

9 Taking methodological stock (III)

> [I]ntellectual experiments...are necessary to sort out the questions involved in analysing complicated processes.
>
> Robinson (1980a: 20)

The general outlines of the various strategies of theory development were discussed in Chapter 6. But strategies have to be implemented. This is the level that we will look at in the following paragraphs, the level of tactics. This will be followed by a discussion of the status of the probability judgments that are frequently encountered in the debate. The chapter concludes with a summary of the relations between PIM and AIM.

1 Tactics and moves

Samuelson's conjecture that reswitching cannot occur in a fully integrated production system (i.e. when the technique of production can be described by indecomposable matrices) is an instance of a strategy which attempts to reveal an idealizing condition of models that had been developed already. Samuelson thinks that the absence of reswitching can still be proved, but from stronger conditions than were previously assumed. Thus, in terms of AIM, he points the way to a heuristic strategy. But as Samuelson considered indecomposability to be an economically relevant condition[1] which had wrongly been neglected, his heuristic strategy is not *ad hoc*. If he had been right, he would have made a discovery, namely that it matters whether or not a production system is indecomposable. The curious thing about Levhari's proof of Samuelson's conjecture is, however, that it makes no use of such economic considerations. Let us first have a closer look at the structure of the proof, because it shows Levhari's tactics.

Levhari's proof procedure consists of the following moves:

1. Formulate the production model in matrix terms so as to be able to handle complete sets of production techniques (and indecomposability).
2. State the economic condition for non-reswitching. In Levhari's model this is the price inequality $p_a \leq p_b$.

3   Rewrite the matrix analogues of the relations that, for instance, Samuelson (1962) had used, namely the wage–interest rate relations for two techniques of production, in terms of these output prices.
4   Rewrite the non-reswitching equation in a suitable form by the appropriate mathematical transformations.
5   State the mathematical property that this form must have in order to preserve the price inequality. The property is that the form is a monotone non-decreasing function of the interest term.
6   Prove that this form has the required mathematical property.
7   State the mathematical steps and lemmas that are required for the proof in lemmas. There is one such lemma, asserting the existence of a vector with particular properties.
8   Interpret the lemma in economic terms.
9   Interpret the result of the proof in economic terms.

It is quite clear that the proof relies heavily on formal, mathematical devices. The reader is not even told what, if any, is the economic relevance of the manipulations with the non-reswitching equation. More precisely, the crucial lemma, stating the existence of a vector with particular properties, seems to be dictated by the requirements of the mathematical proof only. Corroboration for this hypothesis is provided by the gingerly way in which Levhari offers the economic interpretation: 'The condition has *some* economic meaning'. (Levhari 1965: 105, emphasis added). The main, if not sole, reason why the lemma is stated is that it is needed to complete the proof. It is *proof generated*, to use Lakatos' term.[2]

This might give rise to the suspicion that Samuelson, too, did not have sound economic arguments for his conjecture. For surely, if he did, either he or Levhari should have been able to explain the occurrence or absence of reswitching by economic considerations, and there would have been no need for the sort of mathematical proof that Levhari provides. However, formal proofs cannot be dismissed so easily. For it is perfectly conceivable that, if the conjecture had been true, the proof might have succeeded using purely mathematical considerations. From the point of view of economic theory, this might have been considered unsatisfactory, but the proof would have been valid. Moreover – and this would have made the situation more satisfactory in terms of economic theory – it is also conceivable that an economic interpretation for the mathematical, proof-generated concepts had been found later. But all of this is hypothetical twice over, since Samuelson's conjecture is false. The same goes for Levhari's mathematical, proof-generated lemma: in general no vector with the properties needed to prove the result exists.

Bruno, Burmeister and Sheshinski (BBS) examine the properties of a model that is a generalization of Levhari's model: it includes both circulating and fixed capital, and any number of sectors of production instead of two, in the shape of capital inputs in earlier periods and intermediate capital goods. The generalization is tantamount to a factualization in terms of PIM. This may be seen from the move by which fixed capital is introduced. In Levhari's model the depreciation factor, μ, was assumed to have the value 1. BBS generalize the model by replacing this fixed parameter by a variable which may take all values. The result they prove about the model in which μ may take *any* value is certainly valid for a model in which $\mu = 1$. So, they strengthen Levhari's position before criticizing it.

They prove Levhari's result if it is *assumed* that his lemma is true. This is a weaker result than the one obtained by Levhari, as the latter stated that the vector with the required properties always exists. So, BBS do not leave their criticism at the mathematical point of the non-existence of the vector. They demonstrate that if the vector exists, the prediction can indeed be derived. If interpreted in economic terms, a consequence of the assumption is that switches of technique involving one activity are ruled out. And these switches are normal. So, the economic domain is restricted, too.

Why are switches involving one activity the normal case? This assertion of BBS is not based on empirical evidence. Rather, it is part of another *theorem*, the relevant part of which reads:

> 'Adjacent' techniques on two sides of a switching point will usually differ from each other only with respect to *one activity*. Techniques in general may differ with respect to *m activities* $(n \geq m > 1)$ only if certain *m* independent polynomials happen to have a common root at that switching point.
>
> (Bruno, Burmeister and Sheshinski 1966: 542)[3]

In the (intricate) proof no mathematical (or empirical) reasons are given why the rather suggestive words 'usually' and 'happen' are used. It seems to me that the first sentence of BBS's theorem is no more than a definitional or tautological statement, which amounts to stating that the smallest distance ('adjacent') between any two techniques is one activity. This is true by the definition of a technique in terms of activities. The second sentence seems to me to be a purely mathematical theorem which derives from the way in which techniques are modelled mathematically.

Again, BBS add an argument for the restrictiveness of the condition that is couched in economic language:

> Economically the sufficiency condition implies ... that there exists one level of operation for which one technique uses at least as much of all inputs as the other techniques and definitely more of one input; moreover, the latter must hold for *any* pair of techniques that appear on the factor-price frontier.
>
> (Burno, Burmeister and Sheshinski 1966: 543–4)

The underlying idea is apparently that the probability that this condition will be met in the case of two (or more) activities at the same time is even smaller.

They then prove non-reswitching from an alternative sufficiency condition. This condition is weaker or less restrictive because it does allow changes of single activities. But it is still restrictive because it relies on the possibility that techniques can be ordered as to capital intensity. BBS state that this is only possible under 'highly exceptional circumstances' (ibid.: 545). Apparently, the exceptionality judgment is based on purely theoretical considerations. This may be gathered from the clear distinction that is made between theoretical acceptability ('reswitching is, at least theoretically, a perfectly acceptable case' (ibid.)) and empirical likelihood ('there is an open empirical question as to whether or not reswitching is likely to be observed in an actual economy' (ibid.: n. 2)). Both the theoretical and the empirical questions are left open.

Hicks is not interested in the reswitching of techniques as such, but rather in the relation between a change in the rate of profit and the capital intensity of the technique that is chosen. He distinguishes two effects: a substitution effect, which is the joint result of a change in the capital coefficient in the capital good industry and a change in the labour coefficient in the consumer good industry; and a composition effect, which measures the change in the relative capital intensity of the two production sectors. The inverse relation between the rate of profit and the capital intensity of the production technique is preserved when the capital intensities of the production techniques are the same – which was the conclusion of Garegnani's criticism of Samuelson (1962) – or – and this is Hicks' discovery – in case the capital intensities differ but the relative capital intensity remains constant before and after the switch of techniques. What Hicks effectively does is to generalize the known result: it is not so much the linearity of the wpf's as their constant curvature before and after the switch that is relevant for the inverse relation between the rate of profit and capital intensity to be preserved.

What Hicks shows further is that, once the relative capital intensity and thus the curvature of the wpf's changes, the preservation of the inverse relation between profit rate and capital intensity depends on the behaviour of one coefficient in each of the sectors, coefficients which are incommensurable. Of the substitution and the composition effects that Hicks distinguishes, it is the latter that 'breeds exceptions. Not a very satisfactory situation, but one that has parallels in other parts of economic theory.' (Hicks 1965: 154). Hicks' result amounts to a refinement of the conditions from which capital intensity uniqueness can be proved. In my reconstruction, what Hicks has achieved is that he shows that the result that was known so far, the one obtained by Samuelson and criticized by Garegnani,[4] was a special case which relied on a tacit assumption about the curvature of the wpf's. By proving a more general result, namely that it is the constancy of the curvature rather than their linearity, Hicks shows this assumption to be an idealizing assumption. In doing this he follows a heuristic strategy which factualizes Garegnani's result, at the same time partly 'reversing' Garegnani's domain strategy.

Hicks also proves that if the wpf's are not constant, another factor is relevant for the prediction of the profit–capital intensity relation, namely the behaviour of the two incommensurable production coefficients. But here Hicks' development strategy comes to a halt. He cannot say more about the relation between the rate of profit and the capital intensity of the production technique because the ordering of production techniques as to capital intensity is incomplete. Hicks' 'two rules' only say something about the ordering of techniques by the capital–capital coefficient a and the labour–consumer coefficient β, and not by the remaining two coefficients.

Brown integrates these two coefficients, the labour–capital coefficient b and the capital–consumer coefficient α, in the analysis by the tactic of constructing a composite parameter y that is made up of their product. He justifies this procedure by observing that the dimension of the composite parameter is the same as that of β. So, his purely formal step of constructing a composite parameter makes the coefficients commensurable, so that the sets of production parameters (a, β, y) can be used to order different techniques as to their capital intensity. The composite production coefficient is subsequently provided with several different economic interpretations. This suggests that the composite coefficient is proof generated.

As a next move, the composite coefficient is used to analyze, by purely mathematical means, the ratio of the relative changes in β and a, the two coefficients figuring in Hicks' two rules, in terms of the ratio of the relative changes in m, the measure of the curvature of the wpf's, and a. This enables Brown to determine the relative magnitudes of the composition and substitution effects that preserve capital intensity uniqueness. He summarizes the results in a classification of four cases, which state the conditions for capital intensity uniqueness (and its absence) in purely formal terms. No economic reasons or explanation are given for these cases. This becomes also apparent from the conclusion 'that sufficient substitution ensures CIU' (Brown 1969: 342), which seems rather global and vague after such a detailed analysis of the relative magnitudes of the composition and substitution effects. Yet, despite the constructed nature of the composite parameter y (which, as was suggested above, has the appearance of being proof generated), Brown argues that the y parameter is more crucial than m, the measure of the relative capital intensity of the sectors and the measure of the curvature of the wpf's.

His first argument is not convincing. If we look at equation (16) in Chapter 8, which is obtained from (15) by tautological transformations, we might just as well conclude that the parameter that is ultimately responsible for CIU is m. And if the argument really is that y is a *component* of m, it may be objected that m and y are definitionally equivalent parameters. $m = y/a\beta$ holds no priority whatever over $y = ma\beta$. The second – empirical – argument is not convincing, either. It may be just as valuable to empirically examine the role of changes in relative factor intensities between sectors as to examine changes in the composite effect y. Moreover, as y has several interpretations, it seems that an empirical application will run into identification problems.

According to Ferguson and Allen (F&A), Samuelson yielded to criticism too easily by accepting the implications of reswitching as one of the 'facts of life' (Samuelson 1966: 584):[5]

> One such fact is the dependence of relative commodity demand upon relative commodity price and the relation of the latter to factor endowments and factor prices. When this fact is respected and appraised, the likelihood that the neoclassical relation between factor proportions and factor prices holds is much greater than it would otherwise seem.
>
> (Ferguson and Allen 1970: 108–9)

They factualize the assumption of the habitual model that relative commodity price is constant and examine how this affects the prediction about the relation between the rate of profit and capital intensity. Thus, they follow a heuristic strategy. But they do not do so blindly. For in neoclassical theory, relative prices and changes in relative prices have a crucial allocative function. Thus, their heuristic strategy receives, so to speak, programmatic guidance, and the introduction of relative prices is not programmatically *ad hoc*. As was noticed above, the authors recognize that this fact may contribute to their results being not convincing to critics who do not share the neoclassical background. We may make this a bit more precise by observing that, whereas all critics, including opponents of neoclassical production models, may concede the truth of the conclusions F&A reach on the local level of technical analysis, they will probably refuse to accept them for the same global reason that would make them perfectly acceptable to neoclassical economists: the fact that they are in the spirit of the neoclassical research programme.

F&A's analysis contains a move whose status is not immediately clear: the introduction of a critical rate of interest. On the one hand, the concept seems to be purely proof generated in the context of an attempt to differentiate between reswitching and capital reversing. On the other hand, the arguments for its existence consist of, or follow from, steps in the analysis, each of which makes economic sense. I think the conclusion must be that F&A, in the course of their heuristic strategy, have discovered a relevant factor that had been overlooked so far: whether or not the economy has passed the critical rate of interest, i.e. the rate of interest for which two alternative techniques of production have the same capital–labour ratio. So, not only has the heuristic strategy allowed a refinement in the sense that the dependence of the prediction on the factualization of part of the antecedent has been examined, it has also led to the discovery of a relevant factor which is introduced as a new condition in the antecedent. Thus, starting from the factualization of one idealizing assumption (the constancy of relative commodity price) of the models used until then in the debate, F&A revealed that these models contain yet another, as yet unsuspected, idealizing assumption, namely that there is no critical rate of interest, or that the critical rate of interest is negligible. But they give no arguments as to why the existence of this critical interest rate is not *ad hoc*, either in the programmatic sense or in the sense of being independently testable.

2 Strategies and likelihoods

I have observed that F&A follow a heuristic strategy. But their intention is to show that the domain in which the prediction of an inverse relation between the profit rate and capital intensity can be proved to exist is more encompassing than the critics have tried to demonstrate. If this is taken to mean that F&A proved the relation from weaker conditions, this seems a straightforward procedure. However, the article abounds with judgments of the probability or likelihood or possibility of the relation's occurrence. Clearly, what is meant is not empirical likelihood, since no empirical results are quoted. Is there perhaps a logical probability model justifying these judgments, one that assigns equal a priori chances to all possible states of the world? In the article there is evidence neither for nor against this view.

The most innocent reading of the probability-like statements is that, once more relevant factors are taken into account, the prediction may have to be modified. This is how one may read the passage that was already quoted above:

> There is a possibility that at some wage–rate of interest configuration, the neoclassical relation will not hold. However, when one considers the interrelations among factor endowments, factor prices, and commodity prices, the probability does not appear to be so great as some of the Cambridge critics would imply.
>
> (Ferguson and Allen 1970: 108)

Changes in relative prices are relevant – in the neoclassical programme. But no empirical evidence is given for their relevance. It seems that not only are the modifications of the model guided by the research programme, but so are the probability judgments.

I offer the following hypothesis for this use of probability language. F& A, and other authors as well, conduct their analysis in purely theoretical and a priori terms: they use arguments and devices that are either derived from formal mathematics or from economic theory. No empirical arguments that refer to observation statements that may be used in empirical tests are ever invoked. The authors seem to feel uneasy about this, apparently because they think capital theory ultimately has to have empirical import. But they do not develop their models in such a way that they become applicable to reality, and hence empirically testable. Instead, as a sort of second-best strategy, they resort to rather *ad hoc* and unsystematic 'factual' observations of a common-sense nature, or 'factual' observations that are not *ad hoc* because they refer to facts that are facts within the context of a particular theory or research programme yet are not empirical facts. They are what Kaldor has called 'stylized facts' (Kaldor 1957: 2). These 'factual' observations are couched in the form of probability judgments, which have the appearance of preserving some measure of empirical relevance. Likelihood statements are an attempt to resolve the tension felt by the authors between their formal analysis and their empirical pretensions declared, which are never realized. But the attempt is not successful. The reason for the tension, and whether or not it is rightly felt are matters that we will go into in more detail in Chapter 12.

3   AIM and PIM reconsidered

The participants in the debate suffer from the same empiricist bias that we found in AIM. Once more, Musgrave has proved himself to be a philosopher of science who is sensitive to the concerns of the subjects populating his domain of study. But the analysis of the case studies has made it clear that the empiricist bias unnecessarily restricts the applicability of AIM. The strategies of theory development as Musgrave sees them are (1) *parts of immunizing stratagems*, i.e. moves designed to decrease a theory's content under the force of criticism. And this is indeed one of the uses to which AIM's strategies may be put. But they can also be used in two other ways which Musgrave does not recognize. The domain strategy may serve as (2) *an instrument of criticism*, as we have seen in several case studies and most clearly of all in the discussion of Garegnani (1970). And finally, the strategies may be (3) *vehicles of progress*. In the case studies this was shown by the examples of Brown (1969) and Ferguson and Allen (1970). But we can also see how this last use of AIM's strategies operates when we compare them with the strategies of PIM.

All three strategies that AIM discerns are heuristic strategies. This can be seen most clearly if we translate them into the formalism of PIM, as was done in Chapter 6. Domain and negligibility strategies are special cases of the heuristic strategy. Their differences are not syntactical but pragmatic. If we translate AIM's strategies in terms of PIM, we obtain the following correspondences:

Strategies of theory development

AIM	PIM
Heuristic	Either a factualization or a correspondence strategy
Negligibility	Idealization plus approximation
Domain	Idealization

The scheme summarizes the discussion of some of the relations between both models: AIM offers an extension of PIM as it takes pragmatic considerations into account; and PIM demonstrates that the scope of AIM is not restricted to immunizing stratagems but also covers critical and progressive strategic intentions.

4   Weapons

In the above, the various strategies were discussed in terms of moves or tactics. But how do they operate in the field? The story as told so far seems to indicate that formal, mathematical arguments are very important weapons in the tactics used. Many of the results proved in the articles which were discussed seem to follow neatly from particular mathematical operations. Mathematical operations, for instance, allowed BBS to generalize Levhari's model, and it allowed them and others to find neat results proving or disproving particular 'theorems' or predictions. But does it always work so smoothly? And, to raise a different question, is mathematics a neutral instrument of analysis that serves economists as a tool for proving their economic theorems? Again, the way in which BBS use mathematics may suggest that it is. But, on the other hand, some doubt is cast on this matter by the examples of Levhari, Brown and F&A, some of whose results seem to be heavily dependent on conditions that were generated by mathematical proofs. All these matters deserve more attention. The next chapters are devoted to them.

Notes

1 If we are to believe Solow and Burmeister, Bruno and Sheshinski. See note 11 of Chapter 7. Samuelson's own recollection seems a bit different; he speaks of decomposability as a 'singularity'. Cf. the same note.

2 See Lakatos (1976: 144ff.).

3 Remember that one technique consists of, or is defined by, a number of activities. So, if one of the activities is replaced by another, we have to speak of a different technique.

4 Because there is no evidence that Hicks reacted to Garegnani's criticism of Samuelson (1962) – which, after all, was not published till 1970 – I stress that this is a methodological reconstruction, not a historical one.

5 Ferguson changed his mind after his 1969 publication, where he commented on the passage in Samuelson (1966) referred to in the text: 'At present, it seems that little can be added to this evaluation.' (Ferguson 1969: 270). Thus, it may appear that the introduction of relative commodity prices into the model follows on a real discovery or revelation of an idealizing condition in previous models. But the idea that changes in relative commodity prices are relevant is mentioned already in Ferguson (1969: 258), though it is not worked out there. Apparently, it took some time for his neoclassical consciousness to fully wake up.

10 The role of mathematics

It is better to be left with an empty mind than with one filled with nonsense....

Samuelson (1976: 11)

In previous chapters, but particularly in Chapters 7 and 8, we have seen that mathematics has a very important role to play in the strategies of theory development which are followed in the debate. The present chapter is devoted to a more explicit examination of the way in which mathematics operates in the debate, and perhaps in economics in general, and of the ways economists *think* it operates. I will start by giving four traditional views that seem to be quite widely held. These views share the idea that mathematics is a neutral instrument which is entirely subservient to economic analysis. Then I shall describe a different conception of the role of mathematics in economic analysis, one which parts with the neutrality idea. Next, another set of case studies will be presented, the first of which discusses one more defence against the criticism on neoclassical production models, an article by Lowell Gallaway and Vishwa Shukla. This article demonstrates very clearly how a particular application of mathematical methods may go wrong. Also included are the descriptions of two reactions to this article, by Kazuo Sato and Pierangelo Garegnani, both of whom have a very different style of using mathematics. The chapter ends with some conclusions that are based on my analysis of the debate.

1 Mathematics as a neutral instrument

Mathematics as an instrument for resolving disputes

From what economists themselves say about their methods, one might easily get the impression that mathematics is a neutral instrument of analysis. They seem to think that if different people start from the same economic assumptions, they must, by applying logic and mathematics without making mistakes, arrive at the same conclusions. This is a typically rationalist ideal: reduce the argument to a purely non-personal and objective sphere.[1] We may call this the Leibnizian ideal. A lucid characterization is given by Russell, who says of Leibniz (the only philosopher about whose thought Russell claimed to have any *real* expertise):

> he cherished throughout his life the hope of discovering a kind of generalized mathematics, which he called *Characteristica Universalis*, by means of which thinking could be replaced by calculation. 'If we had it', he says, 'we should be able to reason in metaphysics and morals in much the same way as in geometry and analysis.' If controversies were to arise, there would be no more need of disputation between two philosophers than between two accountants. For it would suffice to take their pencils in their hands, to sit down to their slates, and to say to each other (with a friend as witness, if they liked): 'Let us calculate.'
>
> (Russell 1961: 572–3)

This idea of mathematics as a neutral instrument for resolving differences of opinion, if not of economists as accountants, is quite common among economists. Thus, Joan Robinson says:

> How is it possible to have a controversy over a purely logical point? When various theorists each set out their assumptions clearly, after eliminating errors, they can agree about what conclusions follow from what assumptions. They have then prepared the ground for *a discussion, not a controversy*, about the relevance of various models to an explanation to whatever situation it is that they are trying to explain.
>
> (Robinson 1975c: 32, emphasis added)

Wicksell is another representative of this type of rationalism:

> One must, of course, beware of expecting from this [mathematical] method more than it can give. Out of the crucible of calculation comes not an atom more truth than was put in. The assumptions being hypothetical, the results obviously cannot claim more than a very limited validity. The mathematical expression ought to facilitate the argument, clarify the results, and so guard against possible faults of reasoning – that is all.
>
> It is, by the way, evident that the *economic* aspects must be the determining ones everywhere: economic truth must never be sacrificed to the desire of mathematical elegance. In my opinion, neither Jevons nor Walras has transgressed this rule, but their German follower Launhardt has done so several times.
>
> (Wicksell 1954: 53)

Wicksell makes it quite clear that mathematics is purely subservient to economics. And a similar view was held by Carl Menger, who in a letter to Walras[2] says that mathematics is a means of exposition and proof, not of scientific discovery.

Mathematics as an instrument for unification

Menger's view hints at a different use of mathematics, namely as a means for synthesizing existing bits of knowledge in order to obtain one unified structure. In this view, mathematics serves the purpose of presenting the results of economic research in an economical and systematic manner. A prominent representative of this tradition is Samuelson's *Foundations*, whose goal it is to bring out the common mathematical structure of much of economic theory. In its purest form this approach can be found in axiomatic presentations of economic theory; the most impressive example is probably Arrow and Debreu's general equilibrium theory. And of course most, if not all (non-Austrian), textbooks use mathematics in this way. Wicksell is another representative of this tradition. Cf. what Shackle says about him:

> Wicksell had in a supreme degree the urge and the power to synthesize, to see economic theory as a comprehensive unity where every important economic phenomenon must find an explanation at least compatible with that of every other such phenomenon. His mathematical training, or perhaps the natural aptitude and proclivity that had led him to seek such a training, must have been a powerful factor in this drive towards synthesis.
>
> (Shackle 1954: 6–7)

It is quite common to find the above two views combined.[3]

Mathematics as a vehicle of quantitative analysis

According to some authors, the application of mathematics in economics is justified by the fact that economic theories are about quantitative phenomena, such as prices and quantities of goods. According to Mirowski this view is defended in Samuelson's 1972 Nobel lecture, where it is traced back to Schumpeter. Mirowski quotes Jevons as holding the same view.

In criticizing this view, we may observe that the models used, though mathematical, are structural or qualitative rather than quantitative; they are algebraic in the sense that they describe relationships between variables. Thus, Samuelson in his *Foundations* uses mathematics for deriving 'meaningful propositions' from economic theory, by which he means that we are able to determine the signs of variables. At the most, mathematically phrased economic theories are 'quantitative' in that they can be used in the construction of numerical (counter) examples.

Mathematics as an instrument for reducing complexity

The ability of mathematics to represent and facilitate the study of structures has been put forward as another argument for its use. It is the science of handling complexity. As such, its help is called in by any discipline that has to deal with complex phenomena in reality, and economics is one of these. This view is defended in Weintraub (1985: c. 11).

2   Mathematics as an integral part of scientific discovery

The four views discussed above all see the relation between science and mathematics as sequential: science poses the problems after which mathematics is

called in for help. The results are then retranslated into science. They leave the problem why are the calculi of mathematics (and logic) applicable to reality unresolved.
So does Popper, who explicitly addresses the question.[4] Eugene Wigner inquired
into 'the unreasonable effectiveness of mathematics in the natural sciences',[5] but
he, too, fails to give the answer.

On the effectiveness of mathematics in science

The French philosopher Emile Meyerson had addressed the problem earlier, and
he did provide an answer. His solution is that as mathematics is undeniably applicable to reality, it must contain an empirical element, but as it is, or appears to be,
purely formal and a priori, it must also have a grounding in the faculty of reason.
The most basic concept of mathematics is that of identity, which is even more
basic than the concept of relation. The application of identity is the essence of all
reason (Meyerson 1934: 154) and 'all that is mathematical . . . in the end resolves
itself in equalities.'[6] However, mathematical reasoning is never completely 'pure';
it always contains empirical elements. This is because mathematical operations
such as addition and subtraction can ultimately only be conceived as operations
on real objects (Meyerson 1934: 153). It could not even be otherwise, because,
in order to make progress, thinking needs a *divers*. But then wherein does this
divers reside in mathematics, from which all experience appears to be absent?
The answer is in the number system: 'the number system is at the basis of all
mathematical truth'.[7] Numbers are abstractions, but these are subsequently transformed by us into something real. This is why we can subject them to operations,
i.e. real actions.[8] The fact that we are led to think that mathematical reasoning
is devoid of empirical content hails from the powerful correspondence between
the rational and the real which characterizes the number system and its properties.
Analogously in geometry: the *divers* hails from the figure, i.e. our spatial intuition.
The ultimate foundations of mathematics are numerical operations and geometrical
axioms that embody human intuitions about space.[9] In mathematical reasoning the
a priori and experience are continuously involved, and their contributions become
intermingled.[10]

Meyerson differs from Kant, for whom number and space are purely a priori.
This, Meyerson observes, is not the view of modern mathematicians. The idea that
mathematics involves free inventions of the mind does not come from mathematicians, but from philosophers of mathematics. Mathematicians feel they *discover*
things. This is sufficient proof that mathematics is not a matter of free creation or
invention, '[b]ecause discovery undoubtedly implies the intervention of a factor
which comes from the outside, from sensory experience, the application of the
intellect to something whose existence preceded its operation.'[11]

Meyerson does not consider fractional, negative, irrational and imaginary numbers and non-Euclidean geometries to be counterexamples to his rejection of the
possibility of free invention. Mathematicians treat irrational numbers and the concepts of non-Euclidean geometries as real numbers and objects. They subject them
to the same categories as they do real objects, and they perform the same operations
on them.[12]

So, mathematics always originates from something empirical, even when the original empirical domain from which a piece of mathematics arose, or for which a particular mathematical apparatus was developed, has been forgotten. This is a justificationist position: the success of mathematics in science is justified by an appeal to an ultimate empirical foundation. I shall call this Meyerson's *justificationist answer* to the question of the applicability of mathematics to empirical reality. We may add to Meyerson's answer that a standard strategy in mathematics is generalization. This means that the original, possibly empirical problem recedes into the background. Particular mathematical results that were obtained through generalization are applied to a different domain from the one that gave rise to it.

Meyerson also gives an answer to the question of the applicability of mathematics that I shall call his *heuristic answer*, as it explains the successful use of mathematics in the day-to-day work of physicists. Meyerson thinks that the effectiveness of mathematics in physics is the result of a process of mutual adaptation. Mathematics may serve as a heuristic, an instrument of scientific discovery. This is what the case studies in capital theory we have seen so far seem to point to. In the debate, mathematics is not only used to gain clarity and resolve differences of opinion, but it is often an integral part of the analysis. In other words, it is used as part of the discovery process, i.e. it is a heuristic.

Mathematics as a heuristic

Except for Meyerson, the heuristic function of mathematics in science and in economics has hardly been studied at all. The few contemporary exceptions have all been inspired by Meyerson. In previous chapters I have already occasionally referred to the work of Lakatos. Though he offers theories about heuristics within mathematics and within science, he does not analyse the heuristic function of mathematics in science. But there appear to be enough elements lying around in his work for making some progress on this point. This will be attempted at the end of this chapter. As a preliminary I will first discuss some of the ideas of Mirowski and Zahar.

Mathematics as a straightjacket for economics

Mirowski (1987)[13] pays explicit attention to the role mathematics has to play in (neoclassical) economics. According to Mirowski, mathematics is a superior method of thinking in metaphors, and thinking in metaphors is an integral part of science. However, in neoclassical economics the pursuit of mathematical goals has become an end in itself, unchecked by economic and empirical constraints:

> [O]nce mathematical expertise has come to be the badge of the theorist in any science, then theory becomes isolated from that subset of the discipline responsible for empirical implementation and experiment. The mathematical

theorist is given carte blanche by her prestige and her separation from the nitty-gritty of everyday observation to prosecute any mathematical analogy and metaphor which captures her fancy. The negative component of any of these metaphors ... can be effortlessly set aside for the time being, or dismissed as irrelevant, impounded in ceteris paribus conditions or otherwise neutralized, because for the theorist, it is only the mathematics that matters.

(Mirowski 1987: 80)

This is a degeneration which amounts to a forgetting of the original – economic – problems. The mathematical models that were originally introduced as metaphors, lost this status and were eventually taken for the literal, economic truth. The phenomena that did not fit into these models were ignored. Apparently, the need for a retranslation (or the possibility of a retranslation) of mathematics into economics was lost sight of. The mathematics has run out of control and taken over from the economics:

It is flatly not the case that neoclassical economists first decided that it was better to think of an economy as an aggregate of invariant preferences rather than a system of persistent social relations [the equilibrium concept that Mirowski attributes to classical economics]; instead, economists baldly mimicked physics and its attendant mathematical formalism, and then only discovered gradually that their world picture had to be strategically stretched and shrunk to conform to the metaphor of the transformation and the conservation of energy.

The transformations in the ideas of order, competition and equilibrium are thus the direct results of the adoption by neoclassicism of its characteristic mathematical techniques.

(Mirowski 1987: 196)

Thus, in general equilibrium theory the 'law of one price' is a mathematical lemma implied by the mathematical concern with constrained maximization.

The fact that it was the mathematics that came first and the economics second is demonstrated by the curiosum that in neoclassical textbooks the motivation for the law of one price is disposed of in a paragraph or less, while any discussion of the identification of equilibrium with the clearing of the market is relegated to the literature of industrial organization or the endless quest for the 'Keynesian synthesis'.

(Mirowski 1987: 197)

I think that Mirowski is right in observing that attempts to solve economic problems were and often are replaced by attempts to solve mathematical problems, and that subsequently either no retranslation to the economic context takes place at all, or that the translation is dictated and constrained by the mathematical results. But that is not always or necessarily the case. And he is too rash in attributing this to the fact that economists uncritically took over their mathematics from classical physics. There is an intermediate step, one that allows us to explain why not all economists adopted mathematics.

3   The adoption of mathematics by economists

Why has mathematics come to be used so generally by economists? I offer the following conjectures:

1. Ever since Ricardo, economics has been a very abstract discipline. It constructs ideal models which are thought to represent some basic relations and mechanisms, and examines to what extent reality conforms to these. The method of reasoning backwards from models to conditions, which we may call the conditional method, is mathematical in spirit. This can be seen from classical mechanics. And the success of classical mechanics led to the adoption of this approach in economics. This was discussed in paragraph 4 of the Introduction.

The introduction of the theory of subjective value added two other relevant factors:

2. The whole of the discipline acquired a strictly unified character, also after the example of physics.[14] The introduction of a very general and abstract unifying theory of all economic phenomena made it necessary to develop ways of connecting it with empirical reality. This introduced a problem that has to this day not been solved in a satisfactory way.[15]

3. The explanatory principle of the subjective-cum-marginal-value approach, which amounts to a consistent and generalized cost-benefit analysis, is almost self-evident. This stimulated a particular approach to economic theorizing: as the ideal cases are so self-evident, there is no incentive for attempts to falsify them. Instead, the whole world is interpreted in terms of the principle. Marginal value theory (or the theory of optimizing behaviour) is considered to be applicable to all situations involving human choice. This favours an attitude of trying to model reality in such a way that it fits the theory. The prediction is, so to speak, already known. What remains for the analysis is to formulate the conditions from which the predictions may be derived. This favours a method which, starting from the predictions, concentrates on finding the conditions from which the prediction follows. The conditions can be conceived as descriptions of the situation. It is this view of economics that inspired Popper's 'situational analysis' methodology of the social sciences.[16]

Mathematics comes into this in several ways. First of all, an idealizing theory, such as marginal value theory, is very suitable for being formulated in mathematical terms. A limited number of central relationships between a limited number of variables or types of variables almost naturally (though not necessarily, as is demonstrated by the rejection of mathematics by many Austrians) calls for a translation into simple functional forms. Second, the content of marginal value theory cries out for a formulation in terms of the calculus. Third, the method of mathematical proofs has long been identified with the method of the systematic finding of necessary and sufficient conditions. The clarity and neatness of mathematical proofs makes the method of mathematics (or at least what was perceived to be the mathematical method[17]) the standard for other disciplines. A fourth reason why mathematics is attractive is that there are certain mathematical theorems that have been firmly established, or proved. If one can translate a proposition of economics into a mathematical form with known and proven properties, one can avoid an argument in purely economic terms that risks being long, messy and complicated. As we have seen in previous chapters, several authors in the capital theory debate follow this course when proving the (non-) monotonicity of a particular function in order to draw conclusions about the conditions under which reswitching can (cannot) occur.[18] This ties in with a fifth reason why mathematics was found to be attractive: it was thought to provide the means of attaining certainty. A sixth and last reason why mathematics is used is that, by formulating a proposition in mathematical terms, one brings out quite clearly the structure of it. This allows one, for instance, to generalize the proposition by filling in different values for the variables. Thus, BBS (1966) gives a price equation characterizing a production process which includes an expression for intermediate goods. Then they prove that this equation can be rewritten in a form which is formally equivalent to the equation for a production process without intermediate goods. One useful, because time and energy saving, conclusion they draw from this is that 'we can ignore the existence of intermediate inputs as they do not alter the formal structure of the capital model.' (BBS 1966: 531).

The picture drawn by Mirowski is too one-sided and too negative. He is wrong in thinking that the mathematics which was taken over from classical mechanics led to the use of the conditional method, as is shown by the examples of Ricardo and Menger, who employed the method without the mathematics. Rather, it is the other way round: the conditional method preceded and stimulated the use of mathematics, as was argued in the Introduction. And there are a number of other reasons that made it quite natural to use mathematics in economics.

As has been indicated at several points of the methodological analysis of contributions to the debate, mathematics is often used as a heuristic. This need not have exclusively negative consequences. Mathematics is more than only a neutral instrument of analysis. This is different from the function of mathematics which is mentioned by Robinson, Menger and Wicksell, and also different from the views of Popper and Wigner. Zahar, on the other hand, takes up Meyerson's heuristic answer to the question of the role of mathematics in science. I will now discuss his analysis.

4 The dialectics of mathematics and science

In 'Einstein, Meyerson and the Role of Mathematics in Physical Discovery' (Zahar 1980), Zahar studies the heuristic use of mathematics in physics. But this does not keep us from using it for organizing our thought about mathematics as a heuristic in economics. Zahar thinks of the relation between physics and mathematics as an interaction:

> In my opinion the relationship between mathematics and physics is best described in dialectical terms as a to and fro movement between two poles. One moves from physical principles to idealising mathematical assumptions; then back to some more physics; then forward to fresh mathematical innovations with ever increasing surplus structure. The so-called harmony between physics and mathematics is not a miracle but the result of an arduous process of mutual adjustment.
>
> (Zahar 1980: 7)

The 'surplus structure' to which he refers consists of the stronger physical assumptions which may result from translating a physical principle into a mathematical form. This may happen when the mathematical form imposes stronger restrictions than the principle as originally stated in physical terms. The physicist uses mathematical notions which are not abstracted directly from experience and

> operates at the mathematical level, hoping that his operations mirror certain features of reality. However, he is not very clear as to how this mirroring takes place, so he lets himself be guided by the syntax, or by the symbolism, of some mathematical system.
>
> (Zahar 1980: 6–7)

Mathematics can have a second fundamental function in the discovery of physical theories: 'through trying to find a *realistic* interpretation of certain mathematical entities which seem at first sight to be devoid of any physical meaning, the scientist may be led to a physical conjecture.' (ibid.: 7). According to Zahar, this may operate in two ways. The first is that the empirical content of a theory may be increased by straightforwardly interpreting part of the 'mathematical scaffolding' realistically. The second is to express a hypothesis in an equivalent mathematical form. Then progress may be made when the following is the case: the equivalent form involves a particular mathematical entity which is interpreted realistically by subsuming it under a philosophical category (such as substance) obeying general laws; and the equivalent formulation is then discovered to violate these laws. Under these conditions a breakthrough may come about when the equivalent formulation is modified in such a way as to be in accordance with these laws. This second sort of situation as described by Zahar does not seem to occur in the capital theory debate at all.

It may be doubted, too, whether the first situation applies to the debate. Because of its highly abstract character, the models used do not seem to have, or to be intended to have, any empirical content. And indeed, they do not in the sense of that expression that is usually associated with Popper's philosophy of science: the class of all statements that are incompatible with the models, where these statements are thought of as observation statements describing singular, possibly measurable, unary (non-relational) states of the world. But they do have content in the abstract sense of Hayek's pattern predictions.[19] Among the consequences that can be derived from the models are statements excluding particular relations between ideal objects or excluding composite states of an idealized world, such as the simultaneous occurrence of a rise in the rate of interest and a rise in the capital intensity of production.

However this may be, if we substitute 'economic' for 'physical', the quotation from Zahar seems an adequate description of what happens in some of the contributions to the capital debate which have been analysed so far. Mathematics serves as a heuristic in that proofs generate mathematical conditions that can, and often are, provided with an interpretation in economic terms. To highlight the heuristic use of mathematics, I will next discuss another episode of the debate, which will conclude our series of case studies. These cases provide us with examples of both unsuccessful and successful heuristic applications of mathematical tools.

5   A case study

Prove in order to save

Reswitching and capital reversing are counterexamples to the existence of a 'well-ordered' neoclassical production function, i.e. a production function that yields an inverse monotone relationship between factor prices and quantities of factors of production. But if these counterexamples can be shown to rest on assumptions that contradict a 'basic assumption' (ibid.: 351) of economics, they can be ruled out as valid criticism.

Gallaway and Shukla (G&S for short) take this line of defence against the numerical examples of the possibility of reswitching in the 1966 *Quarterly Journal of Economics* symposium articles by Bruno, Burmeister and Sheshinski (BBS), Garegnani, and Morishima. The basic assumption G&S refer to *is that commodity prices be positive and finite for all positive values of the interest rate.* G&S's price condition imposes certain restrictions on the parameters of a two-commodity technique of production.[20] Reacting specifically to the counterexamples of Morishima, Garegnani, and BBS,[21] G&S show that these restrictions are not met by at least one of the production activities that these authors use to show the possibility of reswitching. The criticism of these counterexamples is generalized in a 'general nonreswitching theorem', which says that within the constraints which the price condition imposes on the production parameters reswitching cannot occur. They also give a proof showing that the condition that prices be positive and finite for all values of the interest rate is sufficient for ruling out capital reversing. The very technical and intricate proof of both theorems[22] relies entirely on the mathematical properties of the wpf.

A numerical counterexample

From the two-sector production model

$$1 = (1+r)(a_{01}w + m_1 + n_1 p_2), \tag{1}$$

$$p_2 = (1+r)(a_{02}w + m_2 + n_2 p_2), \tag{2}$$

the equation of the wpf is derived:

$$w = \frac{1 - (m_1 + n_2)(1+r) + (m_1 n_2 - n_1 m_2)(1+r)^2}{a_{01}(1+r) + (a_{02}n_1 - a_{01}n_2)(1+r)^2} \equiv \frac{f(r)}{\phi(r)}, \tag{3}$$

where r is rate of interest, a_{0i} is labour input in sector i ($i = 1, 2$), w is wage rate, m is input of commodity 1 (the commodity produced by sector 1), n is input of commodity 2 (the commodity produced by sector 2), p_2 is price of commodity 2; the price of commodity 1 is taken as the numeraire.

The relative price equation is

$$p_2 = \frac{a_{02} + (a_{01}m_2 - a_{02}m_1)(1+r)}{a_{01} + (a_{02}n_1 + a_{01}n_2)(1+r)}. \tag{4}$$

The 'basic assumption' about prices (relative commodity price p_2 be positive and finite for all positive values of the interest rate) imposes the constraints on (4) that

$$a_{01}m_2 - a_{02}m_1 > 0 \tag{5}$$

and

$$a_{02}n_1 - a_{01}n_2 > 0. \tag{6}$$

These constraints are purely formal; no economic interpretation is provided.

G&S show in a numerical example that the examples of the possibility of reswitching given by Morishima, Garegnani, and BBS violate constraint (6).

Two theorems

G&S set out to prove theorems that are emphatically announced as general.

Non-reswitching   In the proof of the non-reswitching theorem the conditions for reswitching are tested for consistency with the constraints imposed by the price condition within a model with two production techniques that have one activity in common. The wpf's for the production techniques are $f(r)/\phi(r)$ and $f_1(r)/\phi_1(r)$ respectively.

Two lemmas[23] are established: (a) either (A) $\phi(r) > \phi_1(r)$, or (B) $\phi(r) < \phi_1(r)$ for all positive values of r; (b) out of all the possible (eight) configurations of $f(r)$, $\phi(r)$, $f_1(r)$ and $\phi_1(r)$, only the two depicted in Figure 10.1 are prima facie

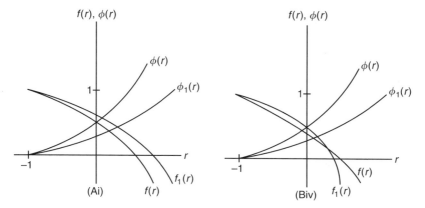

Figure 10.1 Reswitching-consistent wage price frontiers.

consistent with reswitching.[24] These functions are now written as

$$w = \frac{f(r)}{\phi(r)} \equiv \frac{1 - j(1+r) - k(1+r)^2}{s(1+r) + t(1+r)^2} \tag{7}$$

and

$$w_1 = \frac{f_1(r)}{\phi_1(r)} \equiv \frac{1 - j_1(1+r) - k_1(1+r)^2}{s(1+r) + t_1(1+r)^2}, \tag{8}$$

where $j \equiv m_1 + n_2$, $k \equiv n_1 m_2 - m_1 n_2$, $s = s_1 \equiv a_{01}$ (as the systems have one technique in common), $t \equiv a_{02} n_1 - a_{01} n_2$.

Some of the restrictions on j, k, s and t are dictated by the model. In (Ai), $\phi(r) > \phi_1(r)$; and as $s = s_1$, it follows that

$$t > t_1, \tag{9}$$

furthermore, at $r = 0$, $1 - j - k > 1 - j_1 - k_1$, so

$$(j + k) < (j_1 + k_1). \tag{10}$$

But the model does not impose any constraints on the relations between j and j_1, or k and k_1.

For reswitching to exist, the switching equation (as it will be called here)

$$\frac{f(r)}{\phi(r)} - \frac{f_1(r)}{\phi_1(r)} = 0 \tag{11}$$

must have two distinct positive roots, so

$$(1+r)^2 + \frac{s(k_1 - k) + tj_1 - t_1 j}{tk_1 - t_1 k}(1+r) + \frac{s(j_1 - j) + (t_1 - t)}{tk_1 - t_1 k} = 0 \quad (12)$$

must have two distinct positive roots.

The necessary conditions for an equation of the form

$$(1+r)^2 + \alpha(1+r) + \beta = 0$$

to have two distinct positive roots are that $\alpha < 0$ and $\beta > 0$. Whether or not the terms of (12) that correspond to α and β^{25} have the correct signs depends on the relations between j and j_1, and k and k_1. There are four possible combinations:

(i) $j_1 > j$　　(ii) $j_1 < j$　　(iii) $j_1 < j$　　(iv) $j_1 > j$
　　$k_1 > k$　　　　$k_1 < k$　　　　$k_1 > k$　　　　$k_1 < k$,

three of which are eliminated in the first analysis.[26]

This leaves (iv) as 'the most complex of the panel A cases to analyze' (G&S 1974: 353). In order, in this case, to examine the conditions for the switching equation to have two distinct positive roots, (11) is rewritten as

$$\frac{f(r)}{f_1(r)} = \frac{\phi(r)}{\phi_1(r)}. \quad (13)$$

This enables the authors to take limits and evaluate the (asymptotic) behaviour of the functions. The ratios of the functions $f(r)/f_1(r)$ and $\phi(r)/\phi_1(r)$ are drawn as N and D in Figure 10.2. At this point, r^* is rather suddenly introduced as the value of the rate of interest at which $f_1(r) = 0$.[27] This implies that r^* is the value of r for which the wage rate of technique 1 equals zero; but this is not pointed out

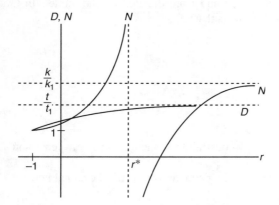

Figure 10.2 Reswitching at the limit (adapted from Gallaway and Shukla 1974: 354).

in the text. It is not until later that this interpretation is given. The way in which this is done has a rather *ad hoc* flavour. It is only after two switch points have been found, in Figure 10.2, that it is observed that

> the second switch point lies beyond $r[*]$ and, therefore, is at a value of w (and w^1) which is negative. Thus, it lies outside the pertinent range of the factor price contour and does not present an instance of reswitching that contradicts the basic neoclassical concept of switching.

> (Gallaway and Shukla 1974: 354)

So, in the diagram the 'economically meaningful' (ibid.: 357) range is bounded by $r = 0$ and r^*. The values $r = 0$ and r^* represent economic constraints. Beyond these values, either $w < 0$ (for all values of $r > r^*$) or $r < 0$.

A necessary condition for reswitching is that D and N intersect at least twice. They do in Figure 10.2; but the second switch point lies beyond r^*, hence outside the positive quadrant of the wpf diagram. In case $k/k_1 < t/t_1$, there is no switch point beyond r^*; but then there can only be one switch point altogether between $r = -1$ and $r = r^*$.

> Thus, in this case the roots of [(13)] consist either of one positive and one negative, two negative, or two complex roots. Whichever is true, reswitching in the range $r = -1.0$ through $r = r[*]$ is ruled out and the last possibility of reswitching occurring within the framework of the panel A assumptions is eliminated.

> (Gallaway and Shukla 1974: 354)

For case (Biv) a similar yet even more complicated procedure is followed to prove that the possibility of 'economically meaningful' (p. 357) reswitching, i.e. reswitching within the range of $r = 0$ to $r = r^*$, is eliminated.

Non-capital reversing The proof of this theorem relies on the fact known at least since Samuelson (1962), that a wpf that is convex to the origin (see Figure 10.3) ensures that there is an inverse relation between the interest rate and the value of capital.

The condition for the wpf to have this shape is

$$\frac{d^2w}{dr^2} > 0. \tag{14}$$

In terms of the model this yields the intricate expression

$$0 < kst(1+r)^2 - jt^2(1+r)^2 + 3t^2(1+r)^2 + 3st(1+r) + s^2, \tag{15}$$

which is satisfied for $0 \leq r \leq r^*$, i.e. the entire economically meaningful range of values of r and w. The expression itself is not given any economic interpretation.

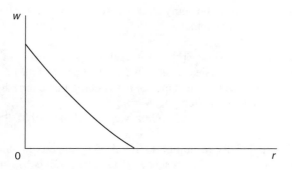

Figure 10.3 The wage price frontier again.

What conclusion do G&S draw from their exercises? They are satisfied with their proofs that the condition for the neoclassical production function to be well ordered is that commodity prices are positive and finite for all positive values of the interest rate. So far, everything seems to be straightforward in economic terms. In their proofs they have made use of constraints on the parameters of the production techniques that were derived from this price condition. These constraints were analysed as to their mathematical properties, and they seem to have served their purpose well: the theorems have been proved. Yet, the authors seem to give expression to a feeling of unease at these purely formal results when they conclude:

> What remains now is to explore the economic significance of the constraints we have imposed on the parameters of production systems in order to obtain these results.
>
> (Gallaway and Shukla 1974: 358)

False proofs don't save. And where is the economics anyway?

Gallaway and Shukla are taken to task on both the economic and the formal mathematical aspects of their proofs. I will discuss two of their critics: Garegnani and Sato.

Garegnani

Garegnani observes that there is no economic justification for the price condition that G&S in the first part of their article claim to be basic to all economic theory, namely that commodity prices be positive for *any* positive value of the interest rate. The economically relevant interval for the rate of interest lies between 0 and r^*, the rate of interest for which $w = 0$. The reswitching examples of BBS, Garegnani and Morishima are perfectly valid within this range. Beyond r^* the wage rate is negative even if commodity prices are positive,[28] as may be seen from Figure 10.4.

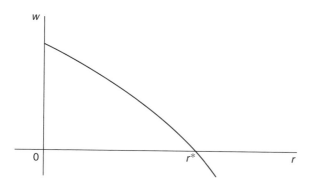

Figure 10.4 A negative wage rate.

But Garegnani does not pursue his criticism along these lines. Instead, he demonstrates that G&S's non-reswitching theorem is false, as even the amended price condition, the one that restricts the economically relevant range to non-negative values of both w and r, does not rule out reswitching. This is demonstrated in a numerical example. The conclusion by G&S that the price condition rules out reswitching is based on an error in their proof.

G&S allege that their price condition is sufficient for ruling out capital reversing as it implies restrictions on the parameters of the production equations that make the wpf convex towards the origin. Garegnani demonstrates that this condition *alone* is not sufficient for ruling out a concave wpf. With the assumption of wages paid at the end of the production period (and not the advanced wages assumed by G&S), the wpf can be concave.

> The convexity of the G–S wage curves is therefore primarily due to the assumption of an 'advanced' wage, which makes the wage an element of capital, additional to the means of production: as the rate of interest rises this (additional) wage element of capital falls, and thus makes for a fall in the value of capital per worker, i.e., makes for the convexity of the wage curve. The G–S constraints ensuring positive prices play only a subordinate role in this respect: the role of preventing the value of the means-of-production element of capital from rising so much, relative to the wage commodity, as to more than compensate the fall in the wage rate.
>
> (Garegnani 1976: 425)

Sato

A variant of Garegnani's first criticism is given by Sato, who criticizes G&S for formulating their price condition in terms of the wrong price ratio. As wages are prices, and as the price system is homogeneous of the first degree, it is not the ratio p_1/p_2 that must be positive, but rather the ratios p_1/w and p_2/w. To be correct, the price ratios that figure in G&S's analysis should be

$$\frac{p_1}{w} = \frac{(y - n_2)a_{01} + n_1 a_{02}}{D} \tag{1'}$$

and

$$\frac{p_2}{w} = \frac{(y - m_1)a_{02} + n_2 a_0}{D}, \tag{2'}$$

where $y \equiv 1/(1 + r)$ and $D \equiv (y - m_1)(y - n_2) - m_2 n_1$.

The price ratio p_1/p_2 may be positive without the p_i/w ratios being positive. In this case the technique is not economically viable as either the wage or at least one of the commodity prices is negative. The implication of this is that the constraints on the production coefficients, on which the proof of G&S's theorem hinges, are irrelevant to the positivity of prices.

Sato rewrites the constraints

$$a_{01} m_2 - a_{02} m_1 > 0 \tag{5}$$

and

$$a_{02} n_1 - a_{01} n_2 > 0, \tag{6}$$

which G&S derive from their price condition without giving them an economic interpretation, as the formally equivalent expression

$$\frac{n_1}{n_2} > \frac{a_{01}}{a_{02}} > \frac{m_1}{m_2} \tag{16}$$

and provides this expression right away with an economic interpretation. He calls it the 'capital intensity condition', which states that each sector is less capital intensive in the use of the product that is produced by itself.[29] This is in sharp contrast with G&S, who *never* interpret the condition in economic terms.

Sato's criticism consists of two steps. First, he constructs a numerical counter example to G&S's general non-reswitching theorem which demonstrates that reswitching *can* occur under the capital intensity condition. The second step involves proving a 'general reswitching theorem'. This says that the capital intensity condition does not eliminate reswitching. Now, this step may seem superfluous because the counterexample has effectively shown G&S's theorem to be false. If this were all there was to it, there would be no justification for discussing it here. But the proof does not serve a merely critical purpose; it is also constructive in the sense that it generates alternative conditions which, unlike G&S's capital intensity condition, are sufficient for ruling out the possibility of reswitching.

When a switch of technique occurs, the two techniques involved are equally profitable at the switch point. So, for *re*switching to occur the output prices of both techniques must be equal at two rates of profit. Sato analyses the conditions for reswitching directly in these terms (instead of in terms of intersecting wpf's, as G&S did).

Setting $w = 1$, and assuming that $n_1 > 0$, he writes the price equations for two techniques (that differ in one activity only, the case that G&S analysed) as

$$p_1 = (1 + r)(m_1 p_1 + n_1 p_2 + a_{01}),$$
$$p_2 = (1 + r)(m_2 p_1 + n_2 p_2 + a_{02}), \tag{17}$$

$$p_1' = (1 + r)(m_1' p_1' + n_1' p_2' + a_{01}'),$$
$$p_2' = (1 + r)(m_2' p_1' + n_2' p_2' + a_{02}'). \tag{18}$$

At a switch point, $p_1 - p_2' = 0$ and $p_2 - p_2' = 0$. Subtracting the corresponding equations (17) and (18) and using the definitions

$$\Delta p_i \equiv p_i' - p_i,$$
$$\Delta a_{0i} \equiv a_{0i}' - a_{0i},$$
$$\Delta m_i \equiv m_i' - m_i,$$
$$\Delta n_i \equiv n_i' - n_i \qquad (i = 1, 2)$$

yields

$$\Delta p_2 = \frac{y - m_1}{n_1} \Delta p_1, \tag{19}$$

$$\Delta p_1 = \frac{n_1(\Delta m_2 p_1 + \Delta n_2 p_2 + \Delta a_{02})}{(y - m_1)(y - n_2')}. \tag{20}$$

At a switch point Δp_1 (and thus Δp_2) $= 0$, which implies that

$$\Delta m_2 p_1 + \Delta n_2 p_2 + \Delta a_{02} = 0. \tag{21}$$

I will refer to (21) as the switching equation.

Now Sato defines two variables

$$X_1 \equiv -\frac{\Delta m_2}{\Delta a_{02}},$$
$$X_2 \equiv -\frac{\Delta n_2}{\Delta a_{02}}. \tag{22}$$

These will be referred to as 'substitution parameters' as they can be interpreted[30] as an expression for the reaction of the capital coefficient to a change in the labour coefficient when a switch is made from one technique to another.[31] Substituting the price equations (17) and (18) into (21) yields an alternative, quadratic form of the switching equation:

$$h(y) = y^2 - Ay - B = 0,$$ (23)

where

$$A \equiv m_1 + n_2 + a_{01}X_1 + a_{02}X_2$$ (24)

and

$$B \equiv (m_2 n_1 - m_1 n_2) + (a_{02} n_1 - a_{01} n_2)X_1 + (a_{01} m_2 - a_{02} m_1)X_2.$$ (25)

The quadratic form is constructed because the conditions for it to have two distinct and positive roots are simple and known. They are that $A > 0$ and $B < 0$. This enables Sato to examine the necessary conditions for the switching equation to have two distinct and positive roots and thus be a *reswitching* equation. If $B > 0$, (23) has only one root, in which case there is just one switch of technique and reswitching is ruled out.

Sato proves that G&S's capital intensity condition is not sufficient for this. The capital intensity condition occurs in (25): the coefficients of X_1 and X_2 are positive, as is the first term on the right-hand side.[32] But (25) shows that the capital intensity condition *alone* is not sufficient for making B positive. For that to be the case the *additional conditions* are needed that X_1 and X_2 be positive as well, so that both $\Delta m_2/\Delta a_{01}$ and $\Delta n_2/\Delta a_{01}$ must be negative.

At this point of his proof Sato provides these conditions with an economic interpretation: capital and labour are substitutes when there is a transition from one technique to the other. $B < 0$, and reswitching occurs, if one of the substitution parameters X_1 and X_2 is sufficiently smaller than zero.[33] A negative value for one of the substitution parameters implies that either $\Delta m_2/\Delta a_{01}$ or $\Delta n_2/\Delta a_{01}$ is positive. This condition is given an economic interpretation, too: one capital good is complementary with labour.

But the condition by itself is not sufficient to ensure that reswitching occurs within the economically feasible range of r. The additional condition is needed that switching equation (23) has two distinct roots for values of r between $r = 0$ and $r = r^*$. In terms of (23) this means that the roots y_1 and y_2 must lie between y^* and 1.[34] Sato examines the necessary and sufficient conditions for this, and expresses them in terms of three inequalities between X_1 and X_2, which are shown in Figure 10.5.

Reswitching occurs if and only if all three inequalities are simultaneously satisfied, in which case the area enclosed by their curves is not empty. Sato states that the slopes of the three curves, $(dX_1/dX_2)_1$, $(dX_1/dX_2)_2$ and $(dX_1/dX_2)_3$, are always such as to enclose a non-empty area. There is only one exception to

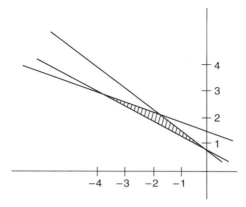

Figure 10.5 Sato's counterexample (adapted from Sato 1976: 432).

this: if the curves have identical slopes, they are parallels and do not enclose any area. This is the case only if the production sectors have the same capital intensity:

$$\frac{n_1}{n_2} = \frac{a_{01}}{a_{02}} = \frac{m_1}{m_2}.$$

In this special case there is no reswitching.[35]

Sato has proved that the capital intensity condition as stated by G&S is not a sufficient condition for non-reswitching. But the condition is not entirely irrelevant, as it puts additional constraints on reswitching equation (23): 'Thus, the capital-intensity condition does not eliminate reswitching, even though it narrows down the area in which reswitching is possible.' (ibid.: 432). From the proof of a variant of his general reswitching theorem (if in a two-sector model both capital goods are substitutes for labour, reswitching cannot occur), Sato concludes 'that substitution–complementarity relationships are much more fundamental to the nonperversity of a neoclassical production system than conditions like the capital-intensity condition.' (ibid.: 430).

Summarized very briefly, Sato's criticism is that G&S's condition for non-reswitching is too weak, derives from the wrong price condition, and is not fundamental.

Notes

1 See e.g. Mirowski (1987: 70).
2 Quoted in Boos (1986: 164).
3 Mirowski lumps the above two views together under the name of 'defence$_2$': 'In this view, mathematical formalism is merely the imposition of logical rigor upon the loose and imprecise common discussion of economic phenomena. The efficacy of this regimen

derives from the discipline of axiomatization.' (Mirowski 1986: 181–2). The defenders of this view are, according to Mirowski, Debreu and Koopmans.

4 In Popper (1963).

5 Wigner (1960).

6 'tout le mathématique . . . se résout en fin de compte en egalités.' Meyerson (1934: 162).

7 'la série des nombres se trouve au fond de toute vérité mathématique' (Meyerson 1934: 155).

8 Cf. Meyerson (1931, para. 233).

9 Cf. Meyerson (1931, para. 241).

10 'Pour nous, . . . *a priori* et expérience interviennent sans cesse l'un et l'autre ici et là et leurs interventions s'enchevêtrent.' (Meyerson 1934: 165).

11 'Car la découverte, assurément, implique l'intervention d'un facteur venant du dehors, de la sensation, l'application de l'intellect à ce qui préexistait à son action.' (Meyerson 1934: 158).

12 Cf., for example, Meyerson (1931: 381): 'en créant ses concepts d'espaces non-euclidiens, le géomètre, par le fait même qu'il les déclare *espaces*, affirme que son intention de les traiter comme nous avons accoutumé de le faire à l'égard de celui de notre perception, sauf, bien entendu, en ce qui concerne les particularités où, en virtu de la définition même par laquelle ils ont créés, ils devront se comporter différemment.' ('When creating his concepts of non-Euclidean spaces, the geometer by the very fact that he declares them to be *spaces* affirms that he intends to treat them just like we are in the habit of doing with the space of our perception. Of course, he does not intend to treat non-Euclidean spaces in this way in as far as they have to behave differently by virtue of their special characteristics or the definitions by which they were created.')

13 Mirowski's *More Heat than Light* (1989) contains a more extensive discussion of the role of mathematics in economics. However, as its subtitle *Economics as Social Physics, Physics as Nature's Economics* indicates, it focuses mainly on the consequences that transferring the mathematics that was used in physics had for economics. I will therefore not discuss it here. My comments on the book can be found in Birner (1993).

14 In the case of Carl Menger this is quite clear. Cf. Birner (1990).

15 This was also discussed in the Introduction.

16 See Popper (1967). See, for a discussion of this article that is also relevant to the present context, Birner (1990).

17 That *in fact* mathematics itself operates by a method of proofs and refutations does not diminish its attraction. One reason for this is that this fact is probably not recognized by many non-mathematicians. Cf. Lakatos (1976).

18 Another example of this is the mathematical theorem that a necessary condition for a quadratic function of the form $y^2 - Ay - B = 0$ to have two distinct positive roots is that $A > 0$ and $B < 0$. As we shall see below, both Gallaway and Shukla, and Sato make use of this mathematical property for proving an economic theorem.

19 See Hayek (1955, 1964).

20 Instead of the generally used terms 'technique of production' and 'activities' (the production functions of the production technique), G&S use 'production system' and 'technique of production'. In the text the more common usage will be followed. Note that G&S assume the wage to be paid in advance.

21 Morishima (1966), Garegnani (1966) and BBS (1966).

22 G&S do not refer to the proposition that capital reversal is ruled out by the price condition as a theorem. But if the non-reswitching theorem is a theorem, then is the latter proposition is one as well.

23 G&S do not use this term.

24 The proof of this lemma is by inspection and elimination. For each of (A) and (B), there are four possible relations between $f(r)$ and $f_1(r)$:

   (i) $f(r) > f_1(r)$ for all r between 0 and r^*, where r^* is the value of r for which $w = 0$.

   (ii) $f(r) > f_1(r)$ for small r, but
      $f(r) < f_1(r)$ for large r as r varies from 0 to r^*.

   (iii) $f(r) < f_1(r)$ for all r between 0 and r^*.

   (iv) $f(r) < f_1(r)$ for small r, but
      $f(r) > f_1(r)$ for large r as r varies from 0 to r^*.

Except for (Ai) and (Biv), which are shown in Figure 10.1, all of these logical possibilities are inconsistent with the existence of two switches, or even one switch of technique.

25 Let us denote them by n_α and n_β.

26 For (i), $n_\alpha > 0$. Possibility (ii) is inconsistent with the condition that makes both w and r positive: (ii) implies that $j_1 - j < 0$ and $k - k_1 > 0$, so $k - k_1 > j_1 - j$. This is inconsistent with $j_1 - j > k - k_1$, which is implied by (10). For (iii), $n_\beta < 0$. So, none of these cases is consistent with reswitching in the positive quadrant of the wpf diagram.

27 Actually, r^* made its first, surreptitious appearance in the proof of the lemmas referred to above; see note 24 above.

28 Garegnani proves the more general proposition that it is impossible for both the wage rate and all prices to be positive if $r > r^*$.

29 This may be made clearer by rewriting Sato's capital intensity condition as

$$\frac{n_1}{a_{01}} > \frac{n_1}{a_{02}} \quad \text{and} \quad \frac{m_2}{a_{02}} > \frac{m_1}{a_{01}}.$$

m is the input coefficient of the good which is produced by sector 1, n is the production coefficient of the good produced by sector 2, and a_{01} are the labour input coefficients.

30 Sato does not offer this interpretation until later in his article.

31 Notice that X_1 and X_2 cannot both be negative because of (21). This result is used in the proof below.

32 The positivity of $m_2 n_1 - m_1 n_2$ is directly implied by Sato's expression of the capital intensity condition.

33 They cannot *both* be negative; see note 31.

34 The relation between r^* and y^* is as follows: r^* is the value of r for which $w = 0$. Rewrite price equations (1') and (2') as $p_i D = wN$, where N is the numerator and D the denominator, $(y - m_1)(y - n_2) - m_2 n_1$. If $w = 0$, then $p_i D = 0$, and as $p_i = 0$, $D = 0$. Write this D as $g(y^*) = y^{*2} - (m_1 + n_2)y^* - (m_2 n_1 - m_1 n_2) = 0$. y^* is the root of this equation.

35 We may observe that this is the surrogate production function model of Samuelson (1962), which was shown to be a special case in Garegnani (1970).

11 Taking methodological stock (IV)

[A]nalysis . . . that avoids the twin dangers of empty formalism and inconclusive anecdote.

Hahn and Matthews (1964: 891)

1 The sorcerer's apprentices

Gallaway and Shukla (G&S) argue that the examples of reswitching that were given during the symposium of the Econometric Society and published in *Quarterly Journal of Economics* in 1966 are inconsistent with an assumption of economic theory which they consider to be 'basic' or fundamental: that commodity prices are positive and finite. So, their criticism amounts to the observation that the examples are *only* formal. Nevertheless, the way in which they attempt to prove their point is almost exclusively formal as well. They come up with purely mathematical constraints without attempting to interpret them in economic terms. The very authors who criticize Bruno, Burmeister and Sheshinski (BBS), Morishima, and Garegnani for violating a fundamental economic assumption confess at the end of their article that they are unable to interpret the formal, mathematical conditions which they have found in their own analysis in economic terms. This means that they cannot exclude that the formal constraints they impose in order to prove their theorems can be given an interpretation which contradicts some (other) basic economic assumption. Indeed, the way in which they manipulate some of their constraints[1] gives rise to the suspicion that they do not have the faintest idea as to how these might possibly be interpreted. Apparently, the aim of proving their theorems formally has taken precedence over the analysis in economic terms. And any reader who fails to see the irony of the situation of his own accord cannot miss it after looking at Sato's reaction. Sato duplicates the structure of G&S's article,[2] but he chooses his mathematical conditions so as to be readily interpretable in economic terms, with the effect that his article reads as a parody of G&S's approach.[3]

On the basis of the procedure they follow, we might impute to G&S a methodology which allows the use of mathematics as a heuristic intermediary between economic premises and economic conclusions; what happens in between does not have to be interpretable in economic terms. But then we have to notice that in their case mathematical analysis has quite clearly taken over from the analysis in economic terms. Instead of being a heuristic that is productive of economic results, the formal apparatus has gotten out of hand, leaving Gallaway and Shukla to gaze like baffled sorcerer's apprentices at the smoke emanating from the phial (or rather, the black box) in which they have tried their new concoction.

Sato does not rest content with pointing out a mistake in the proof of one of G&S's theorems – a mistake that is in all likelihood due to the extremely complicated mathematical and geometrical way in which the theorem is stated – and proving an alternative theorem. Sato's reply is a display of the magisterial powers of one versed in the art of productively applying mathematics to economic argument. G&S, by admitting that the formal conditions which were generated in the proof of their theorem are still awaiting efforts at economic interpretation, are corrected by Master Sato who deploys considerable skill and great care in choosing each formal step in his proof in such a way that it can be immediately provided with economic meaning. For instance, the proof of the alternative theorem employs mathematical devices that are quite explicitly interpreted, one by one, in economic terms – terms, moreover, that fit in closely with the framework of neoclassical theory. Sato seems to advocate a methodology which is radically opposed to the one I attributed to G&S. It amounts to the demand that each and every step in a mathematical proof be interpretable in economic terms.[4]

The contrast could not be greater. G&S blindly rely on proof-generated lemmas and devices; Sato is led by programmatic (if not 'realistic' à la Zahar) considerations when choosing the appropriate mathematical steps. A good example of the way in which Sato derives his guidance from the considerations of the neo-classical research programme is the conclusion he arrives at. On the strength of his proof Sato concludes that it is not the condition of positive commodity prices which is basic (as G&S assert), but rather the extent to which labour and capital are substitutable in production processes.

Now, without further evidence it is impossible to tell to what extent Sato started out with some preconceived notion as to where he wanted to arrive at, and to what extent the process of proving his theorem in mathematical terms gave him economically useful ideas. The idea that substitutability is relevant for the possibility of reswitching and capital reversing had been around for some time[5] and had been used by Sato himself.[6] But even if his formal conditions were initially purely proof generated, he selected those that could be interpreted in terms of substitution. And the fact remains that this is clearly a notion which fits in very well with the corpus and the spirit of the neoclassical research programme.

In order to make some progress in finding out about the heuristic use of mathematics in the debate, I will examine whether there are any systematic relations between formal, mathematical arguments, economic arguments, and the strategies of model development. I will deal with this question in two stages. First, I will discuss whether we can discover any general regularities in the dialectics of mathematics and science, as Zahar calls it. For that purpose I will draw on the work of Lakatos. Then I will make the connection with the specific methodological analysis of the strategies of theory development that has been developed in the previous chapters.

2 From the science of mathematics to the mathematics of science

The recent revival of interest in heuristics, or the logic of discovery, is mainly due to Lakatos. His *Proofs and Refutations* analyses the logic of mathematical discovery, and *Methodology of Scientific Research Programmes* studies the logic of scientific discovery. Unfortunately, no substantial discussion of the role of mathematics in scientific discovery exists in Lakatos' work. I will make an attempt to fill that gap by combining elements of both logics of discovery that Lakatos did write. Now, if there is such a thing as a logic of discovery or a rational heuristics, what may we expect from it? Various demands may be formulated, for instance, that it be non-inductive, or more generally non-justificationist, non-trivial,[7] demonstrably more successful than rivals, capable of accounting for real developments in science and, last but not least, that it give direction to the development of a science. To start with, I will concentrate on the last two demands.

In order to guide research, a heuristics must impose restrictions or constraints. This is argued, for instance, by Nickles, who illustrates this with the example of chemistry.

> [T]he model-building method of doing chemistry was and is also important in a *formal* sense (although not the usual logico-mathematical one) in that it induces a certain structural organization on the body of chemical knowledge, and provides a particularly concrete way to explore the space of possible chemical structures. Chemical knowledge imposes definite limits upon this space, hence, constraints on model building in general. Any specific structural problem imposes additional constraints, as does any hypothesized structural information; so model building is a way to represent the particular research problem with its full array of defining constraints.[8]

The concept of defining constraints is the crux of mathematical proofs. As a first step, let us examine Lakatos' contribution to the methodology of mathematics.

3 Proofs

The logic of mathematical discovery, or the method of proofs and refutations, has been so succinctly stated by Lakatos that it justifies quoting in full. The method, which is also called the method of proof analysis, consists of the following stages:

1 Primitive conjecture.
2 Proof (a rough thought-experiment or argument, decomposing the primitive conjecture into subconjectures or lemmas).
3 'Global' counterexamples (counterexamples to the primitive conjecture) emerge.
4 Proof re-examined: the 'guilty lemma' to which the global counterexample is a 'local' counterexample is spotted. This guilty lemma may have previously remained 'hidden' or may have been misidentified. Now it is made explicit,

and built into the primitive conjecture as a condition. The theorem – the improved conjecture – supersedes the primitive conjecture with the new proof-generated concept as its paramount new feature.

These four stages constitute the essential kernel of proof analysis. But there are some further stages which frequently occur:

5   Proofs of other theorems are examined to see if the newly found lemma or the new proof-generated concept occurs in them: this concept may be found lying at crossroads of different proofs, and thus emerge as of basic importance.
6   The hitherto accepted consequences of the original and now refuted conjecture are checked.
7   Counterexamples are turned into new examples – new fields of inquiry open up (Lakatos 1976: 127–8, italics deleted).

The scheme reads like an accurate description of the episode of the capital theory debate that is discussed in the present study.

- *Primitive conjectures* which were held to be true previous to the debate are the inverse relation between the rate of interest and capital intensity of production techniques, the non-recurrence of the same technique of production at a different interest rate, and the inverse relation between the interest rate and the level of consumption.
- These conjectures were thought to be predicted by, and hence *provable, if not proved, from* the neoclassical production model.
- The *global counterexamples* to the primitive conjectures were found by Robinson, Garegnani, Pasinetti, BBS, and many others.
- This prompted a *re-examination of the proof,* or rather, as the conjectures had been believed to be so much in the spirit of neoclassical production theory that they had not been proved in any detail, an *examination of the proof.*
- The proof of the conjectures is discovered to be premised on *hidden lemmas,* one of which is that the ordering of production techniques as *checking of the hitherto accepted consequences* to capital intensity coincides with their inverse ordering according to the rate of interest at which they are eligible.
- In the debate, discovered lemmas or proof-generated concepts of the crossroads variety did not play any explicit role, though there have been some discussions as to whether the assumption of profit maximizing behaviour was unique to the neoclassical approach or whether it was something that was commonly held by authors working in different theoretical traditions.[9]
- The ways in which, in the capital theory debate, *guilty lemmas are built into the primitive conjecture as conditions* are the different strategies of theory development which we have described in the previous chapters.
- Examples of the *checking of the hitherto accepted consequences* that we have come across are Garegnani (1970), Pasinetti (1966), and BBS (1966).

- We have also encountered instances where *counterexamples were turned into examples which opened up new fields of inquiry*: Brown (1969) and Ferguson and Allen (F&A) (1970).

4   Proofs and programmes

If we look at the details of the proofs given in the debate, we can often observe that purely formal, mathematical steps are used in proving theorems. This was the case not only with Sato and G&S, but also with F&A, Brown, Levhari, and, if we take her literally, Robinson.[10] The primary reason why these steps are included seems to be purely mathematical: they are proof generated. If we kept strictly to the methodology of *Proofs and Refutations*, all we could say about these proof-generated devices is that they help to prove the theorem. Successful proof-generated conditions are their own justification and whether or not they are acceptable depends on the context of the proof: the proof is the only 'problem-background' of proof-generated concepts.[11]

However, in the debate the problem-background of most authors is more complicated than this. Proof-generated concepts are usually not judged by the formal requirements of the proofs only. When deciding whether or not particular proof-generated concepts are acceptable, participants let themselves also be guided by economic-theoretical considerations which are suggested by the research programme in which they are working.[12] Programmatic considerations of this kind constitute the major difference between the method of *Proofs and Refutations* and the methods that are used in the capital theory debate. I refer to this influence as *programmatic guidance*. Clear instances of programmatic guidance can be found in the articles of Sato, F&A, and Brown. Perhaps Levhari's article is another instance, but there it did not lead to the desired result because of a mistake in the formal proof. Clearly, the conditions generated by a mistaken proof can also be subjected to the guidance of an economic research programme under the influence of unjustified wishful thinking.

The method of proofs and refutations offers an accurate general description of the way in which participants in the debate operate. They translate economic problems into mathematical theorems, which they then prove. In order to bring the proof to a successful conclusion, it is often necessary to introduce formal conditions. Sometimes these are blindly proof generated and remain formal. They may also be blindly proof generated and interpreted later in economic terms. But where their choice is guided by considerations of consistency with a particular economic research programme, the analysis of *Proofs and Refutations* (PR) has to be augmented by the idea of programmatic guidance which is taken from *Methodology of Scientific Research Programmes* (MSRP). An economic research programme has a positive heuristic which provides global guidance for the choice and interpretation of lemmas that are needed to prove theorems. What lends thrust, i.e. drive and direction,[13] to the debate are proofs and programmes. By incorporating this element from Lakatos' MSRP into the methodology of PR, we obtain a programme-augmented proofs-and-refutations model of theory development. I will refer to it as PR$^+$.

5 Proofs, programmes, and strategies

Which among the various possible strategies of theory development one chooses depends both on local and global considerations: both the concrete problem situation and the research programme one belongs to. In a situation where a neoclassical production model is criticized, we are not surprised to find a neoclassical author defending the model by means of a heuristic strategy. Nor do we find it odd that an author who belongs to a rival research programme, such as the Sraffian programme, follows a domain strategy when criticizing a neoclassical model. For each local problem situation there is a strategy to follow, depending on whether one wants to criticize or immunize a particular hypothesis or model, or develop it in a progressive way.

In all three cases mathematics may offer valuable help. In the case of a correspondence strategy formulating both the corresponded and the corresponding model in mathematics makes it easier to compare their structures and find out which steps are needed to link them. In the case of a domain strategy, mathematics may play exactly the same part. This is the case where there exists a standard model with a limited domain of application. If one succeeds in showing that another model that has a claim to wider applicability can be reduced without residue to the limited model, one has successfully carried out a domain strategy, and mathematics has the same useful role as in the correspondence strategy. In the case studies which I discussed, Garegnani's strategy of criticizing Samuelson's surrogate model stands out as an example of this: he proved that Samuelson's surrogate production function exactly coincides with the production function of the Clark–Ramsey model. And mathematics may help heuristic strategies by suggesting, through proof-generated lemmas and devices, conditions that are relevant in economic terms but had been overlooked. In the case studies (for instance of Brown and F&A), mathematical proof analysis and programmatic guidance have been seen to conclude marriages that were productive of economic-theoretical offspring.

PR$^+$ in conjunction with the strategies described by PIM and AIM and the distinction between global and local levels of analysis fully accounts for the interaction among economic research programmes, proofs of theorems, and mathematics.

Notes

1 Cf. their n. 7 on p. 350.
2 Including the two steps of a numerical counterexample and the proof of a 'general theorem'.
3 Alternatively, one could say that Sato inflicts a capital punishment on Gallaway and Shukla.
4 According to Jan van Daal, this methodology was defended by the late Willem Somermeyer, the Dutch mathematical economist.
5 For instance, in Hicks (1965) and Brown (1969).

6 In Sato (1974).
7 For this, cf. Musgrave (1989).
8 Nickles (1990: 22).
9 Cf. Kregel (1980).
10 Cf. c. 3, where she is quoted as saying: 'The geometry reveals a curious possibility [of capital reversing].' (Robinson 1953: 106)
11 Cf. Lakatos (1976: 147).
12 Whether a particular condition is originally, as a matter of historical fact, purely proof generated can only be determined from a publication if the proof or its economic interpretation goes wrong, as is the case with Gallaway and Shukla (and perhaps Levhari).
13 I owe this concept of thrust as drive and direction to Neil de Marchi. However, he seems to advocate *Proofs and Refutations* pure and simple, without the programmatic elements that I introduce, as the adequate vehicle for methodological analysis in economics.

12 A final stock-taking

> We do not have the method of the laboratory sciences for settling a dispute by a crucial experiment. Mere logic will never prise a writer off his paradigm until he is ready to drop it himself.
>
> Robinson (1980a: 121)

When I started this inquiry into the relation between idealizing theories on the one hand and factualized models on the other hand, I expected that a clarification of the structure of idealizing theories would provide a direct solution to another problem, the question of why the capital theory debate was felt to be so confusing. But both problems turned out to be more complex than I expected. This forced me to introduce a number of distinctions that clarified their structure. It was thus that I hit upon the distinction between global and local levels of analysis, the distinction between internally and externally generated problems, and the heuristic role of mathematics.

Now that I have come to the end, I will summarize some of the most striking historical features of the development of the debate, and examine whether the methodological apparatus that I have gradually developed enables me to offer some explanations for them. One answer turns out to be the solution to my original problem. This solution can easily be mistaken for a defence of methodological pluralism. It will be argued that such a conclusion would not be justified.

1 Historical ironies

The image that emerges of our historical reconstruction shows is rife with ironies.

1   Robinson discovered reswitching and capital reversing but dismissed them as curiosa and anomalies.
2   Robinson wanted to criticize neoclassical theory. Her own discoveries could have been powerful weapons for that purpose, but she failed to notice.
3   By explaining reswitching and capital reversing and proving that they could only occur within a limited interval of the production function, she had changed their status from anomalies to logical consequences of her own model, but she failed to notice this, too.

4   The situation was practically the opposite in the case of Sraffa. He was fully aware of the critical potential of reswitching, and made it an explicit, important, and even crucial part of his criticism of neoclassical economics. But for some time he was the only one who was aware of this. When finally this was noticed by other economists, it was too late for his arguments to influence the debate.

5   Champernowne used the same apparatus of analysis as later authors and discovered that the possibility of reswitching could only be ruled out by an additional assumption. But this result was never used. It was rediscovered in the debate, as was his observation that reswitching is only problematic in a dynamic context.

6   Robinson later said that she developed the pseudo production function in order to drive home her criticism of the neoclassical approach that comparative statics cannot stand in for dynamics. But this analytical device was taken over by neoclassical authors and incorporated in their defence, starting with Samuelson in 1962. He was inspired by Robinson's construction, and gave a new interpretation to it, namely that it is a useful idealization.[1] (Robinson later admits that she put defenders and critics of neoclassical theory alike on the wrong track for a long time.[2])

7   It was Samuelson himself who, in defending his 1962 surrogate production model, introduced reswitching into the debate by telling Levhari of his conjecture. What two of the staunchest critics of neoclassical economics, Robinson and Sraffa, had failed to achieve, for different reasons, was accomplished by the neoclassic-par-excellence Samuelson: he himself invited a new round of criticism by drawing attention to reswitching.[3]

8   Solow and other neoclassics later came to the conclusion for themselves that the fundamental problem in the debate was the use of static models to make statements about processes in time. Solow denies that it was Robinson who first saw this. He is wrong. But he is right in thinking that she did not make this the main point of her criticism until the early 1970s.[4]

9   The current interest in evolutionary models in economics may be interpreted as a recognition of the fact that 'logical time' is no substitute for 'real time'. This point had been emphasized by Robinson for a long time, but there are no signs that evolutionary economics owes anything to her.

10 The greatest irony of all is that, although the capital theory debate is one of the few examples where economists have discovered 'hard facts', they continue to ignore them in their theoretical and empirical work.

2   The ironies explained: sleepwalking on the object level

How may the ironies be explained? That Samuelson takes over Robinson's pseudo production function hardly needs an explanation. This is something that may happen in any debate. But in all other cases, the sleepwalker effect accounts for what happened. Everybody, or almost everybody,[5] was busy solving local problems, often of a technical nature, whose solutions in their turn created further problems, which were largely of the internally generated variety. This had the consequence of keeping the debate on the local level of economic analysis.

The fact that the debate did not take off after the publication of Champernowne's 1953 article is due to something else. For a phenomenon to turn from a curiosum into an issue, the theoretical context, on the global level of economic analysis, has to change. This change was later provided by the increased interest in empirical growth theory, and Samuelson's defence of Solow's work on aggregate models in particular. Debates do not start unless they have a focal point, and this was provided by Samuelson's defence of his 1962 surrogate model. By introducing the analytical apparatus of the two-sector fixed-coefficients production model and the wage-profit frontier, Samuelson set the terms of the debate.[6] Once Samuelson's model (which turned out, moreover, to be Sraffa's as well) was accepted as the vehicle of analysis, the 'local' course of events was determined by the strategies of theory development. This is true of both defenders and critics of neoclassical production theory.[7] One of the advantages of the distinction between local and global levels in science is that it leaves room for such historical contingencies, which are often important if not crucial for the development of a debate.

3   Empirical versus formal arguments: sleepwalking on the meta level

In the debate the sleepwalker effect seems to be operative on the methodological level, too. Participants are confused in their attitudes towards the formal arguments they offer. They show signs of a guilty conscience about the use of formal arguments in criticism and defence alike. Apparently, they think that it is really the empirical arguments that should count: they are subject to the empiricist bias. Take Ferguson, who observes on the 'Cambridge Criticism':

> Its validity is unquestionable, but its importance is an empirical or an econometric matter that depends upon the amount of substitutability there is in the system. Until the econometricians have the answer for us, placing reliance upon neoclassical economic theory is a matter of faith. I personally have the faith; but at present the best I can do to convince others is to invoke the weight of Samuelson's authority . . .
>
> (Ferguson 1969: xv–xvi)[8]

This type of argument is echoed in the title of Brown (1973), 'Toward an Econometric Accommodation of the Capital-Intensity-Perversity Phenomenon'.[9] Empirical tests are *said* to be important. But no one actually carries them out. Instead of empirical arguments and econometric tests we find probability judgments of an a priori character. In order to understand why these strange likelihood observations are made, it is useful to reinvoke Worralls' distinction: is an idealizing theory a true theory about ideal phenomena, or a false theory about real phenomena? Musgrave thinks the latter, and the participants in the debate seem to agree if we are to go by their *obiter dicta*. But the way they behave in the debate is different: they prove theorems about ideal phenomena. The truth of theories of ideal phenomena obviously cannot be empirical truth. Rather, it is mathematical truth in the sense of provability from particular axioms. The ideal that economists seem to have is to design an axiomatic system from which they can prove their theorems. In order to reach that goal, they try to find both the necessary and sufficient conditions for the theorems. It is the theorems that are central. They state particular convictions economists have about the state of the world, however stylized. This talk about deriving theorems (to which usually is added 'deductively') has obscured the view of what is really happening. Theorems are stated, and then one tries to find ('derive'[10]) conditions for them. The conditions may be proof generated, suggested by an economic research programme, or both. In all cases, it is the theorems (or rather predictions) that come first, and the conditions are found by working one's way backward to the axioms of a theory or model.[11]

The participants in the debate waver between both interpretations of the status of idealizing models. This is also apparent from the fact that quite often likelihood or probability judgments are given that are based on purely formal conditions. It is clear that factual considerations or considerations of common sense are involved. But these are relevant on a different level. On the one hand, participants act as if they want to prove results for ideal models. On the other hand, they talk as if they find the applicability and testability in empirical domains important. But one cannot have it both ways. The wavering explains the appeals to empirical tests without carrying them out and the occasional apologetic remarks about the formality of the results obtained. So, the confusion follows from the fact that participants in the debate do not fully recognize the status of idealizing models. They fail to recognize that *for improving a theory, formal counterexamples and conditions may have the same – critical – function as empirical counterexamples and tests*. While empirical tests are to be sought after where possible, they are by no means the only possible tests. This is implicitly recognized by the methods and arguments that are *de facto* utilized; they are of a formal character.

The case studies dealing with the earlier articles show that what happens in the course of the debate is the *differentiation of the problem*. It is gradually discovered that there is a difference between reswitching and capital reversing, and it is discovered how they are related. This 'mapping of the problem', the analysis of its structure, is a valuable enterprise in its own right as it helps to clarify the structure and possible implications of a particular type of model. True, this may detain participants for too long. In that case they end up doing nothing but analyzing the properties of a particular model and solving local and internally generated puzzles while forgetting the original problem that started the debate. This situation may last until someone comes along who derives a suggestion from a particular research programme for revealing a relevant idealizing assumption. This was the case with Ferguson and Allen (F&A).

The importance that is attached to non-empirical analyses and tests is not unique to economics. In every discipline, sticking to the empiricist bias would mean that rational scientific research would grind to a halt if it were impossible to obtain, or create, new empirical test results. Is this inevitable? Not so, says physicist and 1999 Nobel laureate Gerard 't Hooft. He discusses one of the unresolved problems of modern physics, the relation between quantum mechanics and the theory of gravitation. In order to study the effects of the behaviour of very small particles, the domain of quantum mechanics, on the macro-phenomena of gravitation empirically, small particles would have to be given sufficient mass by means of a very great acceleration, greater than existing particle accelerators are capable of. Even if and when it is physically impossible to construct such powerful particle accelerators, or if and when society finds them too expensive to build, and either moment may soon be reached, that would not mean the end of elementary particle physics. In such a case a theoretical formalism would have to be developed for carrying out thought experiments. The combination of imagination and mathematics would still allow physicists to calculate the effects of the small on the big.[12] Only, the growth of particle physics would then acquire the character of the growth of mathematics, a legitimate and rational enterprise. To draw the line at empirical tests as motors of change is far too restrictive; science is much more complex and comprises more than empirical testing.

4 What do research programmes do?

But even if empirical tests had played any part in the debate, could refutations of factualized neoclassical models have led to a refutation of the idealizing theory that lies at the core of the neoclassical research programme? Before answering this, I propose that we have a look at the methodological function and the logical status of research programmes.

Heuristic guidance: the power of the programme

Idealizing theories belong to the global level of research programmes. They guide research by telling what factors are relevant and what factors can be factualized. The programmatic or heuristic guidance provided by neoclassical theory is an important factor in the development of the debate. This may be seen from the ways in which, for example, Brown and F&A react to criticism. This 'power of the programme' has been recognized by one of the critics of neoclassical marginal value theory, Pasinetti. He distinguishes two research programmes in economics: the production or industry approach as can be found, for instance, in the work of Sraffa, and the neoclassical programme. He compares the situation of the critics of neoclassical theory in the capital theory debate[13] with the position of the defenders of 'marginalism'.

> [I]t is not difficult to see that all the contributions to economic theory just mentioned stem from what has been called above the production or industry approach to economic reality, as opposed to the optimum allocation of resources approach. But their authors themselves did not perceive this very

clearly. Each of those theories has been presented under the compulsion of certain facts, which current theory was unable to explain. As a consequence, they have been presented independently of one another, without an explicit relation to any unifying principle. This has made things easier for the Marginalists. It seemed natural to look for a unifying theoretical framework and marginal economics had one to offer. Although the authors of new theories have, most of the time, strongly protested that their theories had nothing to do with Marginalism, the Marginalists have been at an advantage. *They have had the advantage of synthesis.* For they have always clearly presented their arguments around a unifying problem (optimum allocation of scarce resources) and a unifying principle (the rational process of maximization under constraints).

(Pasinetti 1981: 18–19, emphasis added)[14]

Pasinetti recommends the same strategy to the critics of neoclassical economics. We may add that the unifying power of the neoclassical research programme has been reinforced by the use of mathematics. The examples that spring to mind are the work of Wicksell[15] and Samuelson's *Foundations* (Samuelson 1983).

Irrefutability: the tenacity of the programme

Pasinetti may be right about the power of programmes. But is not their very tenacity a disadvantage? It has been argued that idealizing theories[16] as elements of the superstructure of a research programme cannot be refuted on the basis of negative results obtained with empirical, hence necessarily factualized, models. The following arguments have been put forward:

1   The Duhem–Quine thesis. As theories are complex entitities, and as theories are connected with empirical models through a host of auxiliary theories, we do not know which element of this network is to blame for empirical refutations.
2   Boland argues that neoclassical theory is irrefutable because of the logical form of its central lawlike statement, which is a mixed universally-existentially quantified statement.[17]
3   The argument from instrumentalism: theories are instruments for generating predictions, and instruments cannot be refuted. At the most, they can be judged to be unsuitable for particular purposes.
4   From PIM we can derive another, independent argument as to why idealizing theories in the superstructure of research programmes cannot be refuted by results obtained on the level of more factualized models.

The argument is *that the logical relation between idealizing theories and factualized models is not of the kind that allows falsifications obtained on the level of factualized models to be 'retransmitted' to idealizing models.* For this to be the case, factualized models would have to be logically entailed by, or deductively derivable from, idealizing models. But as we have seen in the discussion of PIM, it is the other way around: idealizing models are logically entailed by, or deductively derivable from, factualized models (plus idealizing conditions).[18]

Krajewski was quoted as saying that this goes against the deeply entrenched intuition that idealizing theories explain factualized models, which in a deductive-nomological model of explanation implies that factualized models are logically entailed by idealizing models. This also seems to be an idea which is common among economists[19] and which is that one somehow 'derives' models from (idealizing) theories. So we have a contradiction, or at the very least a paradox.

5   Presuppositions as heuristics

This negative result is as far as we can get with PIM. But the methodological apparatus that I have developed is capable of resolving the paradox. It may be resolved if we interpret the widely held intuition not in terms of the logic of explanation but in terms of priority. The intuition that idealizing theories are somehow prior to factualized models certainly seems correct. For idealizing theories do provide heuristic guidance for factualizations. *But this correct intuition was projected on the wrong relationship: instead of on the heuristical relation between idealizing theories and factualized models, it was projected on their logical relationship.*

The distinction between logical and heuristical relations has removed the paradox. But is not the price we have to pay a weakening of what has long been considered the attraction of the standard view of science: that we can characterize the relations between theories and models in logical terms? Is the concept of a heuristic not uncomfortably vague? Let us go back to the sense of paradox that may easily arise out of the confrontation of the logical relation between idealizing and factualized models that obtains according to PIM, and the idea that idealizing models are prior to factualized models. We feel a comparable sense of paradox when we are told by a logician that we can describe the presuppositions of a proposition as the logical *consequences* of that proposition.[20] For our intuition is that somehow presuppositions are prior to the propositions that they are presuppositions of. But if we consider an example from one of the case studies, it will be noticed that the idea that presuppositions are necessary conditions is not so counterintuitive after all. Champernowne discovered that the ordering assumption (the ordering of production techniques according to capital intensity is the inverse of their ordering according to the rate of interest) is a necessary condition for ruling out reswitching. In common language, too, this is equivalent to saying that non-reswitching *presupposes* that techniques are ordered in the specified way.

I suggest that we take the analogy literally: *idealizing theories are among the presuppositions of factualized models,* and the logical relation between idealizing and factual models reflects the presupposition relation. The same is true of other elements that belong to the core of a research programme, such as metaphysics; they are all presuppositions of the factualized models that are associated with the programme. Idealizing theories are very much like the metaphysics which form a component of each and every scientific theory.[21]

6   Modelling presuppositions

There have been several attempts to model the presupposition relationship as intended here. The most interesting are discussed below.

Bunge on priority and presuppositions

The idea that one theory or model acts as a presupposition of another has been advocated by Bunge. Bunge deals, inter alia, with the priority relation that may exist between pairs of theories. This relation is a pragmatic or psychological relation, while the logical relation between the theories is a presupposition relation which may 'run in the opposite direction'.

> Thus mathematics presupposes logic from a semantic point of view but mathematics usually comes first both historically and methodologically, in the sense that it has motivated most of modern logic and that it still provides the major control and the chief justification for it. Quite often, the semantic relation of presupposition runs counter to the pragmatic or historical direction.
>
> (Bunge 1970: 301)

An equivalent way of stating the relation between theories or disciplines such as mathematics and logic is to say that one is based on the other.

> To say that a theory A is *based on* another theory B means that A presupposes B . . . And a theory A *presupposes* another theory B just in case the following conditions are met:
> (a) B is a necessary condition for the meaning or verisimiltude of A, because A contains concepts that are elucidated in B, or statements that are justified in B, and
> (b) B is not questioned while A is being built, worked out, criticized, tested, or applied . . .
>
> (Bunge 1970: 300)

Item (a) is said to capture the logical and semantic aspects of presuppositions, and (b) the methodological ones. Bunge observes that the concept of presupposition is to be kept distinct from the one of entailment, whether syntactic or semantic.

> If [B] is deducible from [A] then obviously A presupposes B in our sense, for B is a presupposition under which A holds. But the converse need not hold: A may not follow from its background B alone – and as a matter of fact in general it does not. Thus set theory, which presupposes logic, is not entailed by the latter. Likewise mechanics does not follow from mathematics alone,

and relativistic kinematics requires postulates of its own in addition to those of classical electromagnetic theory.

(Bunge 1970: 301. I have replaced the first occurrences of A and B by B and A, as otherwise the passage becomes unintelligible)

In a note Bunge briefly discusses Van Fraassen's analysis of presuppositions in terms of semantic entailment. This approach, initially proposed by Strawson, defines presuppositions as follows: a sentence A presupposes a sentence B iff both A and non-A semantically entail B. Bunge has three criticisms to offer: '(a) this definition does not recapture the intuitive notion of presupposition; (b) A might entail only a part of its background B: if it did not, it would add nothing to B; (c) the meaning ingredient is not taken care of.' (ibid.: 315, n. 12). He does not elaborate, and the gist of the second and third points of his criticism is not very clear. In what follows I will examine whether the semantic definition of presuppositions for the modelling of relations among theories is as counterintuitive as Bunge thinks, and what possible other merits and demerits it has.

Semantic entailment

Let p and q be sentences. The semantic definition of presupposition is

p presupposes q iff $p \models q$ and $\neg p \models q$.

How could this be applied to the relation between an idealizing theory (T) and a factualized model (M)?

1   Consider a model to be a (set of) sentence(s).
2   Then M presupposes T iff $M \models T$ and $\neg M \models T$.
3   The model mentions relevant factors.
4   The theory T tells us what the (basic) relevant factors are.
5   The negation $\neg M$ of the model M mentions the same relevant factors as does M.

But what can the negation of a model possibly mean? Again, I take an example from the capital theory debate. The discovery that reswitching could occur was used by certain critics of neoclassical economics to conclude that neoclassical economics was refuted. To this Solow replied:

Professor Robinson seems to think that the discovery of the logical reswitching phenomenon is destructive of 'neoclassical economics'. In this context I take neoclassical economics to be the working out of the logical consequences of the two principles of cost minimization and no pure profit, especially in steady states. It is certainly not the adoption of one-sector or two-sector models.

In that sense – which may not be hers – the whole discussion IS neoclassical economics. The possibility of reswitching is a theorem of neoclassical economics, even if it was first pointed out by opponents of the theory.

(Solow 1975: 49–50)

Both reswitching and non-reswitching presuppose (the truth of) neoclassical economic theory (NCET). We may render the original neoclassical model and its prediction as[22]

M : $(x)((\text{Technique})x \ \& \ (\text{Ordering})x \rightarrow \text{no reswitching})$,

and the criticism as

$\neg M$: $\neg (x)((\text{Technique})x \ \& \ (\text{Ordering})x \rightarrow \text{no reswitching})$,

and both $M \models \text{NCET}$ and $\neg M \models \text{NCET}$.

A well-known problem with the semantic-entailment view of presuppositions is that it is either trivial or leads to contradictions. If we hold on to the principle of bivalence (every sentence is either true or false), then the semantic definition states the triviality that every sentence presupposes only tautologies. However, in reality many sentences have false presuppositions. If the sentence q is the presupposition of a sentence p, from the falsity of q and the semantic definition of presupposition, it follows (by modus tollens and $p \models q$) that $\neg p$, and (by modus ponens and $\neg p \models q$) that q, so that we have the contradiction $q \& \neg q$. Solutions have been proposed in terms of three-valued logics, but these have the disadvantage that not all the 'classical' logical theorems are valid. Van Fraassen has developed the so-called supervaluations approach,[23] which preserves all of the classical laws of logic except the law of bivalence. In Van Fraassen's system, sentences may be neither true nor false. This is notably the case for sentences with presuppositions that are not true: if a sentence has a presupposition which is not true, then that sentence is neither true nor false.

The choice for the first horn of Worrall's dilemma, that idealizing theories are true theories of ideal phenomena, has in some cases given rise to the view that idealizing theories are tautologies (Ludwig von Mises, Hayek in his well-known 'Economics and Knowledge'[24]), or are at the very least very much like tautologies (Carl Menger). Whatever the merits or demerits of these positions, in these cases the semantic definition of presuppositions seems to model the relation between idealizing theory and factualized model adequately without the need to give up the principle of bivalence.

If we choose the second horn of Worrall's dilemma, that idealizing theories are false theories about real phenomena, Van Fraassen's system seems like a plausible way of modelling the relation between theory and model. When we read for 'neither true nor false' 'inapplicable', then from the falsity of the idealizing theory conceived of as being among the presuppositions of a factualized model, we conclude that both the model and its negation are inapplicable. A related intuition that seems to be captured by the supervaluations version of the semantic definition of presuppositions is the notion of 'what it is like to do X' or 'what it means that a particular model is a model of X', where X may be any discipline or theory. For instance, different geometries all share the axioms that constitute so-called natural geometry.[25] So it can be maintained that both Euclidean geometry and geometries that deny the axiom of parallels all presuppose natural geometry. Whether or not you maintain these axioms determines whether or not you are doing geometry. The same analysis seems to apply to neoclassical economics: whether or not one presupposes the truth of a maximizing hypothesis determines whether or not one is doing neoclassical economics. This is reminiscent of Menger's classification of the sciences according to fundamental factors. One places oneself outside a particular discipline if one abstracts by isolating abstraction from certain fundamental factors.

I can imagine that the notion of the negation of a model still meets with conceptual difficulties. Let me offer another tentative argument in its favour. In PIM, a model is formalized as a universally quantified conditional statement

$$(x)(Cx \rightarrow Px).$$

Its negation is

$$\neg(x)(Cx \rightarrow Px),$$

which is equivalent to

$$(\exists x)\neg(Cx \rightarrow Px).$$

Now this seems to be the basis of an apt description of one of the strategies of criticism that is followed in the capital theory debate and in theoretical economics in general. The strategy consists of proving that a model for which universal validity was claimed, is only valid in a limited domain. An extreme case of this strategy is proving that the domain of the model is empty. This amounts to finding an impossibility theorem:

$$\neg(\exists x)(Cx \rightarrow Px).$$

Scientific explanations as answers to questions

Another proposal to apply the notion of presupposition to the analysis of scientific theories and their relations is made by Matti Sintonen.[26] He conceives of scientific explanations as answers to questions, and analyzes explanations with the means of erotetic logic. He distinguishes two types of presuppositions of questions. One type comprises logical (or syntactic) and pragmatic presuppositions. The second type is analyzed in terms of beliefs and subjective probabilities and I will not dwell upon these. The first type seems more relevant to the present context: 'presuppositions$_1$ of a question are logical entailments of the question sentences.

Or rather, if only declarative sentences can have entailments, presuppositions$_1$ are logical entailments of the essentially syntactically chosen declarative counterparts of the question sentences.' (Sintonen 1984: 45). Sintonen (1985) contains a further discussion which relies on the so-called structuralist analysis augmented by elements from the traditional statement approach.[27]

The questions a scientist asks are, in part at least, defined by his theoretical framework, which in a structuralist analysis consists of so-called basic theory elements and specialized elements: 'In a quite natural sense a scientist... who holds a Kuhn-theory presupposes the basic theory-elements as well as the specialized elements at t, and these presuppositions provide the background for his questions in any problem contexts.' (Sintonen 1985: 31). Sintonen applies the analytical instruments of the logic of questions and answers to presuppositions, which act as constraints on the answers that are admissible.

> In standard erotetic logic the notion of a presupposition is defined as follows: a proposition p is a presupposition of a question q if and only if the truth of p is necessary for the question to have a (direct) answer... The presupposition of a question thus rules out as inappropriate all responses which violate the presupposition.
>
> (Sintonen 1985: 32)

This is consistent with the idea of a logic of discovery as a set of constraints,[28] and the example he gives expresses the same idea of the delimitations of a particular theory or group of theories that was discussed above.

> But even the Ptolemaic research tradition fits the model to some degree. There was a fundamental law or basic theory-core. Although there was no one single solution to the problem of the planets, all specific theories contained a system of earth-centered circles and major epicycles.... A Ptolemaic astronomer thus *presupposed* the core, the Aristotelian physics and cosmology, the values as well as the theory-net specialization at hand.
>
> (Sintonen 1985: 34, emphasis added)

Sintonen also addresses the dynamics of theories.

> [T]he evolution of a Kuhn-theory brings forth new constraints in this sense: any solution to a problem for a specialized element... must accord with the special laws (and constraints) of its predecessor elements.... In question-theoretic terms this is: a querier who holds ('works with') [a specialized theory element] presupposes$_2$ the predecessor elements.
>
> (Sintonen 1985: 36)

The way in which Sintonen describes the correspondence principle is very similar to the one in para. 5 above augmented by the notion of idealizing theories as constraints or presuppositions: 'The predecessor theory serves as a constraint on further theorizing: any potential theory T_n must have its predecessor theories T_{n-1} etc. as limit cases.' (Sintonen 1985: 39). The notion of syntactic entailment in Sintonen's analysis may be more suitable than semantic entailment (and pragmatic presuppositions, or presuppositions$_2$) for disciplines such as theoretical economics, where the provability of theorems rather than the truth of predictions is important.

7   Presuppositions and the logic of discovery

The interpretation of the relation that obtains between idealizing theories and factualized models as a presupposition relation makes it susceptible to logical analysis and allows us to characterize the concept of idealizing theories (and other elements of the core of a research programme) acting as a heuristic in very definite terms. Their heuristic guidance consists of the attempts on the part of theorists to construct their models in such a way that the idealizing theories and other hard-core elements be entailed by the conjunction of the models and the appropriate idealizing assumptions. In this way, the idealizing core acts as a set of constraints on factualized models. Both the semantic entailment view and Sintonen's analysis which involves the notion of syntactic entailment have this in common. The unity of the class of factualized models that is associated with a particular research programme resides in the fact that they all presuppose the same idealizing theories (and perhaps the same metaphysics). This is a feature that is shared by the two approaches just mentioned and the one advocated by Bunge.

The introduction of presuppositions as crucial elements in the logic of discovery enables me to complete the scheme that was given above.

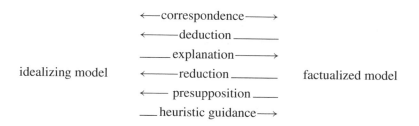

This heuristic function of an idealizing theory acting as a presupposition that must be related to factualized models by a logical entailment relation can be summarized in the methodological rule:

Construct models that are in a relation of correspondence to the basic theory

This regulative principle is central to the logic of discovery that has been called 'conservative induction' by Heinz Post.[29] Post, and his student Noretta Koertge,[30] present a number of case studies showing the operation of this rule. They advance the very strong empirical claim that in the history of science *all* successful theories, or successful parts of theories, were preserved in later theories.[31] This is called the *General Correspondence Principle*, and the similarities with the logic of scientific discovery that is described here warrant an extensive quotation.

> (a) There is a rationale of scientific discovery, over and above mere trial and error. There is a series of restrictions . . . which render the activity of the scientist constructing new theories essentially different from that of a clueless rat trying one trapdoor after another (a remark probably also applying to any actual rat). 'In der Beschränkung zeigt sich der Meister.
>
> (b) These restrictions are 'theoretic', that is, based on internal analysis of available theory.
>
> (c) The procedure is inductive, in the sense of leading from a weaker to a stronger theory ('weaker' at least in the sense that the successful part S^* of the old theory is less precise or less general than the successful part of the new theory L).
>
> (d) It is also essentially inductive in retaining the old theory in a certain sense: it is conservative (as every good scientist is).
>
> (Post 1971: 218)

The interpretation of the logical relation that obtains between idealizing theories and factualized models as a presupposition relation allows us to characterize the concept of idealizing theories (and other elements of the core of a research programme) acting as a heuristic in very definite terms. Their heuristic guidance consists of the attempts on the part of theorists to construct their models in such a way that the idealizing theories and other hard-core elements be logically derivable from them by making the appropriate idealizing assumptions. The unity of the class of factualized models that is associated with a particular research programme resides in the fact that they all presuppose the same idealizing theories and the same metaphysics.

8   Methodological spin-off

The conception of idealizing theories as presuppositions that are semantically or syntactically entailed by factualized models has a couple of unintended methodological advantages. It provides a reinforcement of one of the central ideas of Lakatos' *Methodology of Scientific Research Programmes* (MSRP). According to MSRP, the hard core of a theory is irrefutable *as a matter of convention*. In the present analysis, the hard core is irrefutable *as a matter of logic*. The only way in which idealizing theories could conceivably be tested empirically is via various factualized models (FM_i), but both the idealized theories presupposed by the factualized models and the empirical consequences of these models are among the consequences, not the premises, of the models.

This gives us an answer to a question that has exercised many a critic of neoclassical economics: why did neoclassical theorists not give up neoclassical theory?

The answer is that, even if neoclassical economists had not had recourse to any of the strategies of theory development that I have described, then still, as a matter of logic, negative formal or possibly empirical test results obtained with factualized models could not, as a matter of logic, have served to refute the associated idealizing theory. If we depict the relation of logical derivability by arrows, the relations among a sequence of factualized models, their predictions, and the idealizing theory they are factualizations of may be shown as the following network.

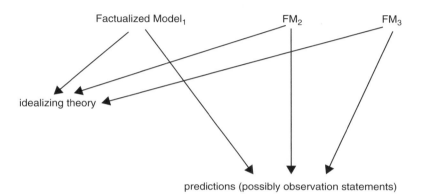

But if idealizing theories cannot be rejected on the basis of tests in factualized models, how can we choose between theories?

9 Different models for different purposes? Three types of pluralism

If idealizing theories have the same status in research programmes as metaphysics, how can we solve the problem of the choice of theories? We have already seen one solution, Musgrave's advocacy of being satisfied with domain strategies as far as they lead to theories that are weaker but have more truth content than their predecessors that were stronger but had less truth content.[32] A consequence of putting this policy into practice is that one could easily end up with a number of true theories that have limited domains of application, and which are not related to one another by any theory.

This is a brand of theoretical pluralism that we find in the Sraffian tradition to which many of the critics of neoclassical production theory belong, such as Garegnani and Pasinetti, and Sraffa himself. According to Gram we can distinguish two types of model. On the one hand the neoclassical model, which is a miniature general equilibrium model of the Walrasian type. And on the other hand the book-of-blueprints model, which is best seen in the context of the capital theory controversy as a general equilibrium model of the classical type, in the spirit of Marx, von Neumann and Sraffa.

The important question thrown up by the capital theory controversy concerns the usefulness of this distinction between classical and neoclassical models of general equilibrium, an issue that turns on the nature of the problem under consideration. If capital theory is to focus primarily on problems associated with the efficient allocation of resources over time, then dynamic generalizations of the Walrasian model will be the most appropriate vehicle of analysis. On the other hand, if the dynamic character of specifically capitalist economies is of primary interest, then models of the Marx–von Neumann–Sraffa type suggest that the assumption of a uniform rate of profit can be shown to bear a particular relationship to the classical concepts of surplus and exploitation ... The difficulty, then, in finding a consensus among the protagonists in the capital theory controversy may be traced to the fact that the general equilibrium structure of their models has not been sufficiently articulated to show that the problem of efficiency and the concept of scarcity is paramount in one set of models, while that of accumulation of a surplus in a specifically capitalist mode of production takes center stage in another set of models.

(Gram 1976: 184, note deleted)

This is a defence of the different-models-for-different purposes pluralism that is consistent with Musgrave's view. On the face of it, Gram's position is similar to what Robinson says in the Preface of her *Accumulation of Capital*. There, she, too, seems to be defending theoretical pluralism:

Economic analysis, serving for two centuries to win an understanding of the Nature and Causes of the Wealth of Nations, has been fobbed off with another bride – a Theory of Value. There were no doubt deep-seated political reasons for the substitution but there was also a purely technical, intellectual reason. It is excessively difficult to conduct analysis of over-all movements of an economy through time, involving changes in population, capital accumulation and technical change, at the same time as an analysis of the detailed relations between output and price of particular commodities. Both sets of problems require to be solved, but each has to be tackled separately, ruling the other out by simplifying assumption. Faced with the choice of which to sacrifice first, economists for the last hundred years have sacrificed dynamic theory in order to discuss relative prices.

(Robinson 1956: v)

But Robinson's defence is different. She does not think that an entirely different theory is needed. All she seems to advocate here is the methodological strategy of separating the influence of relative price changes from the factors influencing accumulation and growth by means of an idealizing strategy. Her introduction of idealizing assumptions seems to rest on more pragmatic, instrumental considerations, and not on the idea that fundamentally different mechanisms are involved that require fundamentally different theories. She just thinks it is time to start examining the other prong of the idealizing fork.

A third, more radical reaction to the problem of theory choice is the sort of instrumentalism that takes as its only criterion a theory's predictive power, a view that is often ascribed to Friedman. This methodology, too, allows a number of theories to be maintained side by side, as each theory may yield the best predictions in specific situations.

Is pluralism of any of the above varieties the last word?

10   Idealization: between instrument and explanation

In the discussion of PIM we have seen that in the course of the development of a discipline, factors may be discovered that till that moment were not taken into account in explanations. From the moment of their development, the models that were used and did not account for the effect of the newly discovered factor, were often considered to be true, factual models. With the discovery of the new factor, their status changes into idealizing models that are related by correspondence to the new models. In a way, the old models have been superseded. But this does not mean that we have to stop using them. They may still be used instrumentally in the domain where they produce acceptable results. Apparently, this type of situation was one of the things Samuelson had in mind when he wrote his 'Parable and Realism'. But Garegnani proved that the domain in which the model obtained the desired results exactly coincided with the ideal domain that was specified in the model's initial conditions. Outside that domain, there was no reason to believe that the predictions would hold even by approximation. The model corresponded only to itself.

The strategies followed by Hicks and F&A lead to different results. They distinguish different cases, and stop there. This is a situation that may be characterized as being of the different-models-for-different-purposes kind. Brown constructs a model that corresponds with Hicks', but then he, too, stops at a classification of four cases describing the possible relative magnitudes of two effects, the substitution and the composition effect. The distinction of cases is an indication that we are still at a rather low level of analysis. The cases have to be explained in order to make theoretical progress. This is what Brown does with Hicks' model. Notice that the explanation is purely formal and a priori, though programme guided. But in principle, a further correspondence step to a model explaining when which effect occurs, is not excluded.

Notice that Solow's and Burmeister's observation (quoted in the Introduction) that the phenomena of production, capital accumulation, and choice of technique that were discussed in the debate cannot suitably be analyzed by means of steady-state models, have the same flavour as the views of Robinson (1956): one has to make the correct idealizations and factualizations. What Solow's and Burmeister's conclusion amounts to is the idea that the debate has remained on the wrong level of analysis for too long, and that the model that was generally used was based on idealizations that made it inappropriate to the problems. By factualizing that model so as to obtain a corresponding, non-steady-state model, these problems might be tackled more successfully.

In the debate empirical predictions play no part, although participants occasionally observed that the conditions that were found had to be tested empirically. But for the course of the debate this would not have made much difference. The formal counterexamples and conditions played the same role that empirical refutations would have played: they prompted revisions of the model. Therefore, Musgrave's insistence[33] on Popper's *principle of empiricism* 'which asserts that in science only observation and experiment may decide upon the *acceptance or rejection* of scientific theories' (Miller 1983: 101) is unduly restrictive. But even if empirical predictions had been generated, ending up with several models each predicting well in a specific empirical domain would not have excluded the possibility of finding another model that tells us why each earlier model predicted as well as it did.

The various brands of pluralism may look different. But according to the analysis presented here, there is no fundamental difference among them. Independently of whether the different-models-for-different-purposes idea is inspired by considerations of methodological expediency, by the conviction that entirely different mechanisms are at work which require different theories for their explanation, or by considerations of predictive power, all three leave open the correspondence strategy of finding a theory that tells us which model applies when. Attempts to do this as much as or perhaps even more than the empirical testing of models are signs that economics is a mature science.

11   Conclusion

So to what conclusions about the capital theory debate does the whole analysis lead? Apart from the influence of the analytical apparatus, including the type of mathematics employed, which I have shown, the previous discussion of Menger (in the Introduction) allows us to state the conclusion very succinctly. In terms of Menger's model, those who tried to defend the neoclassical model (such as Samuelson and BBS) confused two types of idealizations (to substitute that word for Menger's 'abstractions'). Their mistake, as was pointed out later, for instance by Robinson, was to think, or take for granted, that the introduction of time would not change the structure of the model or theory in any important way. In other words, they thought that timeless models were an instance of emphasizing idealization or abstraction. The criticisms showed that this was wrong: abstracting from time was an instance of isolating abstraction. Time is a fundamental factor, the abstraction from which (or if we start from the other end: the introduction of which) changes the predictions of the model or the theory in important ways. Time is one of the 'fundamental causes', to express ourselves once more in Mengerian terms. The introduction of time does not lead to a difference in the extent to which the predictions change, but it changes the content of the predictions. However, time was treated, mostly by the neoclassical economists, as one of the disturbing factors. Perhaps now, with the growing importance of evolutionary models in economics, the time has come to wake capital theory from the slumber in which it has fallen back after the rude but inconsequential awakening from the episode of somnambulism that the debate between the two Cambridges was.[34]

Notes

1 This is confirmed by Samuelson in a letter to the author of 25 August 1989: 'My Surrogate Capital effort...arose from my realization, as I listened to Joan talk about heterogeneous capital goods and separate pages of her blue-print book of techniques, that sometimes a model like hers would produce *aggregate* relations like those in the Leets neoclassical parable. I quickly sketched an instance that looked like a 2-sector neoclassical model but was actually an *n*-good Sraffa model.'

2 Cf. Robinson (1980: 221): 'I confess that I was the first to draw [a pseudo production function]...'. She observes it is not a legitimate construction; it was meant as a protest against a production function with putty capital, but this criticism did not go far enough. It led on to a protest against confusing comparisons of imagined equilibrium positions with movements through historical time. Cf. also ibid.: 223: 'The analysis of comparing technologies has unfortunately run up the blind alley of the pseudo production function, which has held up the development of long run theory for the last twenty years.'

3 This suggests that the debate was between Samuelson and himself, as Steve Rankin commented on an earlier version of Chapter 3. But that seems a little too simple. My historical reconstruction is incomplete, as it does not cover what happened between 1962 and 1964. It seems that in that crucial period there were frequent contacts between Samuelson and economists from Cambridge, UK. Sometime in that period, reswitching started to play a prominent part in the discussion. It is impossible to find out from published material how this came about. But the fact remains that the debate did not take off until Levhari published a theorem about the impossibility of *reswitching*.

4 Well before they themselves reached this conclusion.

5 Cf. what was said about Garegnani in Chapter 11.

6 There is no reason to believe in a conscious plot. This seems to be different in another debate, that between monetarists and Keynesians. Friedman understood the mechanism of persuasion very well, and he quite consciously forced the discussion in the empirical domain, as he judged – correctly as it turned out – the global situation to be such that empirical arguments would be better received than theoretical ones. Cf. Desai (1981: 64): 'As often happens in scientific controversies, the dominant theory defines the ground on which the battle is to be fought by any rival challenger. To counter Keynesian theory, Friedman had to have a theory of income determination [which was lacking]. But Friedman was successful in taking the attack into the econometric/empirical area. Thus...he shifts the argument about the quantity theory to an empirical one about the stability of the demand for money function.' Desai argues that Friedman 'kept the battle there by a bold stroke', that is, by engaging Keynesians and monetarists alike in a ten-year discussion of the question which was more stable: the demand for money or the consumption function.

7 Cf. Kregel (1973: 204): 'Much of the post-Keynesian analysis has suffered from being a negative rather than a positive approach, that it has spent as much effort trying to solve neoclassical puzzles as it has trying to work out its own methods.'

8 Cf. also: 'The crucial point to emphasize is that the validity of neoclassical theory is an empirical, not a *theoretical*, question.' (ibid.: 258). For the point of Samuelson's authority it is perhaps good to remember that Garegnani's criticism of Samuelson (1962) had not been published yet.

9 Notice by the way that Brown in this article follows a heuristic strategy on Samuelson (1962): 'The approach taken in the paper first specifies a model which is formally identical to Samuelson's... surrogate production function model.... It departs from

the Samuelson approach in allowing the capital intensities between the consumption and capital good producing sectors to differ.' (p. 937). But what he comes up with is a restatement of his earlier, 1969 results, cast in terms like 'misspecification bias'. No econometric model is developed let alone tested.

10 Strictly speaking, only necessary conditions can be logically derived from theorems. But the big prize goes to him or her who succeeds in finding the sufficient conditions, and the biggest prize to whoever states necessary *and* sufficient conditions.

11 Blaug calls this method 'going round the back door', and he thinks it is used only where the analysis is very complicated. I quote the passage in full, as it contains an account of what happens in the debate that is not subject to a full empirical bias, though it is far too simplified: 'Is it true that economies can switch very often from one technique to another?

Now it is amazingly difficult to answer this question, and whenever economists are faced with this very difficult question, they usually try to answer it by going round the back door. That's what people have done in this case: well, maybe I cannot show whether switching has happened in the past or is likely to happen now in the real world, but perhaps I can construct a model in which I look at what has to be true to rule out switching, that is, a kind of model in which switching is impossible, and then I can ask myself whether such a model is realistic.' See Caravale (1976: 24).

12 Cf. 't Hooft (1987).

13 Pasinetti also discusses contributions that fall outside the scope of my sample of publications.

14 Notice that Pasinetti gives an illustration of the local character of the activities of authors working in the tradition of the industry approach.

15 I refer the reader to the passage from Shackle on mathematics as 'a powerful factor in this drive towards synthesis' which was quoted at the beginning of Chapter 10.

16 The fact that most theories are idealizations has not received much attention in the philosophy of science. Most discussions are about 'theories' tout court.

17 See Boland (1981). For a general analysis of this type of statement cf. also Watkins (1958).

18 See the paragraph on Correspondence and factualization of Chapter 4.

19 For a catalogue of the ideas about 'assumptions' and their relations to other theory elements, cf. Hamminga (1984, Appendix J).

20 Cf. Sintonen (1984), who conceives of scientific explanations as answers to questions, and analyzes explanations with the means of erotetic logic. He pays attention to the presuppositions of questions, and he distinguishes two types: logical (or syntactic) and pragmatic presuppositions. The second type is analyzed in terms of beliefs and subjective probabilities and need not detain us. But the first type is relevant to the present context. See Sintonen (1984: 45): 'presuppositions$_1$ of a question are logical entailments of the question sentences. Or rather, if only declarative sentences can have entailments, presuppositions$_1$ are logical entailments of the essentially syntactically chosen declarative counterparts of the question sentences.'

21 This is what Watkins calls a theory's M-component. Cf. Watkins (1975). For the idea of metaphysics as belonging to scientific theory's presuppositions, cf. also de Vries and van Hezewijk (1978, para. 3.3). Neither article works out the logical aspects of this idea.

22 Assuming that the ordering assumption was implicitly made. If we do not assume this, we get a different model from the one of the critics.

23 Cf. Van Fraassen (1968).

24 Hayek (1937).

25 I owe this example to Henk Visser.

26 Cf. Sintonen (1984).

27 'because it best suits the intuition that problems are literally *questions*. (For this reason also I adopt the statement view for *theories*: theories must be linguistically formulated because we want (the presuppositions of) theories to make logical contact with certain presuppositions of questions.)' Sintonen (1985: 28).

28 Cf. 'What is crucial for a logic of discovery is the possibility of limiting the set of specific questions that arise in a problem context.' Sintonen (1985: 36).

29 Cf. Post (1971).

30 In Koertge (1969).

31 'Quite generally, the thesis may be put this way: no theory that ever "worked" adequately turned out to be a blind ally. Once a theory has proved itself useful in some respects, has shown its semantic simplicity or explanatory power, it will never be scrapped entirely. Even the phlogiston theory had features that were useful scientifically in its day, and those features translate smoothly into present theory.' Post (1971: 237).

32 See above, Chapter 6.

33 In Musgrave (1981) and again in his letter of 20 November 1988 from which I quoted earlier.

34 For a suggestion for the direction capital theory should take, cf. Birner (1999).

Bibliography

Akyüz, Y., 1972, 'Income Distribution, Value of Capital, and Two Notions of the Wage–Profit Trade Off', *Oxford Economic Papers*.

Albin, P., 1975, 'Reswitching: An Empirical Observation', *Kyklos*.

Arrow, K. J. and Levhari, D., 1969, 'Uniqueness of the Internal Rate of Return with Variable Life of Investment', *Economic Journal*.

Asimakopoulos, A., 1988, 'Joan Robinson and Economic Theory', in Asimakopoulos, 1988a.

Asimakopoulos, A. (ed.), 1988a, *Investment, Employment and Income Distribution*, Polity Press, Oxford.

Asimakopoulos, A. and Harcourt, G. C., 1974, 'Proportionality and the Neoclassical Parables', *Southern Economic Journal*.

Bartley III, W. W., 1984, 'Knowledge is a Product not Fully Known to its Producer', in Leube and Zlabinger, 1984.

Batóg, T., 1976, 'Concretization and Generalization', *Poznan Studies*.

Bernholz, P., Faber, M., and Ross, W., 1978, 'A Neo-Austrian Two-Period Multisector Model of Capital', *Journal of Economic Theory*.

Bernstein, M. A., 1985, 'The Methodological Resolution of the Cambridge Controversies: A Comment' (on Cohen, 1984), *Journal of Post Keynesian Economics*.

Bhaduri, A., 1966, 'The Concept of the Marginal Productivity of Capital and the Wicksell Effect', *Oxford Economic Papers*.

Bhaduri, A., 1969, 'On the Significance of Recent Controversies on Capital Theory: A Marxian View', *Economic Journal*.

Bhaduri, A., 1970, 'A Physical Analogue of the Reswitching Problem', *Oxford Economic Papers*.

Bharadwaj, K., 1970, 'On the Maximum Number of Switches Between Two Production Systems', *Schweizerische Zeitschrift für Volkswirtschaft und Statistik*.

Birner, J., 1985, 'Keynes versus Hayek: interne en externe factoren in een controverse in de economie', *Kennis & Methode*.

Birner, J., 1989, 'Idealizations and the Development of Capital Theory', *Poznan Studies*.

Birner, J., 1990, 'A Roundabout Solution to a Fundamental Problem in Menger's Methodology and Beyond', *History of Political Economy*.

Birner, J., 1993, 'Neoclassical Economics as Mathematical Metaphysics', *History of Political Economy*.

Birner, J., 1993a, 'Testing Economic Theories Empirically: The Contribution of Econometrics', *Oekonomie und Gesellschaft*.

Birner, J., 1994, 'Idealizations and Theory Development in Economics. Some History and Logic of the Logic of Discovery', in Hamminga and de Marchi, 1994.

Birner, J., 1996, 'Cambridge Histories True and False', in Marcuzzo *et al.*, 1996.

Birner, J., 1997, 'Between consensus and dissent. The intellectual styles of Keynes and Hayek', Working Paper 14/97, ICER, Turin, Italy.

Birner, J., 1999, 'The Place of the Ricardo Effect in Hayek's Economic Research Programme', *Revue d'économie Politique*.

Birner, J., 2002, 'A conservative approach to progress in economics', in Boehm, Gehrke and Kurz, 2002.

Blaug, M., 1975, *The Cambridge Revolution; Success or Failure*, IEA.

Bliss, C. J., 1970, 'Comment on Garegnani', *Review of Economic Studies*.

Bliss, C. J., 1975, *Capital Theory and the Distribution of Income*, North-Holland.

Boehm, S., Gehrke, C., and Kurz, H., 2002, *Is there progress in economics?*, Edward Elgar.

Boland, L., 1981, 'On the Futility of Criticizing the Neoclassical Maximization Hypothesis', *American Economic Review*.

Boos, M., 1986, *Die Wissenschaftslehre Carl Mengers*, Böhlau.

Bose, A., 1964, 'The "Labour Approach" and the "Commodity Approach" in Mr. Sraffa's Price Theory', *Economic Journal*.

Bose, A., 1964a, 'Production of Commodities – A Further Note', *Economic Journal*.

Brems, H., 1975, 'The Cambridge Controversy: A Cambridge, Massachusetts View of Cambridge, England', *De Economist*.

Brems, H., 1977, 'Reality and Neoclassical Theory', *Journal of Economic Literature*.

Bronfenbrenner, M., 1977, 'Ten Issues in Distribution Theory', in Weintraub, 1977.

Brown, E. C. and Solow, R. M. (eds), 1983, *Paul Samuelson and Modern Economic Theory*, McGraw-Hill.

Brown, M., 1969, 'Substitution–Composition Effects, Capital-Intensity Uniqueness and Growth', *Economic Journal*.

Brown, M., 1973, 'Toward an Econometric Accommodation of the Capital-Intensity-Perversity Phenomenon', *Econometrica*.

Brown, M., 1980, 'The Measurement of Capital Aggregates – A Post Reswitching Problem', in Usher, 1980.

Brown, M. and Chang, W. W., 1976, 'Capital Aggregation in a General Equilibrium Model of Production', *Econometrica*.

Brown, M., Sato, K., and Zarembka, P. (eds), 1976, *Essays in Modern Capital Theory*, North-Holland.

Bruno, M., 1969, 'Fundamental Duality Relations in the Pure Theory of Capital and Growth', *Review of Economic Studies*.

Bruno, M., Burmeister, E., and Sheshinski, E., 1966, 'The Nature and Implications of the Reswitching of Techniques', *Quarterly Journal of Economics*.

Bruno, M., Burmeister, E., and Sheshinski, E., 1968, 'The Badly Behaved Production Function: Comment', *Quarterly Journal of Economics*.

Bunge, M., 1970, 'Problems Concerning Intertheory Relations', in Weingartner and Zecha, 1970.

Bunge, M., 1973, *Method, Model and Matter*, Reidel.

Burmeister, E., 1968, 'On a Theorem by Sraffa', *Economica*.

Burmeister, E., 1974, 'Synthesizing the Neo-Austrian and Alternative Approaches to Capital Theory: A Survey', *Journal of Economic Literature*.

Burmeister, E., 1975, 'Comment: This Age of Leontieff . . . and Who?', *Journal of Economic Literature*.

Burmeister, E., 1975a, 'Many Primary Factors in Non-joint Production Economies', *The Economic Record*.

Burmeister, E., 1976, 'Real Wicksell Effects and Regular Economies', in Brown, Sato and Zarembka, 1976.

Burmeister, E., 1977, 'The Irrelevance of Sraffa's Analysis without Constant Returns to Scale', *Journal of Economic Literature*.

Burmeister, E., 1977a, 'On the Social Significance of the Reswitching Controversy', *Revue d' Economie Politique*.

Burmeister, E., 1980, *Capital Theory and Dynamics*, Cambridge University Press.

Burmeister, E., 1980a, 'Comment', in Usher, 1980.

Burmeister, E., 1984, 'Sraffa, Labor Theory of Value, and the Economics of Real Wage Rate Determination', *Journal of Political Economy*.

Burmeister, E. and Hammond, P. J., 1977, 'Maximin Paths of Heterogeneous Capital Accumulation and the Instability of Paradoxical Steady States', *Econometrica*.

Burmeister, E. and Kuga, K., 1970, 'The Factor-Price Frontier, Duality and Joint Production', *Review of Economic Studies*.

Burmeister, E. and Laing, N. V., 1977, 'On Some Unresolved Questions in Capital Theory: An Application of Samuelson's Correspondence Principle', *Quarterly Journal of Economics*.

Burmeister, E. and Turnovsky, S. J., 1972, 'Capital Deepening in a Model with Many Capital Goods', *American Economic Review*.

Campbell, D. M. and Higgins, J. C. (eds), 1984, *Mathematics; People–Problems–Results*, Wadsworth.

Caravale, G. (ed.), 1976, *The Cambridge Debate and the Theory of Capital and Distribution*, Università di Perugia.

Cartwright, N., 1983, *How the Laws of Physics Lie*, Oxford, Clarendon.

Cartwright, N., 1989, *Nature's Capacities and their Measurement*, Oxford, Clarendon.

Cartwright, N., 1999, *The Dappled World. A Study of the Boundaries of Science*, Cambridge University Press.

Champernowne, D. G., 1953, 'The Production Function and the Theory of Capital: A Comment', *Review of Economic Studies*.

Champernowne, D. G., 1958, 'Capital Accumulation and the Maintenance of Full Employment', *Economic Journal*.

Cigno, A., 1972, 'The Theory of Economic Growth', in Napoleoni, 1972.

Cohen, A. J., 1984, 'The Methodological Resolution of the Cambridge Controversies', *Journal of Post Keynesian Economics*.

Cohen, A. J., 1985, 'Issues in the Cambridge Controversies', *Journal of Post Keynesian Economics*.

Collard, D., 1963, 'The Production of Commodities' (rev. of Sraffa, 1960), *Economic Journal*.

Collard, D., 1964, 'Production of Commodities – A Rejoinder', *Economic Journal*.

Collard, D., 1973, 'Léon Walras and the Cambridge Caricature', *Economic Journal*.

Compaijen, B., 1981, *Kapitaal, rendement en tijd*, Wolters-Noordhoff.

de Marchi, N. B. and Blaug, M. (eds), 1991, *Appraising Economic Theories: Studies in the Methodology of Scientific Research Programmes*, Edward Elgar.

Desai, M., 1981, *Testing Monetarism*, Frances Pinter.

Diamond, P. A., 1965, 'Technical Change and the Measurement of Capital and Output', *Review of Economic Studies*.

Dixit, A., 1977, 'The Accumulation of Capital Theory', *Oxford Economic Papers*.

Dobb, M., 1970, 'The Sraffa System and Critique of the Neo-Classical Theory of Distribution', *De Economist*.

Dobb, M., 1973, *Theories of Value and Distribution since Adam Smith*, Cambridge University Press.

Dobb, M., 1975, 'Revival of Political Economy: An Explanatory Note', *The Economic Record*.

Dougherty, C., 1972, 'On the Rate of Return and the Rate of Profit', *Economic Journal*.

Dougherty, C., 1980, *Interest and Profit*, Methuen.

Dow, S. C., 1979, 'Methodological morality in the Cambridge Controversies', *Journal of Post Keynesian Economics*.

Dow, S. C., 1982, 'Neoclassical Tautologies and the Cambridge Controversies – Reply' (to Salanti, 1982), *Journal of Post Keynesian Economics*.

Eatwell, J. L., 1977, 'The Irrelevance of Returns to Scale in Sraffa's Analysis', *Journal of Economic Literature*.

Eichner, A. S. and Kregel, J. A., 1975, 'An Essay on Post-Keynesian Theory: A New Paradigm in Economics', *Journal of Economic Literature*.

Faber, M., 1980, 'Relationship between Modern Austrian and Sraffa's Capital Theory', *Zeitschrift fur die gesamte Staatswissenschaft*.

Faber, M., 1981, 'Modern Austrian Capital Theory and Orosel's Standard Neoclassical Analysis: A Reply' (to Orosel, 1981), *Zeitschrift für Nationalökonomie*.

Feinstein, C. H. (ed.), 1967, *Socialism, Capitalism and Economic Growth; Essays Presented to Maurice Dobb*, Cambridge University Press.

Feiwel, G. R. (ed.), 1989, *Joan Robinson and Modern Economic Theory*, MacMillan.

Ferguson, C. E., 1969, *The Neoclassical Theory of Production and Distribution*, Cambridge University Press, 1979.

Ferguson, C. E., 1971, 'Capital Theory Up to Date: A Comment on Mrs. Robinson's Article', *Canadian Journal of Economics*.

Ferguson, C. E., 1972, 'The Current State of Capital Theory: A Tale of Two Paradigms', *Southern Economic Journal*.

Ferguson, C. E. and Allen, R. F., 1970, 'Factor Prices, Commodity Prices, and Switches of Techniques', *Western Economic Journal*.

Ferguson, C. E. and Nell, E., 1972, 'Two Books on the Theory of Income Distribution: A Review Article', *Journal of Economic Literature*.

Fine, B., 1980, *Economic Theory and Ideology*, Edward Arnold.

Finley, M. I., 1977, *The World of Odysseus*, Chatto & Windus.

Fisher, I., 1907, *The Rate of Interest*, MacMillan.

Fleming, J. S. and Wright, J. F., 1971, 'Uniqueness of the Internal Rate of Return: A Generalization', *Economic Journal*.

Frey, B. S., 1977 (Discussion contribution to Koopmans, 1977, pp. 175–6), in Harcourt, 1977.

Friedman, M., 1953, 'The Methodology of Positive Economics', in Friedman, 1953a.

Friedman, M., 1953a, *Essays in Positive Economics*, University of Chicago Press.

Gallaway, L. and Shukla, V., 1974, 'The Neoclassical Production Function', *American Economic Review*.

Gallaway, L. and Shukla, V., 1976, 'The Neoclassical Production Function: Reply', *American Economic Review*.

Garegnani, P., 1960, *Il capitale nelle teorie della distribuzione*, Giuffré.

Garegnani, P., 1966, 'Switching of Techniques', *Quarterly Journal of Economics*.

Garegnani, P., 1970, 'Heterogeneous Capital, the Production Function and the Theory of Distribution', *Review of Economic Studies*.

Garegnani, P., 1970a, 'A Reply', *Review of Economic Studies*.

Garegnani, P., 1976, 'The Neoclassical Production Function: Comment', *American Economic Review*.

Garegnani, P., 1976a, 'On a Change in the Notion of Equilibrium in Recent Work on Value and Distribution: A Comment on Samuelson', in Brown, Sato and Zarembka, 1976.

Gavroglu, K., Goudaroulis, Y., and Nicalopoulos, P. (eds), 1989, *Imre Lakatos and Theories of Scientific Change*, Kluwer.

Gram, H., 1976, 'Two-sector Models in the Theory of Capital and Growth', *American Economic Review*.

Gram, H. and Walsh, V., 1983, 'Joan Robinson's Economics in Retrospect', *Journal of Economic Literature*.

Hacking, I., 1981, 'Lakatos' Philosophy of Science', in Hacking, 1981a.

Hacking, I., (ed.), 1981a, *Scientific Revolutions*, Oxford University Press.

Hahn, F., 1972, *The Share of Wages in the National Income; An Enquiry into the Theory of Distribution*, Weidenfeld & Nicholson.

Hahn, F., 1975, 'Revival of Political Economy: The Wrong Issues and the Wrong Argument', *The Economic Record*.

Hahn, F., 1982, 'The Neo-Ricardians' (*Cambridge Journal of Economics*), in Hahn, 1984.

Hahn, F., 1984, *Equilibrium and Macroeconomics*, Blackwell.

Hahn, F. and Matthews, R. C. O., 1964, 'The Theory of Economic Growth: A Survey', *Economic Journal*.

Halévy, E., 1972, *The Growth of Philosophic Radicalism*, Faber.

Hamminga, B., 1983, *Neoclassical Theory Structure and Theory Development*, Springer.

Hamminga, B. and de Marchi N. (eds), 1994, *Problems of Idealisation in Economics, Poznan Studies*.

Harcourt, G. C., 1970, 'Reply', *Journal of Economic Literature*.

Harcourt, G. C., 1971, 'Reply to Ng', *Journal of Economic Literature*.

Harcourt, G. C., 1972, *Some Cambridge Controversies in the Theory of Capital*, Cambridge University Press.

Harcourt, G. C., 1975, 'The Cambridge Controversies: The Afterglow', in Parkin and Nobay, 1975.

Harcourt, G. C., 1975a, 'Decline and Rise. The Revival of (Classical) Political Economy', *The Economic Record*.

Harcourt, G. C., 1975b, 'Revival of Political Economy: A Further Comment', *The Economic Record*.

Harcourt, G. C., 1976, 'The Cambridge Controversies: Old Ways and New Horizons – Or Dead End?', *Oxford Economic Papers*.

Harcourt, G. C. (ed.), 1977, *The Microeconomic Foundations of Macro-economics*, MacMillan.

Harcourt, G. C., 1977a, 'Introduction', in Harcourt, 1977.

Harcourt, G. C., 1977b, 'The Theoretical and Social Significance of the Cambridge Controversies in the Theory of Capital: An Evaluation', *Revue d' Economie Politique*.

Harcourt, G. C., 1982, *The Social Science Imperialists*, edited by Kerr, P., Routledge & Kegan Paul.

Harcourt, G. C., 1982a, 'Capital Theory, Much Ado about Something', in Harcourt, 1982.

Harcourt, G. C., 1986, *Controversies in Political Economy, Selected Essays by G. C. Harcourt,*, edited by Hamouda, O. F., Harvester.

Harcourt, G. C. and Laing, N. F. (eds), 1971, *Capital and Growth; Selected Readings*, Penguin.

Harcourt, G. C. and Massaro, V. G., 1964, 'Mr. Sraffa's Production of Commodities', *The Economic Record*.

Harris, D. J., 1973, 'Capital, Distribution, and the Aggregate Production Function', *American Economic Review*.

Harris, D. J., 1980, 'A Postmortem on the Neoclassical "Parable"', in Nell, 1980.

Harrod, R. F., 1939, 'An Essay in Dynamic Theory' (*Economic Journal*), in Sen, 1970.

Harrod, R. F., 1949, *Towards a Dynamic Economics*, MacMillan, London.

Harrod, R. F., 1961, rev. of Sraffa, 1960, *Economic Journal*.

Hatta, T., 1976, 'The Paradox in Capital Theory and Complementarity of Inputs', *Review of Economic Studies*.

Hausman, D. M., 1981, *Capital, Profits, and Prices; An Essay in the Philosophy of Economics*, Columbia University Press.

Hayek, F. A., 1937, 'Economics and Knowledge', *Economica*.

Hayek, F. A., 1941, *The Pure Theory of Capital*, Routledge & Kegan Paul.

Hayek, F. A., 1942, 'The Ricardo Effect', in Hayek 1949.

Hayek, F. A., 1949, *Individualism and Economic Order*, Routledge & Kegan Paul.

Hayek, F. A., 1955, 'Degrees of Explanation', in Hayek, 1967.

Hayek, F. A., 1964, 'The Theory of Complex Phenomena', in Hayek, 1967.

Hayek, F. A., 1967, *Studies in Philosophy, Politics and Economics*, University of Chicago Press.

Hayek, F. A. (ed.), 1968, *Carl Menger, Gesammelte Werke*, Mohr.

Hegeland, H. (ed.), 1961, *Money, Growth and Methodology; Essays in Honour of J. Åkerman*, C. W. K. Gleerup.

Hemming, M. F. W., 1962, rev. of Sraffa, 1960, *Journal of the Royal Statistical Society*.

Hicks, J. R., 1937, 'Mr. Keynes and the "Classics": A Suggested Interpretation', *Econometrica*.

Hicks, J. R., 1960, 'Thoughts on the Theory of Capital – The Corfu Conference', *Oxford Economic Papers*.

Hicks, J. R., 1965, *Capital and Growth*, Oxford University Press.

Hicks, J. R., 1975, 'Revival of Political Economy: The Old and the New', *The Economic Record*.

Hintikka, J. and Remes, U., 1974, *The Method of Analysis*, Reidel.

Hintikka, J. and Vandamme, F. (eds), 1985, *Logic of Discovery and Logic of Discourse*, Plenum Press.

't Hooft, G., 1987, 'Elementaire deeltjes en spookverhalen', Diesrede, Universiteit van Utrecht.

Howard, M. C., 1980, 'Austrian Capital Theory: An Evaluation in Terms of Piero Sraffa's Production of Commodities by Means of Commodities', *Metroeconomica*.

Jaeger, K., 1973, 'A Comment on Y. Akyüz: Income Distribution, Value of Capital, and Two Notions of the Wage-Profit Trade-Off', *Oxford Economic Papers*.

Jaeger, K., 1974, 'Profitrate und Reswitching', *Zeitschrift für Wirtschafts- und Sozialwissenschaften*.

Johnson, H. G., 1962, rev. of Sraffa, 1960, *The Canadian Journal of Economics and Political Science*.

Jones, R. W., 1965, 'The Structure of Simple General Equilibrium Models', *Journal of Political Economy*.

Kaldor, N., 1957, 'A Model of Economic Growth', *Quarterly Journal of Economics*.

Kaldor, N., 1961, 'Capital Accumulation and Economic Growth', in Kaldor, 1978.

Kaldor, N., 1966, 'Marginal Productivity and Macroeconomic Theories of Distribution' (*Review of Economic Studies*) in Harcourt and Laing, 1971.

Kaldor, N., 1972, 'The Irrelevance of Equilibrium Economics', *Economic Journal*.

Kaldor, N., 1978, *Further Essays on Economic Theory, Vol. 5 of Collected Economic Essays*, Duckworth.

Kamarck, A., 1983, *Economics and the Real World*, Blackwell.

Koertge, N., 1969, 'A Study of Relations between Scientific Theories: A Test of the General Correspondence Principle', Ph.D. thesis, University of London.

Koestler, A., 1964, *The Sleepwalkers; A History of Man's Changing Vision of the Universe*, Penguin.

Koopmans, T. C., 1977, 'Examples of Production Relations Based on Microdata', in Harcourt, 1977.

Körner, S., 1963, 'Deductive Unification and Idealisation', *British Journal for the Philosophy of Science*.

Körner, S., 1966, *Experience and Theory*, London.

Krajewski, W., 1977, *Correspondence Principle and Growth of Science*, Reidel.

Krajewski, W., 1987, 'Explanation, Truth and Idealization' (Review of Cartwright, 1983), *Dialectics and Humanism*.

Kregel, J. A., 1973, *The Reconstruction of Political Economy*, MacMillan, London.

Kregel, J. A., 1980, 'The Theoretical Consequences of Economic Methodology: Samuelson's Foundations', *Metroeconomica*.

Kregel, J. A., 1980a, 'Economic Dynamics and the Theory of Steady Growth: An Historical Essay on Harrod's "Knife-edge" ', *History of Political Economy*.

Krelle, W., 1977, 'Basic Facts in Capital Theory. Some Lessons from the Controversy in Capital Theory', *Revue d'Economie Politique*.

Lachmann, L. M., 1973, *Macro-economic Thinking and the Market Economy: An Essay on the Neglect of the Micro-foundations and its Consequences*, IEA.

Laibman, D. and Nell, E., 1977, 'Reswitching, Wicksell Effects, and the Neo-classical Production Function', *American Economic Review*.

Laing, N. F., 1969, 'Two Notes on Pasinetti's Theorem', *The Economic Record*.

Lakatos, I., 1970, 'Falsification and the Methodology of Scientific Research Programmes', in Lakatos and Musgrave, 1972.

Lakatos, I., 1976, *Proofs and Refutations; The Logic of Mathematical Discovery*, edited by Worrall, J. and Zahar, E., Cambridge University Press.

Lakatos, I., 1978, *The Methodology of Scientific Research Programmes; Philosophical Papers* Volume I, edited by Worrall, J. and Currie, G., Cambridge University Press.

Lakatos, I., 1978a, *Mathematics, Science and Epistemology; Philosophical Papers Volume II*, edited by Worrall, J. and Currie, G., Cambridge University Press.

Lakatos, I., 1978b, 'The Method of Analysis-Synthesis', in Lakatos, 1978a.

Lakatos, I. and Musgrave, A. (eds), 1972, *Criticism and the Growth of Knowledge*, Second improved edition, Cambridge University Press.

Lange, O., 1938, 'The Rate of Interest and the Optimum Propensity to Consume', *Economica*.

Laudan, L., 1977, *Progress and its Problems*, Routledge & Kegan Paul.

Laymon, R., 1980, 'Idealization, Explanation, and Confirmation', *Philosophy of Science Association*.

Lerner, A. P., 1965, 'On Some Recent Developments in Capital Theory', *Proceedings of the American Economic Association*.

Leube, K. and Zlabinger, A. (eds), 1984, *The Political Economy of Freedom; Essays in Honor of F. A. Hayek*, Philosophia Verlag.

Levhari, D., 1965, 'A Nonsubstitution Theorem and Switching of Techniques', *Quarterly Journal of Economics*.

Levhari, D. and Samuelson, P. A., 1966, 'The Nonswitching Theorem is False', *Quarterly Journal of Economics*.

Levine, A. L., 1977, 'The Irrelevance of Returns to Scale in Sraffa's Analysis: A Comment', *Journal of Economic Literature*.

Little, I. M. D., 'Classical Growth', *Oxford Economic Papers*.

McKenna, J. P., 1960, rev. of Sraffa, 1960, *Southern Economic Journal*.

McManus, M., 1963, 'Process Switching in the Theory of Capital', *Economica*.

Makower, H., 1957, *Activity Analysis and the Theory of Economic Equilibrium*, MacMillan.

Malinvaud, E., 1953, 'Capital Accumulation and Efficient Allocation of Resources', *Econometrica*.

Marcuzzo, C., Pasinetti, L., and Roncaglia, A. (eds), 1996, *The Economics of Joan Robinson*, Routledge.

Massaro, V. G. and Harcourt, G. C., 1964, 'A Note on Mr. Sraffa's Sub-Systems', *Economic Journal*.

Meade, J., 1966, 'The Outcome of the Pasinetti-Process: A Note', *Economic Journal*.

Meek, R. L., 1961, 'Mr. Sraffa's Rehabilitation of Classical Economics', *Scottish Journal of Political Economy*.

Menger, C., 1871, *Grundsätze der Volkswirtschaftslehre*, Vol. I of Hayek, 1968.

Menger, C., 1883, *Untersuchungen über die Methode der Socialwissenschaften und der Politischen Oekonomie insbesondere*.

Meyerson, E., 1931, *Du cheminement de la pensée*, Alcan.

Meyerson, E., 1934, 'Les mathématiques et le divers', in Meyerson, 1936.

Meyerson, E., 1936, *Essays*, Vrin.

Miller, D., (ed.), 1983, *A Pocket Popper*, Fontana.

Mirowski, P., 1986, 'Mathematical Formalism and Economic Explanation', in Mirowski, 1986a.

Mirowski, P. (ed.), 1986a, *The Reconstruction of Economic Theory*, Kluwer.

Mirowski, P., 1987, 'Shall I Compare Thee to a Minkowski–Ricardo–Leontieff–Metzler Matrix of the Mosak–Hicks Type?', *Economics and Philosophy*.

Mirowski, P., 1989, *More Heat Than Light: Economics as Social Physics, Physics as Nature's Economics*, Cambridge University Press.

Mirrlees, J. A. and Stern, N. H. (eds), 1973, *Models of Economic Growth*, MacMillan.

Morgan, M., 1991, 'The Stamping Out of Process Analysis in Econometrics', in de Marchi and Blaug.

Morishima, M., 1964, *Equilibrium Stability, and Growth; A Multi-sectoral Analysis*, Oxford University Press.

Morishima, M., 1966, 'Refutation of the Nonswitching Theorem', *Quarterly Journal of Economics*.

Moss, S., 1980, 'The End of Orthodox Capital Theory', in Nell, 1980.

Mukherji, B., 1982, *Theory of Growth and the Tradition of Ricardian Dynamics*, Oxford University Press.

Musgrave, A., 1981, ' "Unreal Assumptions" in Economic Theory: The F-Twist Untwisted', *Kyklos*.

Musgrave, A., 1989, 'Deductive heuristics' in Gavroglu *et al.* 1989, pp. 15–32.

Napoleoni, C., 1972, *Economic Thought of the Twentieth Century*, Martin Robertson.

Nell, E. J., 1967, 'Theories of Growth and Theories of Value' (*Economic Development and Cultural Change*), in Harcourt and Laing, 1971.

Nell, E. J., 1967a, 'Wicksell's Theory of Circulation', *Journal of Political Economy*.

Nell, E. J., 1970, 'A Note on Cambridge Controversies in Capital Theory', *Journal of Economic Literature*.

Nell, E. J., 1973, 'The Fall of the House of Efficiency', *Annals of the American Academy of Political and Social Science*.

Nell, E. J., 1975, 'The Black Box Rate of Return', *Kyklos*.

Nell, E. J. (ed.), 1980, *Growth, Profits, and Property. Essays in the Revival of Political Economy*, Cambridge University Press.

Newman, P., 1962, 'Production of Commodities by Means of Commodities', *Schweizerische Zeitschrift für Volkswirtschaft und Statistik* (rev. of Sraffa, 1960).

Ng, Y. K., 1971, 'A Note on "Some Cambridge Controversies in Capital Theory"', *Journal of Economic Literature*.

Ng, Y. K., 1974, 'Harcourt's Survey of Capital Theory', *The Economic Record*.

Ng, Y. K., 1974a, 'The Neoclassical and the Neo-Marxist–Keynesian Theories of Income Distribution: A Non-Cambridge Contribution to the Cambridge Controversy in Capital Theory', *Australian Economic Papers*.

Nickles, T., 1990, 'Logics of Discovery', *Philosophica*.

Nowak, L., 1980, *The Structure of Idealization. Towards a Systematic Interpretation of the Marxian Idea of Science*, Reidel.

Nuti, D. M., 1970, 'Capitalism, Socialism and Steady Growth', *Economic Journal*.

Nuti, D. M., 1971, 'Vulgar Economy in the Theory of Distribution', *Science & Society*.

Nuti, D. M., 1973, 'On the Truncation of Production Functions', *Kyklos*.

Nuti, D. M., 1974, 'On the Rate of Return on Investment', *Kyklos*.

Nuti, D. M., 1977, 'Price and Composition Effects and the Pseudo-Production Function', *Revue d'Economie Politique*.

Orosel, G. O., 1979, 'A Reformulation of the Austrian Theory of Capital and its Application to the Debate on Reswitching and Related Paradoxes', *Zeitschrift für Nationalökonomie*.

Orosel, G. O., 1981, 'Faber's Modern Austrian Capital Theory: A Critical Survey', *Zeitschrift für Nationalökonomie*.

Orosel, G. O., 1981a, 'Faber's Capital Theory: A Rejoinder', *Zeitschrift für Nationalökonomie*.

Ott, A. E., 1963, rev. of Sraffa, 1960, *Jahrbücher für Nationalökonomie und statistik*.

Parkin, M. and Nobay, A. (eds), 1975, *Issues in Contemporary Economics*, Manchester University Press.

Pasinetti, L. L., 1962, 'Rate of Profit and Income Distribution in Relation to the Rate of Economic Growth', *Review of Economic Studies*.

Pasinetti, L. L., 1966, 'Changes in the Rate of Profit and the Reswitching of Techniques', *Quarterly Journal of Economics*.

Pasinetti, L. L., 1966a, 'New Results in an Old Framework. Comment on Samuelson and Modigliani', *Review of Economic Studies*.

Pasinetti, L. L., 1969, 'Switches of Technique and the "Rate of Return" in Capital Theory', *Economic Journal*.

Pasinetti, L. L., 1970, 'Again on Capital Theory and Solow's "Rate of Return"', *Economic Journal*.

Pasinetti, L. L., 1972, 'Reply to Mr. Dougherty', *Economic Journal*.

Pasinetti, L. L., 1974, *Growth and Income Distribution. Essays in Economic Theory*, Cambridge University Press.

Pasinetti, L. L., 1977, 'On Non-substitution in Production Models', *Cambridge Journal of Economics*.

Pasinetti, L. L., 1977a, 'Le choix des techniques et les théories du capital, des prix et la répartition du revenu', *Revue d'Economie Politique*.

Pasinetti, L. L., 1978, 'Wicksell Effects and Reswitching of Techniques in Capital Theory' (*Scandinavian Journal of Economics*), in Ström and Thalberg, 1978.

Pasinetti, L. L., 1981, *Structural Change and Economic Growth*, Cambridge University Press.

Patryas, W., 1979, 'Concretization and Entailment', *Logique et Analyse*.

Pen, J., 1971, *Income Distribution*, Penguin.

Pietruska-Madej, E., 1978, 'Anomalies and the Dynamics of Scientific Theories', *Poznan Studies*.

Popper, K. R., 1963, *Conjectures and Refutations*, Routledge & Kegan Paul.

Popper, K. R., 1967, 'The Rationality Principle', in Miller, 1983.

Popper, K. R., 1976, *Unended Quest; An Intellectual Autobiography*, Fontana.

Post, H. R., 1971, 'Correspondence, Invariance and Heuristics: in Praise of Conservative Induction', *Studies in the History and the Philosophy of Science*.

Quandt, R. E., 1961, rev. of Sraffa, 1960, *Journal of Political Economy*.

Randall, J. H., 1961, *The School of Padua and the Emergence of Modern Science*, Antenore.

Randall, J. H., 1962, *The Career of Philosophy*, Columbia University Press.

Reddaway, B., 1936, 'The General Theory of Employment, Interest and Money', *The Economic Record*.

Reder, M. W., 1961, 'Review of "Production of Commodities by Means of Commodities: Prelude to a Critique of Economic Theory" by Piero Sraffa', *American Economic Review*.

Ricardo, D., 1821, *The Principles of Political Economy and Taxation*, Everyman, 1973.

Rivett, K., 1970, 'Suggest or Entail', *Australian Economic Papers*.

Robinson, J., 1936, *Essays in the Theory of Employment*, Hyperion Press (1980 reprint of 1947 Blackwell Second edition).

Robinson, J., 1952, *The Rate of Interest; and Other Essays*, MacMillan.

Robinson, J., 1953, 'The Production Function and the Theory of Capital', *Review of Economic Studies*, also in Harcourt and Laing, 1971.

Robinson, J., 1955, 'The Production Function and the Theory of Capital – A Reply' (to Solow, 1955), *Review of Economic Studies*.

Robinson, J., 1956, *The Accumulation of Capital*, Third edition, MacMillan, 1969.

Robinson, J., 1958, 'The Real Wicksell Effect', *Economic Journal*.

Robinson, J., 1959, 'Accumulation and the Production Function', *Economic Journal*.

Robinson, J., 1961, 'Prelude to a Critique of Economic Theory', *Oxford Economic Papers*.

Robinson, J., 1962, 'The Basic Theory of Normal Prices', *Quarterly Journal of Economics*.

Robinson, J., 1962a, *Essays in the Theory of Economic Growth*, MacMillan.

Robinson, J., 1965, 'A Reconsideration of the Theory of Value' (*New Left Review*), in Robinson, 1975, Vol. III, pp. 173–81.

Robinson, J., 1966, 'Comment on Samuelson and Modigliani', *Review of Economic Studies*.

Robinson, J., 1970, 'Capital Theory Up to Date', *Canadian Journal of Economics*.

Robinson, J., 1971, 'Capital Theory Up to Date: A Reply', *Canadian Journal of Economics*.

Robinson, J., 1971a, 'The Measure of Capital: The End of the Controversy', *Economic Journal*.

Robinson, J., 1971b, *Economic Heresies*, Basic Books.

Robinson, J., 1972, 'The Second Crisis of Economic Theory', *Proceedings American Economic Association*.

Robinson, J., 1974, 'History versus Equilibrium', in Robinson, 1975, Vol. V.

Robinson, J., 1975, *Collected Economic Papers*, Cambridge University Press.

Robinson, J., 1975a, 'Introduction 1974. Reflections and Reminiscences', in Robinson, 1975, Vol. II.

Robinson, J., 1975b, 'Comments and Explanations', in Robinson,1975, Vol. III.

Robinson, J., 1975c, 'The Unimportance of Reswitching', *Quarterly Journal of Economics*.

Robinson, J., 1975d, 'Reswitching: Reply', *Quarterly Journal of Economics*.

Robinson, J., 1977, 'Q'est-ce que le capital?', *Revue d'Economie Politique*.

Robinson, J., 1978, 'The Organic Composition of Capital', *Kyklos*.

Robinson, J., 1979, 'Misunderstandings in the Theory of Production', *Greek Economic Review*.

Robinson, J., 1979a, *The Generalization of the General Theory; and Other Essays*, MacMillan (reprint, with the order of the chapters altered, of Robinson, 1952).

Robinson, J., 1980, 'Time in Economic Theory', *Kyklos*.

Robinson, J., 1980a, *Further Contributions to Modern Economics*, Blackwell.

Robinson, J. and Naqvi, K. A., 1967, 'The Badly Behaved Production Function', *Quarterly Journal of Economics*.

Roncaglia, A., 1978, *Sraffa and the Theory of Prices*, Wiley.

Rosser Jr, J. B., 1978, 'Continuity and Capital-Reversal: Comment', *Economic Inquiry*.

Rowthorn, R. E., 1974, 'Neo-classicism, Neo-Ricardianism and Marxism', *New Left Review*.

Russell, B., 1961, *History of Western Philosophy*, Allen & Unwin.

Salanti, A., 1982, 'Neoclassical Tautologies and the Cambridge Controversies', *Journal of Post Keynesian Economics*.

Samuelson, P. A., 1949, 'Abstract of a Theorem Concerning Substitutability in Open Leontief Models', in Stiglitz, 1966.

Samuelson, P. A., 1957, 'Wages and Interest: A Modern Dissection of Marxian Economic Models', *American Economic Review*.

Samuelson, P. A., 1959, 'A Modern Treatment of the Ricardian Economy: I. The Pricing of Goods and of Labor and Land Services. II. Capital and Interest Aspects of the Pricing Process', *Quarterly Journal of Economics*.

Samuelson, P. A., 1961, 'A New Theorem on Nonsubstitution' (originally in Hegeland, 1961), in Stiglitz, 1966.

Samuelson, P. A., 1962, 'Parable and Realism in Capital Theory: The Surrogate Production Function', *Review of Economic Studies*.

Samuelson, P. A., 1963, 'Comment on Ernest Nagel's "Assumptions in Economic Theory"', *American Economic Association Papers and Proceedings*.

Samuelson, P. A., 1966, 'A Summing Up', *Quarterly Journal of Economics*.

Samuelson, P. A., 1972, Nobel Lecture, *American Economic Review*.

Samuelson, P. A., 1975, 'Steady-state and Transient Relations: A Reply on Reswitching', *Quarterly Journal of Economics*.

Samuelson, P. A., 1976, 'Interest Rate Determinations and Oversimplified Parables: A Summing Up', in Brown, Sato and Zarembka, 1976.

Samuelson, P. A., 1983, *Foundations of Economic Analysis*, Enlarged Edition, Harvard University Press.

Samuelson, P. A., 1989, 'Remembering Joan', in Feiwel, 1989.

Samuelson, P. A. and Modigliani, F., 1966, 'The Pasinetti Paradox in Neoclassical and More General Models', *Review of Economic Studies*.

Samuelson, P. A. and Modigliani, F., 1966a, 'Reply to Pasinetti and Robinson', *Review of Economic Studies.*

Samuelson, P. A. and Solow, R. M., 1956, 'A Complete Capital Model Involving Heterogeneous Capital Goods', *Quarterly Journal of Economics.*

Sandelin, B., 1980, 'Wicksell's Missing Equation, the Production Function, and the Wicksell Effect', *History of Political Economy.*

Santiago Valente, W., 1980, 'Is Frank Knight the Victor in the Controversy between the Two Cambridges?', *History of Political Economic.*

Sato, K., 1974, 'The Neoclassical Postulate and the Technology Frontier in Capital Theory', *Quarterly Journal of Economics.*

Sato, K., 1976, 'The Neoclassical Production Function: Comment', *American Economic Review.*

Say, J.-B., 1880, *A Treatise on Political Economy*, Kelley edition of the New American Edition.

Saylor, S., 2000, *Last Seen in Massilia. Mysteries of Ancient Rome*, Constable & Robinson.

Schouten, D. B. J., 1961, rev. of Sraffa, 1960, *De Economist.*

Sen, A. (ed.), 1970, *Growth Economics*, Penguin.

Sen, A., 1974, 'On Some Debates in Capital Theory', *Economica.*

Shackle, G. L. S., 'Foreword', in Wicksell, 1954.

Shephard, R., 1953, *Cost and Production Functions*, Princeton University Press.

Sintonen, M., 1984, *The Pragmatics of Scientific Explanation, Acta Philosophica Fennica*, Vol. 37.

Sintonen, M., 1985, 'Separating Problems from their Backgrounds: A Question-Theoretic Proposal', in Hintikka and Vandamme, 1985.

Sneed, J. D., 1979, *The Logical Structure of Mathematical Physics*, Reidel.

Solow, R. M., 1955, 'The Production Function and the Theory of Capital', *Review of Economic Studies.*

Solow, R. M., 1956, 'A Contribution to the Theory of Economic Growth', (*Quarterly Journal of Economics*), in Sen, 1970.

Solow, R. M., 1962, 'Note on Uzawa's Two-sector Model of Economic Growth', *Review of Economic Studies.*

Solow, R. M., 1963, *Capital Theory and the Rate of Return*, North-Holland.

Solow, R. M., 1963a, 'Heterogeneous Capital and Smooth Production Functions: An Experimental Study', *Econometrica.*

Solow, R. M., 1967, 'The Interest Rate and Transition between Techniques', in Feinstein, 1967.

Solow, R. M., 1970, 'On the Rate of Return: Reply to Pasinetti', *Economic Journal.*

Solow, R. M., 1975, 'Brief Comments', *Quarterly Journal of Economics.*

Solow, R. M., 1983, 'Modern Capital Theory', in Brown and Solow, 1983.

Solow, R. M., 1985, 'Economic History and Economics', *American Economic Review.*

Solow, R. M., 1988, 'Growth Theory and After' (Nobel lecture), *American Economic Review.*

Spaventa, L., 1968, *Realism without Parables in Capital Theory*, Recherches récentes sur la Fonction de Production, Centre d'études et de recherches universitaire de Namur.

Spaventa, L., 1970, 'Rate of Profit, Rate of Growth, and Capital Intensity in a Simple Production Model', *Oxford Economic Papers.*

Spaventa, L., 1973, 'Notes on Problems of Transition between Techniques', in Mirrlees and Stern, 1973.

Sraffa, P., 1951, 'Introduction', in Sraffa, 1951a.

Sraffa, P. (ed.), 1951a, *The Works and Correspondence of David Ricardo*, Cambridge University Press.

Sraffa, P., 1960, *Production of Commodities by Means of Commodities*, Cambridge University Press.

Sraffa, P., 1962, 'Production of Commodities: A Comment' (on Harrod, 1961), *Economic Journal*.

Starrett, D. A., 1969, 'Switching and Reswitching in a General Production Model', *Quarterly Journal of Economics*.

Stiglitz, J. E. (ed.), 1966, *The Collected Scientific Papers of Paul Samuelson*, Vol. I, MIT Press.

Stiglitz, J., 1973, 'The Badly Behaved Economy with the Well-Behaved Production Function', in Mirrlees and Stern, 1973.

Stiglitz, J., 1973a, 'Recurrence of Techniques in a Dynamic Economy', in Mirrlees and Stern, 1973.

Stiglitz, J. E., 1974, 'The Cambridge–Cambridge Controversy in the Theory of Capital: A View from New Haven: A Review Article', *Journal of Political Economy*.

Streissler, E., 1963, rev. of Sraffa, 1960, *Zeitschrift für Nationalökonomie*.

Streissler, E., 1969, 'Hayek on Growth: A Reconsideration of his Early Theoretical Work', in Streissler, 1969a.

Streissler, E. (ed.), 1969a, 'Roads to Freedom; Essays in Honour of Friedrich A. von Hayek', Routledge & Kegan Paul.

Ström, S. and Thalberg, B. (eds), 1978, *The Theoretical Contributions of K. Wicksell*, MacMillan.

Swan, T. W., 1956, 'Economic Growth and Capital Accumulation', *The Economic Record*.

Thomas, E. C., 1975, 'On Technological Implications of the Wage-Profit Frontier', *Journal of Economic Theory*.

Tietzel, M., 1987, 'Idealisierte Erklärungen', *Zeitschrift für allgemeine Wissenschafts–theorie*.

Usher, D. (ed.), 1980, *The Measurement of Capital*, Chicago University Press.

Uzawa, H., 1962, 'On a Two-sector Model of Economic Growth', *Review of Economic Studies*.

Van Fraassen, B., 1968, 'Presupposition, Implication, and Self-Reference', *Journal of Philosophy*.

Vellupillai, K., 1975, 'Irving Fisher on "Switches of Technique": A Historical Note', *Quarterly Journal of Economics*.

de Vries, R. P. and van Hezewijk, R., 1978, 'Systems Theory and the Philosophy of Science', *Annals of Systems Research*.

Watkins, J. W. N., 1958, 'Confirmable and Influential Metaphysics', *Mind*.

Watkins, J. W. N., 1975, 'Metaphysics and the Advancement of Science', *British Journal for the Philosophy of Science*.

Watkins, J. W. N., 1978, 'Minimal Presuppositions and Maximal Metaphysics', *Mind*.

Watkins, J. W. N., 1984, *Science and Scepticism*, Hutchinson.

Weingartner, P. and Zecha, G. (eds), 1970, *Induction, Physics, and Ethics*, Reidel.

Weintraub, E. R., 1985, *General Equilibrium Analysis; Studies in Appraisal*, Cambridge University Press.

Weintraub, S. (ed.), 1977, *Modern Economic Thought*, University of Pennsylvania Press.

von Weizsäcker, C. C., 1983, 'On Ricardo and Marx', in Brown and Solow, 1983.

Wicksell, K., 1923, 'A Mathematical Analysis of Dr. Åkerman's Problem', *Ekonomisk Tidskrift*, also in Wicksell 1934, Vol. 1, pp. 274–99.

Wicksell, K., 1934, *Lectures on Political Economy*, 2 Vols., Routledge & Kegan Paul.
Wicksell, K., 1954, *Value Capital and Rent*, tr. by Shackle, G. L. S., Allen & Unwin, pp. 274–99.
von Wieser, F., 1914, 'Theorie der gesellschaftlichen Wirtschaft', in *Grundriss der Sozialökonomik*.
Wigner, E., 1960, 'The Unreasonable Effectiveness of Mathematics in the Natural Sciences' (*Communications in Pure and Applied Mathematics*), in Campbell and Higgins, 1984.
Worrall, J., 1982, 'Scientific Realism and Scientific Change', *The Philosophical Quarterly*.
Worrall, J., 2000, 'The Scope, Limits, and Distinctiveness of the Method of "Deduction from the Phenomena": Some Lessons from Newton's "Demonstrations" in Optics, *British Journal for the Philosophy of Science*.
Wright, J. F., 1975, 'The Dynamics of Reswitching', *Oxford Economic Papers*.
Yeager, L. B., 1976, 'Toward Understanding Some Paradoxes in Capital Theory', *Economic Inquiry*.
Yeager, L. B. and Burmeister, E., 1978, 'Continuity and Capital Reversal: Reply', *Economic Inquiry*.
Zahar, E., 1980, 'Einstein, Meyerson and the Role of Mathematics in Physical Discovery', *British Journal for the Philosophy of Science*.

Index

DISCARDED
CONCORDIA UNIV. LIBRARY

CONCORDIA UNIVERSITY LIBRARIES
SIR GEORGE WILLIAMS CAMPUS
WEBSTER LIBRARY